Destiny Bridge

destiny bridge

FRANK WORTHEN

A Journey Out of Homosexuality

forever books
WINNIPEG, CANADA
www.foreverbooks.ca

Destiny Bridge
Copyright © 2010 by Frank Worthen

ISBN: 978-1-926718-17-0

Cover Design: Yvonne Parks Design
Book Design: Andrew Mackay
Managing Editor: Rick Johnson

Published by

Forever Books

WINNIPEG CANADA
www.foreverbooks.ca

Printed in the U.S.A.

Some names have been changed to ensure the privacy
of the persons involved

Dedication

*This book is dedicated to these three precious gifts
from God, who have so blessed my life:*

*Anita, my wife, who is everything I ever
wanted and more;*

*Mike Payton, who led me down the Lord's path
to new life; and*

*Mike Riley, Senior Pastor of Church of the Open
Door, who has defended and championed this ministry for 30-plus years. He has been a friend and
counselor to me, and also to the countless men and
women who have come to this ministry for help.*

ACKNOWLEDGEMENTS

*Many thanks to Lela Gilbert, who took an almost
endless manuscript and produced a book.
Excellent work, Lela.*

*To Tim Wilkins, who helped me to see the potential
in my manuscript and believed in my work
even more than I did.*

*To my helper friends,
Alan Medinger, Arla Bonnett,
Barbara Driskill, and Chris Cheney.*

Contents

Prologue

The sun was beating through the window and had raised the temperature of my office to an uncomfortable degree, defeating the best efforts of the air conditioner. I was fighting off an overwhelming feeling of drowsiness, trying my best to focus my full attention on "Brad," the young man who sat across the desk from me. He was pouring out his frustrations and I knew he was counting on me to listen. I fixed my eyes on his sad face, thinking how similar his story was to that of literally hundreds of other troubled men I'd talked to over the years—men who had struggled with homosexuality and gender confusion.

"Tell me about your parents," I said, paying close attention now not only to his words but also to his facial expression and body language.

Over several decades, innumerable young men had sat where Brad was sitting. The faces had changed, the circumstances of their lives had varied, but the basic story remained all-too familiar. I studied Brad's boyish face and saw how nervously he was gesturing with his hands. Tears welled in his eyes as he answered my question, but his voice remained as clear as it was dramatic. "My father never understood me. Never! We always have had a terrible relationship. To be honest..." He paused.

"Yes?"

"To be honest, I have always hated my father! I wish he was *dead*!" Now his voice broke. I waited for a moment or two and then quietly urged him to continue, "And your mother...?"

Brad told me that he loved his mother. She had always come to his defense. She was the one who knew and understood him when his father didn't even try. Even when he had told his mother about his homosexual orientation, she had comforted him and vowed, "I promise not to tell Dad!"

Then the young man said something that seemed shocking to him, but didn't surprise me at all. "Even though I love my mother," he hesitated briefly before continuing, "I know this is weird, but I also hate her!" He went on to explain that what he really hated was the control she exerted over his life. Would she ever allow him to grow up and make his own decisions? But that wasn't the only reason he "hated" his mother.

Ever since early childhood, like so many other young men who struggle with same-sex attraction, Brad had taken upon himself the responsibility for his mother's happiness and security. "Somehow, someway, she always drove me to take care of her. She leaned on me, and we are tied together in a kind of mutual bondage. I feel like I've somehow stepped into my father's shoes. He was never there for her, but I am!" Then he added, "...whether I want to be or not!" He talked more about protecting his mother from neglect and abuse. He wished he could be free, but deep inside he knew that only her death would free him from the chains of this responsibility.

"That's not the only thing," Brad went on, "I have always had trouble with other guys—guys my own age in school and in the neighborhood where I grew up. They called me a fag, a queer, a sissy. They hated me for no reason!"

Brad choked back tears again as he told me that he had loved a boy in one of his classes, but this boy had never once acknowledged that Brad even existed. Lonely and depressed, desperate for male affection and attention, Brad had begun to search for love and attention elsewhere. Before long, he found older men in parks who wanted him. Brad had given himself away, freely and without restraint. Eventually he had become so obsessed with anonymous sex that he had taken deadly risks, and had finally been arrested on lewd-conduct charges.

Suddenly, he stopped talking, looked over at me and said, "But you don't understand either."

In fact, Brad could not have been more wrong. I wasn't like the other counselors and pastors he had talked to—nothing like them at all. Why? Because I had walked in his shoes. Oh, had I ever! I understood all too well what Brad was saying. It may have been the story of countless other young men, but it was my story, too. Looking into his disbelieving face, I adamantly assured him that, yes, I did understand.

After offering him what help I could at that time, the session was soon over. I walked Brad to the door just as the staff was leaving. It was five o'clock. I gave him a hug and bade him farewell. There might have been a time when I would have hugged him for all the wrong reasons but, by God's grace, that was all behind me. Now I hugged him because I knew very well what he was facing. As he walked away, I was left to my own reflections. Like Brad, I had known rejection, humiliation, insecurity, lack of male affirmation, loneliness, and self-hatred. These all had played a major role in my past life.

Now writing these words, I am 80 years old. There have been many young men like Brad who imagined I could never understand. And so, for the benefit of the countless strugglers I've met and worked with, and because of the wonderful way the Lord has used my past weaknesses to give others strength for the present and the future, I have recorded my long and difficult spiritual journey in the pages that follow. I hope it will be of help to others who struggle with homosexual issues. And also, I hope that it will bring to those who love them, some understanding of the causes of homosexuality and of the difficult journey "gay" people face. Homosexuality is often called "Father Replacement Search" and, sadly, most of the time the facts bear out the validity of this theory. I pray that reading about my journey will be a blessing to all.

The Boy in the Attic

I was born in 1929—the year of the great stock-market crash—an exceedingly bad year to be born. The first and only child in my family, I arrived twelve years after my parents were wed. Before I came along, during better days, my father had purchased an enormous old Victorian house in San Jose, California, for just $2,000. He had always intended to upgrade the place and he had the skill and know-

Frank Worthen at 8. (1937)

how to do so. However, with the Great Depression bearing down with full force on everyone, there was no money even to

15

paint it. The house grew progressively darker and uglier as my childhood passed. As I grew, the ornate trim around the eaves gradually fell off, the paint faded and peeled, and our family home looked increasingly grotesque and shabby. It became an eyesore in a neighborhood of fashionable bungalows—at least in part—because of my raging vandalism and uncontrollable destructive impulses.

But of course my first memories are not of our family home's deterioration. Like most children, my earliest recollections are of my parents. I think my mother was about 32 years old when I was born. At 5'6", she often complained of being too tall—women were shorter in those days. And although she must have been pretty as a young girl, I always recall her as weary and haggard. She was a study in contradictions—sometimes fun and a bit on the wild side, but most often morose, depressed, and very bitter. She kept a long list of the wrongs she had suffered at the hands of others. And from one day to the next, I never quite knew which side of her personality to expect.

From all indications, at the time of their marriage, my parents were a fun-loving couple, carefree and enthusiastic adventurers on my father's motorcycle. Somewhere along the way, however, the fun stopped and the hard realities of life brought an end to any dreams Mother may have had. She had turned into a typical housewife and young mother, shackled to the enormous Victorian house that she hated—the completion of which was one of my father's innumerable unfulfilled goals. Mother was also chained to her own squabbling, hard-scrabble family, trying to keep them a safe distance from her husband, who disliked them all intensely.

As for my father's personality, he had a creative imagination and never stopped dreaming. He was a good-looking, rugged type of man who delighted in sports and loved being surrounded by his buddies. Besides being a local sportsman, he was a skilled mechanic and carpenter, and for some years held down a good job with Pacific Gas and Electric (P.G. & E.), our local utility company. Father was never rowdy or reactive. With other men, he never shouted, but handled them firmly, able to take charge in any situation. This, along with his skilled work, made him a valuable employee.

However, my parents' financial situation became disastrous during the Depression—and they weren't the only ones. In those days, it was not unusual to see whole families trudging along the highway with all their belongings, searching unsuccessfully for shelter. I remember as a small boy watching them in amazement, noticing that they were covered with dust. In fact, the dust of the Depression hung over all of our lives like a dark, gritty cloud, obscuring any opportunity for happiness. The desperate poverty we faced in the 1930's would be unimaginable today except in the poorest developing countries. Like so many others, wondering where the next meal would come from was our family's primary anxiety.

Not long after Wall Street crashed, my father's salary was cut in half. Because of his skills, he was able to get a second job. During the summer and fall months, he would work for P.G. & E. by day, and then moonlight at a local cannery in the evening, oiling and maintaining food-processing equipment. In my earliest years, my father was a shadow figure, one who would arrive at the house late at night after I was in bed, and leave before I got up.

Occasionally, Father came home for dinner before heading out to his second job. I remember eagerly waiting for him at the gate, longing for his attention. When he finally arrived, he would absently pat me on the head and head for the kitchen. From that point on, I was left out of the picture because, besides whatever food she may have prepared, my mother always had a litany of complaints for her exhausted husband. I stayed out of the kitchen until I was called to dinner. By then, Mother had usually burned the food and she and Father weren't talking to each other. After a silent and uncomfortable dinner, he would leave for the night shift, slamming the door behind him.

Around this time, I began to develop the fine art of destructive manipulation. Before Father got home, I got involved in some sort of mischief—usually breaking something—just before he arrived. That meant my mother had me to complain about, and I successfully got my father's attention. He'd drop my pants and spank me on my bare bottom. It hurt, but it was still attention. I longed for his touch and was willing to pay the price to get it.

Although Father worked hard, he played hard, too. He was the star of his baseball team and was also quite a gambler. Now and then, he would take me with him to his favorite bar. There he placed bets, drank, and played some kind of game using cups and dice on the countertop. I sat on a barstool watching and listening, and although Father usually forgot I was there, sometimes one of the other men would talk to me and give me small change.

For obvious reasons, my mother was not happy about her husband's gambling habit. I clearly remember watching as she held up a couple of items of her underwear shouting at him, "Look at this! Everything I own is full of holes and I don't have any money to replace them! I'll bet you wasted more money shooting craps tonight than any of this would have cost!" As was her habit, she then pounded her angry fists into his chest. As usual, Father never responded in anger. He just fell silent and went to bed, never acknowledging her complaints one way or another. Occasionally he would win big and come home feeling very justified about his gambling ventures. Unfortunately, however, little of his winnings or his hard-earned money ever filtered down to the family food or clothing budget.

Despite Father's drinking and gambling, as a young boy I held Mother more responsible for my own unhappiness and the disruption of our home life than I did him. I placed the blame on her mostly because she was so vocal and animated. Father didn't handle pressure too well; when difficult circumstances came, he escaped into his world of drinking, gambling, and get-rich-quick ventures. As infuriated as Mother was over his other weaknesses, it was Father's get-rich-quick schemes that drove her crazy. The worst scheme was the "gold mine," his favorite fantasy of them all.

Thanks to Father's search for a pot of gold, part of my early childhood was spent in California's oak-studded "gold country," in the foothills of California's majestic Sierra Nevada mountains. The gold-mine dream was planted in Father's imagination when he heard that there were still vast stores of treasure left, even long after the gold rush era had ended. My father's buddy, Mel, used to hang around our house spinning tales of men panning for gold and finding priceless nuggets in riverbeds. Some ambitious adventurers, Mel claimed, had even hit a rich gold vein after digging a mine!

I liked Mel and looked forward to his visits. He made my father smile and was just as excited about "getting rich, quick" as Father was. Careful not to interrupt their conversation, I sat quietly in the corner of the room with my toys so I wouldn't be told to leave. Mother, on the other hand, was not at all happy about Mel or his fantastic tales. She had a sinking feeling that, yet again, her husband was being seduced by a new, risky adventure. Like Father, she had hopes of paying off our ever-increasing debts. But she knew all too well that Father would have to settle down and work hard for that to happen.

She fought long and hard to dissuade Father from chasing gold, but his mind was already made up. Until that pipe dream arose, he had never shouted at Mother. Now, though, he was fighting for what he thought would be the salvation of the family, the fortune that would solve all our financial problems. I can only guess, but I think he probably imagined that Mother would quiet down, stop complaining, and be a loving wife once the debts were paid and she could buy the things she wanted. Maybe she would have, but that wasn't what happened.

It was against Father's nature to be violent; he never hit her. Now, though, as he defended his new enterprise, he responded to her shouting by shouting back. I was desperate to escape.

One evening I hid behind the door to the attic stairs. Our attic was a dark, forbidding place and I was frightened to go up there, but sitting at the bottom of the stairs, I felt relatively safe. My parents exploded into shouting matches every night. The more I got used to them, the more the attic stairs became comfortable to me. One night in the middle of their fight, they both realized I was missing. "Where is he?" Mother asked. Father went to look in the basement, but Mother found me on the attic stairs.

"What are you doing up here?" she demanded.

"Nothing," I shrugged, as she hauled me off to bed.

Eventually, Mel and Father headed out together to search for the golden cache. Their quest led them to a bar in Columbia, California. Today Columbia is a state park, but in the 1930's it was a lively, functioning city. There at the bar, where they spent most of their time, one story caught their interest. They were told—on the best of authority—that a rich vein of gold ran beneath a local widow's farmland. Fascinated, they searched out this privileged widow. Unaware that they were being set up, they located her and she confirmed the story.

"Yes!" she agreed, "I'll gladly let you mine on my land, but first..."

The "widow lady," as they called her, explained that there were some improvements to her property that she really couldn't afford. If they would fix up her house, she'd let them mine for gold on her land. The deal was made. I remember Father returning home and announcing that he and Mel had found the right place to dig and how this elderly lady knew the exact spot where the gold lay—it had been revealed to her by some spirits. During the next couple of weeks my father set about wiring the clever old lady's house for electricity. He put his skills to work making upgrades, all the while dreaming about the mine. Before he could actually start digging, though, there always seemed to be just one more project to do. Meanwhile Mel, who had initiated all this, began to see through the scam and lost interest. Ignoring Mel's concerns, my undaunted father enlisted my two great-uncles to help so he could work on the repairs and, at the same time, get the mine up and running.

Father spent his vacation time and nearly every weekend in Columbia. Sometimes Mother and I joined him there for a week rather than being trapped in the big San Jose house, with its bill-collectors, and, later on, quarreling family members. So, for several years I spent my summer months in Columbia, and many evenings with Father at the bar. (To my surprise on a recent visit to Columbia, I found that bar still intact. It looks exactly as it did in my early childhood.)

That's where I watched Father grow very excited when one of the regulars announced a fifty-dollar bounty on mountain lions. Everyone's eyes widened and they all agreed to go mountain lion hunting together. I tagged along, and that day has never left my memory as a day of great fear and overpowering sense of abandonment.

As I followed along behind the men, we suddenly heard crashing in some nearby brush. Without warning, all the men ran off, leaving me alone in a clearing. I could hear noises all around me and, above all, I heard many gunshots. I was terrified! In my child's imagination, I could visualize a lion leaping out at me and tearing me apart. I desperately needed my father there to protect me. I may have been alone for only a few minutes, but to me it seemed like hours. Not only was I afraid of the lions, but I was scared of getting shot. Worst of all, I knew if I cried or made any noise, Father would never take me with him again. I remained silent.

Eventually the bedraggled hunters returned without the mountain lion. My father was visibly crushed at coming back from the hunt empty-handed. He had hoped to bag several lions in order to pay off some of the debt the foolish mine-venture had incurred. I had been upset with him for deserting me, but when I saw how disappointed he was, I forgot about being left alone. Instead, I tried in my small way to comfort him. I don't think he noticed.

A couple of times, our family forgot about the mine for a weekend and we went to the beach together. I remember my father holding my hand. He held it tightly in his as we waded out into the surf. He never seemed to notice, however, that when the water was up to his chest, it was several feet above my head. As much as I loved holding his hand, I soon learned to avoid wading with my father.

Still, he was wonderful company. At the beach he seemed more relaxed and, surprisingly, Mother was careful not to ruin this special time away from all our troubles. At the beach she was somehow transformed into a happy little girl, which made the entire experience a happy one. She told me her own father had taken her to this same beach many years before, and that returning there brought back warm memories for her.

During those few days at the beach we were like any ordinary family, having fun and enjoying life together. Both parents gave me all the money I wanted for ice cream, snow cones, and candy bars. Those hours by the seaside remain among my few good memories of childhood. Even today, when driving by that beach, I remember feeling close to my father. I never held it against him that I'd almost drowned while holding his hand. It was a small price for such happiness.

But any occasions of closeness I shared with my father—and they were rare—ceased once the goldmine venture was over. Soon, Mel and Father began another futile venture and Mother was left, again, to manage the home front. Even before the mine, we were hard-pressed for money. Now, with a mountain of debt from that misadventure, we were far worse off than before. Mother had to face all the unhappy people who were unsuccessfully trying to collect on past-due bills.

The only salary bill collectors received during the Depression was a commission, which was calculated from whatever amount they collected. After knocking on the door at the front of our house, they would march into the back yard and pound on the back door. Mother and I had to be silent and invisible, because if they heard or saw us, they would persist. If we had neglected to close the curtains, we had to lie flat on the floor until they left. This constant humiliation drove Mother out of the house. We stayed away for hours, going on picnics, watching local parades, and attending all sorts of free events. For me, those were good days.

Mother was suffering, however, and she was never one to suffer in silence. She was not the quiet type. Whenever Father came home, she sought revenge. If she never had a peaceful minute, neither would he; she'd see to that. As he walked through the doorway, her attack began. She pounded his chest with her fists, screaming at him and raging uncontrollably. Few could say that she wasn't totally justified. She endured much because of his foolishness. But in her vindictive rage, intending to make Father pay for his wayward ways, Mother also was destroying her own life, and mine as well.

Perhaps if he hadn't always been chasing yet another adventure, we might have had a reasonable home life, but that wasn't Father's style. Anyway, by now any hopes of a normalcy were dashed. Sometimes he would stop at the house for dinner before going off with Mel. When he did, the fighting between my parents increased to a new and frightening level. Even sitting on the attic stairs, I could still hear their angry words. Finally, I couldn't stand it any longer. I was ready to brave the dark, frightening attic itself.

There was a single light bulb in the middle of the room and I had to search in the dark for the switch to turn it on. The flooring didn't extend over the entire space and there were sunken areas caused by closets and cabinets below. I felt very much alone, with two very unpleasant options. I could either remain with my parents and endure the sound of their horrifying verbal abuse, or I could hide out alone in the dark and scary attic. I chose solitude.

If my father was around at all, he didn't seem to know I existed—or didn't care. I have since concluded that he was aware that I was bonding more and more with Mother and trying less to relate to him. He must have begun to see me as an appendage of my mother. In any case, he was now rejecting both of us. During those crucial years of needed attachment, I lost all possibility of bonding with my father.

When I was around six years of age, our corner grocery store changed hands and two young men took over. The younger of the two delivered our groceries at the back door. I found myself waiting for hours on the steps for him to appear. He always talked to me and I longed to see him as often as I could. I was starved for male affection even then, although at the time I had no idea why I was so attracted to this delivery boy.

About that same time, I realized that I was ashamed of our family. I was humiliated because of our shabby house, and I was deeply embarrassed by our chronic financial woes. Because the nearby store kept our credit-limit very low, Mother had to continue to search for other grocery stores that would allow us credit, but few took the chance. Every time she was disgraced by another denial of credit, she took it out on Father. I didn't think the anger in our family could get any worse, but it did.

Mother's relatives came to live with us.

I was about seven years old when my mother invited

them—over my father's adamant objections. Just as he didn't listen to her, she didn't listen to him. And, just as she was loud, hot-headed and vocal, so was her family. They constantly fought among themselves. There was, however, a silver lining; I now had a grandfather who allowed me to climb up into his lap.

For a while, Grandpa was a great substitute for my father's love. He delighted in me and told me many stories. He was retired so he had few obligations, and I became an important part of his life. Despite all the quarreling relatives, I was happy to have my grandfather around all the time. About the time I was eight, however, he was rushed to the hospital, where he soon died. This was a tremendous loss to me. Just then, though, another man entered my life. This time it was my Uncle Charlie.

My successful, hardworking Grandpa had been deeply disappointed in his son, Charlie (my mother's brother). He'd had long-cherished hopes that Charlie would make his job at the railroad into a life-long career, but Charlie had other ideas—many other ideas. I knew what my father and the rest of the family thought of him. My father often called him a bum. After losing his railroad job, Charlie took odd jobs, never again finding full-time employment in our hometown. But Uncle Charlie was very good to me. He comforted me during my grandfather's illness and death, and he quickly became my window to the world.

Uncle Charlie was a small wiry man, curious and energetic. Despite his alleged laziness, he had an active and brilliant mind. For example, he was an expert in anything operated by steam. He knew steam engines through-and-through, and was often called upon to repair what others didn't understand and couldn't fix. I imagine he was just reaching his forties when I got to know him. He had never married and, to anyone's knowledge, had never dated, either. He quickly became the most significant person in my growing-up years.

My hometown, San Jose, California, was a small city at that time, with only about 35,000 residents (today its population exceeds a million). My mother seemed willing enough to let Uncle Charlie take me around town. He loved adventure and he planted a love for adventure in me. The thirties were a time when the U.S. government invested large sums of money into infrastructure. Charlie and I watched the new Post Office being built. He knew some of the workmen so we were able to wander around the construction site, which was forbidden to others. We also watched the new Southern Pacific train depot being constructed. We saw an artist working on the large S.P. logo inside the depot and talked to the workmen excavating the tunnels that extended from the depot to the various tracks. Charlie always seemed to know what was new and exciting, and he couldn't wait to take me with him to see the latest and greatest sights in his world. I loved him, but my family members certainly did not. Whenever he was in the house, battles raged for hours.

I never quite knew what the issues were, but later I learned the rest of the family accused him of taking rather than giving. Sometimes they even accused him of theft. I didn't take any sides in battles about Charlie. I never knew whether the others were right, or if they simply hated him; but somehow their disapproval did make my relationship with Uncle Charlie uncomfortable.

When I was with Charlie, he never mentioned anything about the family, never defended himself, or said anything negative about anyone else. Maybe he thought hanging out with me was his contribution to the family, but it seemed to me that he enjoyed it as much as I did. He and I would take streetcar rides to the end of the line, just to pass the time. For a while, he had been a streetcar conductor, and had then moved on to be a railway engineer. He still had friends on the railroad, so at times I got to ride in the cab of a train. The most memorable event of all was being in the cab of the new Daylight train on the Los Angeles run. He allowed me to operate some of the controls and we took the engine out to the limits of the train yard and back. Even today, the Daylight is still viewed as America's most beautiful train.

During those months of turmoil surrounding Uncle Charlie, I was awakened one night by a strange, ominous sound. At first, it sounded like a crowd at a football field or baseball stadium. As I shook off sleep, I clearly heard people outside, running in the streets. My mother rushed into my room, got me up, and took me with her to watch from our front porch. *Where is Father?* I asked myself. For some reason, he had not come home that night.

"What's going on?" Mother shouted to someone running by. The reply was puzzling, "It's a hanging!" "It's a hanging!"

A hanging? I wasn't exactly sure what a hanging was, but my mother knew very well. She was visibly frightened and would not let me off the porch; instead, she grabbed me and held me tightly.

Later on, the terrible story shook our community like an earthquake. Two men had kidnapped the son of a popular local merchant. Although the media of the day, unlike today's media, did not pursue the rape and sexual side of the story, it was still the talk of the town. Everyone was saying, "Those perverts sure got what they deserved!" This was the prevailing justification for the hanging, more than the fact that the pair had murdered the young man. Hate against the perpetrators was running high—hate for what they had done and hate for homosexuals in general. Still a youngster, I knew nothing of homosexuality and only knew that they had killed a boy like me. Why they had done so, I didn't understand until many years later.

When my father returned home in the early morning we learned more details about what had happened. I had never seen him so energized. He described every detail of the dreadful incident, clearly satisfied that the "right thing" had been done. I remember him saying, "If we'd left it to the courts, those men might have gotten away with what they did! But now they are dead; and believe me, that's a good thing!"

It seemed that an angry, vengeful crowd had gathered outside the city jail. Since my father and the sheriff were friends, the sheriff had deputized him, and although we hadn't realized it at the time, he had been on duty that night. Amidst demands that the rapists be handed over to the lynch mob, the sheriff had quietly said to his men, "Leave the cells unlocked; leave all the doors unlocked, and go home."

When the raging crowd saw the police abandon the city jail, they moved in, grabbed the two men from their cells, and dragged them to the park across the street, where they beat them nearly to death. Then someone showed up with a rope. The two rapists were hanged from one of the park's trees. After the hanging, some enterprising man cut the rope into foot-long sections and sold each section for a dollar.

I was just a little boy, but I have never forgotten that night. The horror of what those men did—the torture and brutality— has remained with me all my life. Looking back at it today, you'd think it would have made me afraid of seeking sexual pleasure with older men. It should have, but it didn't.

With my mother's unmanageable family living with us and my father's deliberate neglect, Mother was hungry for affection, so she lavished all her attention on me. Although she wanted to buy me toys and give me parties, she had no money. But one thing we did have was nut trees in our back yard. So Mother would gather up the walnuts and almonds and take them in small bags to a local wholesaler. She would come home with fifty cents or, on a really good day, maybe even a dollar. She was as thrilled as I was to hurry off to the variety store and buy a present for me.

By this time, I had completely given up seeking any relationship with my father. I could only agree with my mother's verdict: Father had abandoned us both, and now we only had each other. But now, I also had Uncle Charlie. Mother wasn't quite comfortable with that relationship, though I didn't know why. Every time I came home from one of my adventures with Uncle Charlie, Mother more or less interrogated me, asking in detail what had happened. Sometimes she even said, "Did he touch you?" I didn't know what she was asking. I can truthfully say that Uncle Charlie was always upright with me; he never touched me in a sexual way. It certainly wasn't the case with a number of other young men who crossed his path, but of course I had no awareness of this.

Before I started school, I did have a few neighborhood friends. We took part in some sexual experimentation, which awakened my desire and awareness, but it was just kids' play. We had no idea what we were doing, except we all somehow knew that it was wrong. When a girl wanted to join in, we sent her home and I immediately tattled on her to my mother. I conveniently left out what we had been doing.

Up to the first day of school, my relationship with other neighborhood kids was that of a normal child. Mother had always watched me like a hawk , but she never discouraged my having friendships. Once I enrolled in school, however, I no longer fit in. My erstwhile friends discovered that I was outside the "inner" circle and they quickly abandoned me, joining the others in taunting me. My first day at school was terrifying. I ended up as a complete outsider, and the first words I heard my teacher say to my mother were, "Your son is very different."

I really don't know what she specifically meant by that; I was certainly shy and frightened. After that terrible introduction to public school, I learned that being different was not a good thing. My mother had dressed me in the best clothes I had, but maybe my clothing was out of style. To this day, I don't know. I do know, though, it certainly would not be the last time that people saw me as "very different."

I was so traumatized, Mother stayed with me that whole day to make sure I would be all right. Later, the teacher informed Mother that I had a speech impediment. My first name was Wesley (which I completely dropped the instant I graduated from high school). Unfortunately, I simply could not pronounce the letter "s," so when asked my name, I responded, "Wetley." There were the usual jokes that I had wet my pants or wet the bed. Also, I think the kids picked up from the teacher the idea that I was somehow unacceptable, and that only increased their ridicule.

From that day on, school became my prison. I desperately wanted to run away. I longed to be safely back home, entertained by my mother, or hanging out with Uncle Charlie. Instead, I had to endure my role as a loser. I became the weak animal that the pack feels duty-bound to destroy. As months went by, there were short intervals when the mood would change. If I had a party and invited my classmates, they showed up. But after the party, they would resume their rejection and ridicule, keeping me out of their circle of friends. Still, now and then, one of them would ask, "When's the next party?"

Even though school was hell for me, I was always at my desk early. I knew that if I came through the door after they were all in class, they would greet me with ridicule. Over the months, I became increasingly sad and silent. I was desperate to escape that very unpleasant environment. The dark, frightening attic of our Victorian home—which had first become my refuge during my parents' worst arguments—now became my universe. Since life was unbearable, I developed a fantasy world.

From my attic, I could hear the muffled sounds of all the fighting going on below, but now I could not make out the words. And I didn't want to—I'd heard enough already. I was beginning to develop a love/hate relationship with my mother. I loved her dearly and she loved me and would do anything for me, but I hated her voice. I hated her anger. I hated her fists that pounded on my father, and the way she screamed at her family members. I wanted to become deaf. I became fiercely attached to that space in the attic and didn't want anyone to invade my territory. It was my only safe place in the world.

Mother tried to entice me to rejoin her downstairs, but I wanted to be alone. She couldn't pry me loose from my attic, so she manipulated my father into building me a very large finished playroom in the attic. He constructed shelves and Mother beautifully wallpapered the walls and ceiling. My room was the size of a small house. I should have been very happy with such a grand room all to myself. Unfortunately, however, neither Mother nor Father knew the extent of the anger that raged inside me, like a red-hot volcano about to erupt. Fury had seethed within me for years, bubbling up with every insult, every family battle, and every hurtful rejection. In truth, I was a very disturbed child.

With increasing frequency, I exploded in fits of rage. These outbursts became my way of expressing the most infuriating questions of my life: Why was I in exile when other kids were out on the streets playing together? Why didn't I have a loving family? Why did my father abandon me? Why did other kids hate me, and what did I do to deserve it?

With no other way to communicate my anguish, I tore apart my surroundings. As I grew older and stronger, I was able to do increasing damage. I dragged my father's sledge hammer from the basement to the attic and wielded it against the shelves and walls my parents had so lovingly built for me. It wasn't long before my beautiful room was a mass of wreckage. I even went to the extent of ripping out the windows from their casings. The neighbors, who thought our house was already an eyesore, must have been quite dismayed by what they heard and saw.

When there was little more I could do with the sledge hammer and wrecking bar, I began to set fires in various areas of the house. My father had just built a new screen porch off the back of the house. That was my primary target. Thanks to my skills as an arsonist, nearly a dozen fires were ignited on Father's beloved porch.

I had no understanding of what I was doing. Meanwhile, unbelievably, my parents were so caught up in their own hostilities that they took little notice of my destructive behavior. I often wonder if they knew it was connected to their own vicious treatment of each other. Now and then, I received a sound beating from my father. In retrospect, I can see that I was longing for physical touch from him, and my vandalism was one way I could control the situation. Although it was negative touch, it was nevertheless touch. But it did little to satisfy the terrible longing in my soul.

I was frighteningly out of control. Some of the things I did were strange, even for someone as disturbed as I was. My mother took my birthday and Christmas gifts to the attic and placed them there for me in boxes. Every day I poured water over them. I found termite-infested wood in the yard and nailed it to the attic beams. Sadly, after I was a grown man, I heard that when the house was finally torn down, a workman fell through the attic floor and broke his leg. The floor had been weakened by termite infestation.

Occasionally my father would threaten me, saying that if I didn't quit my destructive behavior, he would send me to military school. That actually sounded like heaven to me. I wanted so badly to escape all the trauma and rejection, that his warning did nothing but harm. Instead of reforming my behavior, it became much worse. I sawed through the foundations of our house; I found his brace and bit and drilled several dozen three-inch holes in our kitchen floor and, in an all new line of attack, drilled even more in Father's new screen porch.

Uncle Charlie patched up every hole, but no family member ever thanked him for his efforts. In the meantime, I destroyed the roof of our garage; I dug huge holes in our driveway and front lawn; and I ripped off part of our front stairway. When Father confronted me, I defied him. "Okay, I'm ready to go to military school," I challenged.

But I hadn't realized Father had no funds to send me away. He was stuck with me, and I was stuck with my miserable existence. It still strikes me as strange that—apart from my first teacher—no one ever seemed to see how deeply disturbed I was. I was in desperate need of help. The people around me were so wrapped up in their own misery, they barely noticed me or the profound hunger that was eating away at my soul.

From left: Mother, Grandmother, Frank (at age 10), and Father while at the 1939 World's Fair in San Francisco.

Our Victoria House.

Frank Worthen at 14. (1943)

Chapter Two

Family Losses and New Beginnings

Our family's financial problems were staggering. To help alleviate the constant pressure of debt and deprivation, Mother went to work as an Avon Lady. She wasn't the kind of woman who was interested in cosmetics, but she excelled in selling Avon's line of household products—laundry soaps and cleaning supplies. She was quite successful, paying off many of our debts and providing money for food. I enjoyed the arrival of huge boxes of Avon products and helped Mother sort it all out and fill the orders. However, as Mother's business increased, she arrived home later and later. Since my school was over at 3:30 in the afternoon, sometimes I had several hours alone, which gave me time to act out many of my destructive strategies. Nearly every day, when my mother arrived home, there would be some new vandalism waiting to ruin her day.

I loved my mother, but I also held deep resentments against her for driving my father away from our home and, more painfully, from me. On rare occasions, Father came home in a good mood, but inevitably, she would pour out her wrath on him, and he would flee after dinner. I remember watching as his good mood vanished. First, sadness would cross his face, but it soon turned to anger. Sometimes I heard him shout, "What more do you want of me, woman? I'm doing the best I can!" When Father thought of his home life, what could he possibly think of but an ungrateful, demanding wife and a very destructive kid?

My parents must have found a way to be together now and then, because I later learned of a brief pregnancy that took place when I was seven. At that time, of course, I had no awareness of such a tragedy. I do remember that Mother seemed to have slowed down. She took little notice of my daily sabotage, and seemed to have lost her energy. I recall her growing more haggard-looking, and I noticed that she could hardly make it up our long flight of steps. This was just before I demolished Mother's most prized possession, our Queen Anne dining room set. I smashed all the chairs and left them lying in pieces around the table.

When Mother first discovered what I had done, she tried to chase me—intending to beat me. Instead, she suddenly sank to the floor in despair. Then she went to bed. Our next door neighbor, Grace, called the doctor; Mother was sick for several days. I felt very bad that I had caused her so much trouble, but I didn't realize the full extent of her distress. About midnight of the third day, the doctor came again to see her. Later, he carried a cloth filled with blood—containing something solid in the center—through my bedroom. He flushed it down the toilet.

I could hear Mother crying inconsolably. Two days later, she was up, back at work, and no longer so tired. But oh, was she angry with me! Again and again, she shouted at me, "You killed your brother! You killed your brother!"

What was she talking about? A brother? I didn't have a brother, although I wished very much that I did. As a rejected, isolated child, there was nothing I could have wanted more than a brother. So how had I killed him? I had no idea what a miscarriage was. I didn't put the pieces together until I was almost an adult.

This was a traumatic turning point for me. From that time on, I was much less violent. Instead, I become increasingly withdrawn and isolated. I spent longer hours in my attic. My fantasy life now revolved around my brother and what he might have been like. I have carried the regret and remorse of that miscarriage with me my entire life. More than once I have asked myself, *If my brother had lived, would I have taken the path that led me into homosexuality?*

Years came and went. Somehow, I survived the horrors of elementary school and found myself about to graduate from the sixth grade. I was still very much a loner, and my mother was increasingly concerned about my safety. She focused her fears on one particular danger, telling me never to go through the pedestrian subway—a cement tunnel that ran beneath a wide, busy street, its entrance right at the school's front door. This subway was gloomy, poorly-lit, and reeked of urine. Very few students ventured inside it, although it originally had been constructed for their use. Mother insisted that I walk down an entire block to where there was a cross-walk, instead. She didn't give me any explanation, so I pressed her to tell me why I should avoid the subway. Finally, she revealed that a boy had been molested there.

I could hardly believe my ears, and Mother would have been horrified if she could have read my mind. *So there are men who want boys? Boys like me?* I was a boy who wanted men, and I was very interested in finding one who would want me. This naive hope added new fuel to my already-expanding fantasy life, and soon became my favorite story. Again and again, I begged Mother to explain it to me. She must have wondered why I kept asking, but she repeated her warnings, always ending with the same appeal to stay away from the subway.

In my over-active imagination, the filthy pedestrian walkway was transformed into the Subway to Happiness. In real life, I walked through it—slowly and hopefully—every chance I got. Sometimes I lingered there in anticipation. At first, I could hardly stand the foul smell, but it was evidence that perhaps Mother was right; there must have been men in that subway from time to time. If so, where were they now? If Mother had only known how hard those "dirty old men" were to find! It never crossed my mind that one of them might harm me. In my fantasy, they would love and protect me. I was completely innocent about what else they might do to me, or force me to do with them. Mother's entire sexual vocabulary consisted of only three words, "Don't fool around!" She thought this was enough information about sex. If I didn't fool around, what more would I need to know?

Unknown to her, in my short life I had already fooled around a little. For about five years, I had played around sexually with twin boys who had lived next door. As luck would have it, just after these two friends moved away, something weird and alarming happened to me. I was around ten years old when I had an ejaculation. It frightened me, and there was no one to explain what it meant. I could only conclude that my male equipment was permanently ruined.

This strange incident haunted me. *What was wrong with me?* At night, I would break out in cold sweats; the worry of it lay heavily on my mind. I often thought to myself, *Mother was right; I should never have fooled around with myself—now I'm broken for life.* But, then I began to wonder, *If I am broken, why am I not sick?* It would be a long time before I finally understood.

In those lonely years I was afraid of boys, but at least I knew enough not to play with girls—which would have led to even more ridicule. During recess, from some hidden spot in the schoolyard, I quietly observed the boys playing. A few were good-looking and I enjoyed staring at them, but I couldn't help notice how rough and rowdy they all were. Even as a friendly gesture, they whacked each other across the shoulders or shoved and kicked at one another. Occasionally, when someone was hit too hard, a fight broke out and a couple of them were soon pounding each other in the face. I had no desire to experience what I understood to be physical abuse. I kept telling myself, *I don't need them!* However, somewhere in my heart I knew I did need them. I needed to belong. Being an outcast was so hard to bear.

At home, now that vandalizing the house was no longer my favorite pastime, I spent the afternoons reading instead. Grace, our next-door neighbor, had a rather large library with many books written for young boys. She had bought them in years past, to interest her own son in reading. By this time, he was a college student and Grace was more than happy to share his books with me. She gave me every Oz book ever printed, as well as the whole Tom Swift series. These were my favorites.

Then, all at once, my pleasurable reading was interrupted— eclipsed—by something entirely new. My parents bought me a bicycle.

Suddenly I was free. I could explore the world on my own without anyone looking over my shoulder. Several times in the past, my father had taken our family to San Francisco. I had been fascinated by the big city—it seemed magical to me. I was intrigued by the people there. They seemed quite different from those I was used to in San Jose. San Francisco had ragged street people—some of them beggars, people playing instruments on the sidewalks, evil-looking characters in alleyways, and beautifully-dressed men and women in limousines. My father frequented a few working-class bars in San Jose, but in San Francisco, I saw flashy art-deco bars and restaurants.

Market Street was packed with every kind of personality, all of them attractive and captivating, rushing from one place to another.

The noise level of the city added to the excitement. There were cable car bells, chimes from clocks and churches, traffic noises, screaming fire engines, people shouting about Jesus, fog horns, and ferry boat whistles. But above all else, there were men, handsome, successful-looking men. I wanted to grow up quickly and join these men—whoever they were—in their important endeavors. Perhaps here I could find a place of my own. Maybe I would even be accepted as one of them. It was a fantastic city and I wanted to be part of it.

San Francisco was about fifty miles from San Jose, a long way to go on a bike. However, San Mateo was more like 30, and it had a streetcar I could take into the city for only ten cents. Several times I biked to San Mateo, caught the streetcar, and spent the day exploring San Francisco. At this time I was only about twelve years old. One day, my father had to go to into the city on company business and, half-way there, driving along on the Bay Shore Highway, he passed me bicycling at top speed on my way to the same destination. When I got home that night I heard plenty about it from him. But seeing me there had made him secretly proud of me. Later on I learned from others that he bragged about his kid, "...bicycling all the way to San Francisco!" He apparently hadn't guessed about the San Mateo streetcar. That incident somehow changed his mind about me, at least a little. I was now more than just a mamma's boy; I was strong and independent enough to go to San Francisco on my own. Hearing what he had said about me made me feel much closer to him.

However, staying close to Father proved to be an impossible dream. Too often, I found myself caught between him and Mother. Occasionally one of them would ask me, "Who do you love the best?" What a terrible question to ask a child! If I said

"Mother," my father would withdraw, stung that I was siding against him. If I said "Father," my mother would angrily blurt out, "After all I do for you! How can you be so ungrateful?" I could not win. I usually answered, "I love you both," but that wasn't good enough. One or the other would say, "You've got to *choose!*"

How I hated this question when it came up! I think Mother felt ownership of me because Father was always gone, and she had to deal on her own with my emotional outbursts and destructive behavior. I doubt that my father ever really expected me to say that I loved him most. Yet secretly, I did. He was not the one who made my life unpleasant, it was Mother. She always started the fights and—whatever Father's sins were, they happened away from home and out of my sight—I continued to blame her for our unhappy existence.

I have now come to believe that totally absent fathers are less harmful than emotionally absent fathers. When a father is gone, a child can fantasize about what it would be like if he were there. However, with an emotionally absent father, that kind of dreaming is impossible. I think my father was gone enough of the time that I was able to have a few positive fantasies about him.

One day he took me aside and said, "I'm going to divorce your mother." I turned this around in my mind. I would be left alone with Mother. Sure, I loved her, but the primary dream of my life was to have a relationship with my father. I exclaimed, "I will go with you! I'll keep house for you, and I'll take care of you!" He didn't respond. Unfortunately, he hadn't asked if I wanted to go with him. That night, Father packed his bags, said goodbye to Mother and headed down the front steps to his car. I thought surely he would turn around, catch my eye and say, "Frank, are you going with me?" But he didn't; he just got in the car and backed it out of the driveway. My heart was broken. I ran down the steps and after the car crying, "Take me! Take me!"

Father couldn't hear me. Mother was devastated. The question, "Who do you love the most?" had been answered that night, once and for all. Mother had felt entitled to my devotion—she was quite sure she'd earned it. Now, she felt utterly betrayed. It took a long time for that wound to heal, if it ever really did. In a few days, Father returned, as if nothing had happened. As always, the fighting continued. But I never wanted to get close to my father again; that hurt was too deep to mend.

Summer passed, September rolled around again, and the misery of school returned. A furtive glance around homeroom on my first day of junior high school confirmed that some of the kids from grammar school were still there, but many former schoolmates had transferred to other schools. Just as I was wondering who was there and who wasn't—and how those changes might affect my social standing—the classroom door opened and in walked the most beautiful boy I had ever seen. There was a quiet gasp from the girls, and even the boys took notice. With blonde hair and bright blue eyes, he made an immediate impression on everybody. Since he arrived after class had begun, the teacher said to him, "Please introduce yourself to the class."

"My name is Will Connelly," this golden boy said with a smile. "I transferred here from Lowell Grammar School."

For the rest of the week, Will remained the center of attention. Who would he deign to be among his friends? He was cool and confident, giving the impression that he had every situation under control. While he was the primary topic of the girls' conversations, the boys also wanted to be seen with him, to bask in his reflected glory. But Will kept his distance, treating everyone with a cool reserve. His manner seemed to say, "I am self-sufficient; I don't need anybody." At times he was abrupt and rude to the other guys, while he ignored the girls completely.

But to my amazement, a strange thing was happening. It was becoming apparent to everyone that, somehow, I had become Will's friend. I couldn't believe my good fortune. In hindsight, through the eyes of a realistic adult, I'm inclined to think that Will chose me as his friend because he wanted a subordinate—somebody he could use and control. Well, believe me, I was quite willing to be used and controlled, if Will was to be the one doing it. True, he was sarcastic and often belittled me, but from my needy perspective, even his put-downs were treasures.

This new friendship wasn't perfect and caused me more pain and disappointment than I could have predicted, but still, it lasted for the next six or seven years. Will and I shared many exciting adventures together. Devoted as I was to the Tom Swift adventure books, not to mention my own fantasy life, Will became my Tom Swift, and I was his sidekick, Ned Newton.

Mother saw what was happening. She recognized that I was madly in love with Will and she tried her best to keep us apart. She often argued that Will had complete control over my life. Of course, I denied it, but at the same time, I knew she was right. In any case, Will was banned from our house. Mother never invited him to any of my birthday parties; she didn't want to encourage our relationship. Mother was afraid Will would teach me things I shouldn't know, and I was afraid that he wouldn't! Mother had an ally in her battle against Will—Uncle Charlie. Charlie was upset that my time was monopolized by Will and that I wasn't as available to go with him to explore his latest discoveries. In the first years of our friendship, being with Will took precedence over everyone and everything in my life, which bruised Uncle Charlie's feelings.

I recall my twelfth birthday as a big event. Mother had gone all-out, planning and preparing a lavish celebration that featured a variety of desserts, games, prizes, and even a photographer, who sent my picture to the local paper where it was published in the social column. All this was small-town stuff, but it was fun. At twelve, my relatives and my mother's friends pronounced me the most beautiful little boy they had ever seen. My aunts pronounced me "darling" and "a handsome little man."

My thirteenth birthday was another story. There was no party. Just a few relatives showed up, and no one could call me "a handsome little man" any longer. At twelve, I had been a short, sturdy little fellow, with a perfect build. By the time I turned thirteen, the winds of change had not blown favorably upon my body. I was a mess. I was six feet tall, thin as a rail, and my former beautiful complexion had been replaced by a mass of pimples. Worst of all, my nose decided to grow out of all proportion to the rest of my body. If I'd had low self-esteem before, at thirteen, it reached the bottom of the pit.

My thirteenth year was a traumatic in other ways, too. Mother decided that she needed to expand her, "Don't fool around!" message. Nothing had happened to me in the subway, but now that I was more mobile, she broadened the horizons of her fears. She warned me to avoid all parks and railroad tracks. I found this warning to be just as intriguing as the old subway story. So that's where the missing subway men had gone! Now I was bicycling to every park in the city and walking alone down miles of railroad tracks, but to no avail.

Meanwhile, it was a fearful time for America. The war in Europe wasn't going well and everyone was talking about our country being invaded. Hitler had revealed his plans for the American people, and even to me as a kid, his intentions were very frightening. We heard he intended to send all the food in the U.S.A. to Europe, hoping to starve us all to death. As the war progressed, people became increasingly paranoid and neighbors became suspects.

It was rumored that the Japanese gardener who lived around the corner was sending secret signals to Japanese warplanes. He was suspected of cutting the lawns in such a way that they spelled out Japanese characters. When the government suddenly came and hauled him and his family off to an internment center, it appeared that the rumors had been true. Next, the German baker was accused of spying and his store was boycotted. Those were days when mistrust gripped us all.

Meanwhile, San Jose came alive with defense factories and servicemen. Occasionally some of these servicemen would whistle at me. Naturally, I wondered what it meant and asked myself, *Do they think I'm a girl?* I didn't look like a girl, and maybe they were just being friendly, but I remained puzzled.

Since I'd had no consistent male role model in my life, I may have been slightly effeminate, but I wasn't aware of it. Will was a rugged, manly type of guy and I don't think he would have associated with me if I had been overly girlish. Looking back at it now, I would guess that at least some of these service men were gay and recognized something in me that I had yet to realize about myself. This sixth sense is now sometimes called "gaydar."

Gay mannerisms are of two distinct types. One type simply involves effeminate speech and gestures. These come from having only mother as a role model, and can affect gay and straight males alike. The other gay mannerisms involve an array of affectations. These are artificial gestures and patterns of speech, which are intended to attract attention. Effeminacy is next to impossible to change without the intervention of one or several straight males. But the affectations can be ended almost immediately, since they are consciously chosen for effect. I know I had no affectations, but I am unsure about the effeminacy. It is even possible that those sailors were struck by Will's good body and good looks, and I just happened to be there.

By that time, Will and I had been friends for nearly two years. Of course he had noticed the dramatic changes in my physical condition, and decided to do something about it. He had enrolled in the YMCA and was lifting weights and using other exercise equipment, bringing his body nearer to perfection every day. Meanwhile, my string-bean of a body seemed to be going in the opposite direction. Will insisted that I also enroll at the "Y" and begin weight lifting. I wanted to be close to Will, so naturally I agreed. Besides, I didn't want him to be embarrassed to be seen with me. I tried my best to improve my physique and to some extent, I succeeded.

During those years, my relationship with my Uncle Charlie had changed. For one thing, he had moved out. He and my grandmother had found a place to rent for fifteen dollars a month and had left behind the chaos of our home. Because Charlie had lived with us, I think he understood why I was such an isolated, lonely child. He always tried to cheer me up. I loved Uncle Charlie and felt guilty about spending so much time with Will and ignoring him. However, now that I had my bicycle, I could go visit Uncle Charlie when Will had other things to do. I usually found him with teenage boys. One part of me was jealous of these boys, wanting him all for myself, while another side of me also wanted to know these handsome, athletic boys.

Uncle Charlie, however, was determined to keep those other boys and his favorite nephew worlds apart. Our activities now involved visiting museums and events that had a scientific bent. One of the things that attracted people to my uncle was his knowledge of science. In his home, he had a small, working model of a steam engine, along with electrical devices that rang bells and gave people shocks. Uncle Charlie was anything but dull. One day he handed me a brochure announcing that a science exhibition was coming to town.

The folder showed a man standing on a transformer with a million volts of electricity passing through him and great sheets of lightening-like flames flaring out of his upraised hands. This spectacular event was called "Irwin Moon's

Sermons from Science." I could hardly wait to see it. When the night of the show finally arrived, Uncle Charlie and I had excellent seats. I didn't notice that it was sponsored by the Christian business men of our town in conjunction with Moody Bible Institute. We were there because both my uncle and I loved anything that had to do with science.

The show did not disappointment us. It was a thrilling demonstration of electrical wonders. But that really wasn't the point. Irwin Moon was there to introduce a message I had never heard before—that God offered every one of us salvation from sin through His Son, the Lord Jesus Christ. This point came through powerfully. On that special night, while thrilling us with scientific wonders, Dr. Moon also introduced Jesus in a way that cut through all my preconceived ideas about religion. For me, this new revelation did not have much to do with the words that Moon spoke—they were confusing and, truthfully, I had no idea what he was talking about. But the Spirit of the Lord entered my life that night. It was like a river of warmth and comfort flowing into my lonely, rejected heart. I had a feeling of well-being that I'd never experienced before.

Who was this Jesus who promised love, acceptance, and an assurance that things were going to be all right for me? Could that be true, even though I still faced daily ridicule? I had to know more. At the end of his presentation, Irwin Moon called for people to come to the front of the auditorium and "accept Jesus." I was too shy to go forward. Besides, I didn't know what it meant. What would I be getting into? What would my parents, family, and friends think? What about Will? I was quite sure none of them would be the least bit happy about it. Yet, in my heart, I silently responded, *Whoever You are Jesus, I do accept You.*

I left the "Sermons in Science" event determined to find out more about Jesus, but I was immediately in conflict. My hormones were working overtime by then, and I couldn't stop thinking about my sexual cravings. At the same time, I also wanted to know more about Jesus and to find out about that warm, hopeful feeling I'd experienced at Irwin Moon's science event. What had that been all about?

On the last day of school that year, we were released from class at 11 in the morning. Our parents didn't expect us home until early afternoon, so Will suggested that he and I go with two other guys to play poker at John's house. It was only later that he mentioned it would be strip poker, but it was still fine with me. Maybe this would be my chance to get some further information about sex. In the past, I had asked Will a lot of questions, but he would never give me the answers I was looking for. He always said, "Yeah, someday we'll talk about that." I was hoping this strip-poker game might turn out to be that "someday."

I had never played cards before, and the other guys had to show me how. I think they had already agreed among themselves that I would be the loser of the game. I had never heard of strip poker, but I soon found out what it was, because about an hour into the game, I was sitting there completely naked. I was worried that this new game might be for keeps, and I didn't know what I was going to do if I didn't get my clothes back.

Right about then, Will started a conversation about how dumb I was. He mocked me to the others, saying, "Frank doesn't even know what masturbation is." They all looked blank. They wanted to agree that I was dumb, but they weren't willing to admit that they had no idea what Will was talking about either. The next hour was filled with sex-talk, and I learned just about everything I'd wanted to know. Eventually we heard John's mother's car coming up the driveway. There was a mad scramble to get our clothes on and put the furniture back in place. She had a fit about her house being torn up, but didn't seem to have a clue what we had been doing.

I loved Will like I had never loved anyone else, but he and I were not in any way sexually involved. He didn't seem to be sexual with either girls or boys, even though he was very macho. Whether something sexual might have developed during our poker game I will never know, since John's mother cut it short. I was just glad to finally get some answers to my questions about sex.

But I still had questions about Jesus.

Since my tenth year, I had been taking piano lessons. I knew that Mrs. Hughes, my piano teacher, played the organ at her church. I couldn't help but wonder if she might be a Christian. I told her about Sermons from Science and her face brightened up. It was quickly evident that she knew about Jesus. She talked about Him being her "personal Savior" and she explained to me His two great commandments—to love God with all our hearts, and to love other people as we love ourselves. I tried to communicate something of the good feeling I had experienced as I listened to Irwin Moon. Mrs. Hughes understood immediately.

"Jesus came into your heart that night, Frank," she smiled.

This was amazing! She had just confirmed what I'd believed all along—something really had happened to me. "But, Frank," she went on to say, "there's something else you need to do. You must publicly accept Christ into your heart. That's very important." I was trying to imagine how I would do that when she continued, "So, why don't you come to church with me next Sunday? You can sit with me on the organ bench and maybe you'll begin to understand what it means to be a Christian."

That next Sunday I did just that. I went to church with Mrs. Hughes and sat on the organ bench beside her, turning the music pages as she played. There was something about that good-hearted Christian woman that made me feel protected and loved. I never really learned much at church about Jesus or Christianity, but as the weeks went by, Mrs. Hughes explained more and more to me about following Jesus. Throughout my life, I never really lost the longing for Him that had come into my heart the night of the science show.

I loved organ music and begged my mother to let me take organ lessons. It was very difficult for her to come up with money for the additional expense, and at times Mrs. Hughes had to wait to be paid. But, already playing the piano, I now quickly learned how to play the organ. All that time, Mrs. Hughes radiated the love of Jesus. I delighted in the joy and peace that emanated from her personality. I also got acquainted with a few of the church's young people. Although I learned nothing about Jesus from them, in the process I did lose a small part of my emotional dependency on Will.

In a humiliating episode, Will had shamed me one time too many, and I remained very offended with him. I had kept a diary for a few years. In one of our conversations, Will had asked me to tell him what was in it, but I wouldn't tell him. I always kept it hidden because it was full of my secrets, including passages describing how much I loved Will. One day when he was at my house with several of his friends, Will decided to search for my diary. His friends egged him on and he finally found it. I tried to tear it out of his hands, but he was stronger than I. Then, to my abject embarrassment, he proceeded to read it aloud to the other guys. They acted uncomfortable with what he was doing, but made no effort to stop him. At first they laughed, but then the shocking message sank in: Frank is queer. Frank is in love with a boy.

Everyone fell silent. When they stopped giving Will the laughs he wanted, he announced off-handedly that he had to be going. Everyone followed him out the door and I was left feeling ashamed and utterly exposed. While the others may have thought all along that I was queer, I hadn't yet made that determination for myself. I was just a guy in love with a guy. Strangely enough, Will was soon hanging around as if he had done nothing wrong. I continued to spend time with him, but

I never quite recovered from that incident. I found it impossible to trust him again.

Now, however, thanks to Mrs. Hughes and her church, I had a few other people in my life. I was invited to wonderful picnics and barbeques. For the first time ever, I felt accepted and had a sense of belonging. The church's minister, Pastor Turner, was a kindly, very lovable old man. One Sunday he preached about baptism—something I'd never heard about before. I decided that the next time the church had a baptismal service, I would be baptized. When I told my family, not unexpectedly, a huge argument ensued.

My favorite uncle, Charlie, said that I was going in a "dangerous" direction. Uncle Bruce said that religion was sucking me in and that my mother should step in and stop it. Mother, on the other hand, seemed to mildly approve of my new spiritual direction. In fact, one Sunday she talked my father into attending church with her and me. He was very out of place, extremely uncomfortable, and never returned. Mother herself only went to church with me on one other occasion, but she seemed somewhat happy about my involvement there. Perhaps she would have endorsed anything that could keep me away from Will. When my baptism was scheduled, I asked my mother to be baptized with me. To my surprise, she agreed. On a Wednesday night, both my mother and I were baptized. Mrs. Hughes was very excited about all this and she announced that I was also ready to play the organ for a church service. Things were looking up for me, and I was grateful.

Despite my commitment to walking with Jesus, my battle with hormones, same-sex attraction, and temptation had begun in earnest. And unfortunately, it wasn't long before my new church family was no longer a safe haven from homosexuality. A few months after my baptism, the church board decided they needed a younger, more dynamic pastor. After more than twenty years of service to his beloved church, poor old Pastor Turner was fired. The old man who had baptized me was gone and in his place appeared a handsome, 30-year-old, former youth pastor.

Pastor Connors was a short, stocky, dark-haired bundle of energy. If it was change they were after, the church board definitely got what they wanted. Pastor Connors' focal point was *youth*, and to him the older members were only there to finance his projects. Aside from writing tithe checks and providing "special offerings," he thought they should step aside and stay out of his way.

Soon construction workers were building a new wing for youth-group activities. The room once used for adult Sunday school became Pastor Connor's expansive new office. Some of the elderly members who found this youth focus hard to deal with left the church, complaining as they left. Middle-aged members were willing to put up with the inconveniences since they felt the new direction brought energy to the congregation. Pastor Connor also wanted Mrs. Hughes out of the church because she was too old and didn't fit the profile he wanted to project. He was clever about it. When she unwittingly advised him that I was ready to play publicly, he assigned me to the Wednesday night service. He added the promise that I would someday play for the Sunday service as well. I was horrified when I realized that he planned to replace Mrs. Hughes with me.

Pastor Connors gave me permission to practice on the church organ any day of the week, and I often did so after school. There were usually around a dozen young people at church then, some doing special projects, some planning parties and outings, and some just enjoying the social scene. While Pastor Connor didn't welcome adult church members into his office, it was always open to boys. He made sure everything appeared on the up-and-up by consulting with girls downstairs in the foyer. I was probably around more than any of the other young people. Besides practicing on the organ every afternoon I was also there Wednesday nights, Sunday mornings, and at the Sunday evening youth-group meetings. I seemed to be one of Pastor Connors' prime projects. He never failed to ask me how I was doing. "And, Frank," he often inquired, "is there anything personal you'd like to discuss with me? If so, please feel free..."

One afternoon he rounded up all the boys. "I want all of you in my office right now," he announced. Once we got into his office, he began a lengthy talk on how young men need sex education. He went on to say that some boys are born with sex defects that would prevent them from having a normal sex life when they married. He then asked us all to drop our pants so he could examine our genitals. Some he declared normal. Others, he said, would require further study; perhaps they were normal, but perhaps not. I was able to slip out of the room before it was my turn to be examined. Yet at the same time, I saw nothing strange about the pastor's conduct, and assumed that he was just doing his job. I did hope, however, that his examination of private parts would not happen again. I was so grateful to have escaped that embarrassing situation. But in fact, I hadn't.

A few days later, Pastor Connors found me practicing the organ. "I want to talk with you about your playing on Wednesday nights," he said quietly. I was immediately afraid I had done something wrong. Perhaps I had missed some notes and hadn't realized it. Whatever it was, I didn't want to jeopardize my wonderful job, so off to his office I went. Pastor Connors' new shelves were by now filled with books on psychology and a few sex manuals.

He made a brief comment about my Wednesday night organ playing, letting me know he was pleased and that there would be no changes. That was a huge relief to me. Then he asked if I would like to discuss anything of a sexual nature. "No," I told him. He wouldn't take no for an answer and said he needed to examine me. But when he saw that I was resistant, he backed off. He knew just how far he could go, and he didn't want to push it in case word of his "examinations" got out. He talked for awhile about masturbation and ejaculation and then let me go back to my practice session. I hoped he had noticed how uncomfortable he had made me feel, and that he wouldn't bring up sex again. That was not to be the case.

The fact was, since I had come to know Jesus, I was not so interested in men. I had tried my best to put aside my sexual desires. And some of my "deficits" had been resolved. I had male attention from Pastor Connors, and the boys in the church's youth group accepted me as an equal member. Although I continued to have sexual impulses and a fantasy life, many of my needs for love and attention were being filled non-sexually. And I certainly didn't want sex with my pastor; I was wise enough even then to know it would bring about a moral conflict I couldn't handle.

In gym class at school, the other boys called me names. I had no idea what those names meant, although they were clearly ridiculing me. But the church youth group offset the rejection I experienced at school. The church kids recognized that I had a "special relationship" with Pastor Connors, but for some reason they didn't seem to think it was strange. They just tried to get inside information from me about what might happen next in the restructuring of our church.

One evening, I came home to find my whole extended family gathered at our house. They were all shouting and arguing, and it sounded like everyone was talking at once. Clearly something had happened, but no one seemed to want to tell me. I heard my father saying, "Let him rot in jail, the pervert!"

My mother was emphatic, "We just can't do that! We've got to do something to help him."

My grandmother kept repeating that this was all a mistake, that her son wouldn't do any such thing, "You have got to tell them they are wrong!" It seemed everyone was demanding that my father do something, but about what?

Suddenly, I heard Uncle Charlie's name mentioned. I joined in the shouting, "Why is Uncle Charlie in jail? What happened?"

At first no one paid much attention to me or what I was trying to find out. Then my mother took me aside and said, "Uncle Charlie has been arrested for fooling around with boys. You have got to tell me the truth, has Uncle Charlie ever touched you?"

I said, "No!" And that was the truth. But in that same instant, I remembered all the teenage boys who constantly surrounded him. It took several more hours before my father said, "Okay, OKAY! I'll see what I can do, but you know very well that after that kidnapping, rape, and murder affair, nobody in this town wants to help a queer. You can bet on it! And besides, I don't want all this reflecting on our family. I'm going to try to keep it quiet, but to tell you the truth, I don't care what happens to him."

Predictably, the story couldn't be kept quiet. The newspapers printed every detail they could find, and gave a rundown on every person in Charlie's family. All our names were mentioned. After seeing that, Father decided not to help Charlie, and the family arguments started all over again. All the men Father worked with wanted to know more about the case. Father hated queers and he was extremely humiliated. Even my schoolmates were asking me if it was true. I had no idea what to say to them.

Eventually we found out what had happened. Uncle Charlie enjoyed lavishing gifts on boys. I knew it was true—I had often been the beneficiary of his largesse. This generosity, however, had given the impression to two of the boys Charlie had molested that he had money. They had blackmailed Uncle Charlie and he'd had no way of meeting their demands, so they turned him into the police. Finally, my father could bear the disgrace no longer. He told my mother's family that he would intervene and see what he could do.

As it turned out, his special friendship with the sheriff gave him some leverage. So did some very interesting information that Father had never revealed to others outside our family: that the sheriff had ordered the jail doors left unlocked the night of the hanging, thus giving the lynch mob easy access to the two rapist/murderers. After a private discussion with my father, the sheriff quickly arranged to drop the charges against Uncle Charlie, with the understanding that Charlie would leave town and never come back again.

While he was in jail, I sent a letter to Uncle Charlie. I wrote that I felt sorry for him and was not judging him like the rest of the family. I expressed my love and compassion for him and told him that Jesus would forgive him if he asked Him to. I promised to visit him, whether or not he was in jail. And, I vowed that whatever happened, he and I would always be friends. Uncle Charlie kept that letter until he died.

After he was chased out of town, Charlie settled in Oakland, California, where he got the best job he'd ever had. He went to work at the docks, where his engineering skills were just what the shipbuilders were looking for. I visited him as often as my family would let me and he frequently had a box of change waiting for me, sometimes as much as fifteen or twenty dollars. It was a lot of money for a boy my age. He also joined a religious cult in Oakland, but I always held onto the hope that someday he would accept Jesus.

Uncle Charlie never approached me in any sexual way. We never spoke about homosexuality, even though in later years he could see the direction my life was taking. I can't fully explain why Uncle Charlie never molested me, but I think it was because he really loved me and didn't want to face the separation from me if such an offense were discovered. Also, even in the gay lifestyle, there are certain situations that are off-limits. Just as I didn't see Pastor Connors as a potential sexual partner, Uncle Charlie probably didn't see me that way either.

It wasn't long after Uncle Charlie's departure from San Jose, near my fourteenth birthday, that my father came home from work one day in great pain. He had strained himself pushing a heavy cart loaded with iron, which he had done in an act of kindness, trying to help another man who wasn't strong enough for the job.

The next day Father went to the doctor. He was told that he had suffered a simple hernia and that he would be fine after a relatively minor operation and a few days in the hospital. The day of the surgery arrived and after it was over, the doctor left without a word. In a few hours my father regained consciousness and seemed fine. The following day he was in good spirits, and the third day he was asking the nurses if he could go home. But later that afternoon, Father began to feel weak. The duty nurse called the doctor, and after a brief examination he nervously told Mother that he needed to consult a specialist. The following morning, before the out-of-town specialist could arrive, we received a call from the hospital saying that if we wanted to see Father alive, we'd better hurry. We rushed to the hospital.

At first glance, Father seemed all right. He was a little drowsy, but he explained that he was just tired and needed more sleep. He told us not to worry; he would be coming home soon. Then all at once, right in the middle of a sentence, Father lost consciousness. His eyes fixed themselves on the ceiling. A nurse came in, checked his pulse, and gently lowered his eyelids. He was gone.

The specialist arrived, but it was too late. He conferred with the family doctor and afterward they talked to my mother and me. He hadn't said a word about it before, but now our doctor informed us that there had been "something strange" about Father's internal tissue when he was sewing him up; it had been abnormally soft, and the stitches hadn't held properly. He added that if penicillin had been available he probably could have saved Father, but the war had taken all the supplies and it was unavailable for civilian use.

We had questions, theories, doubts, and even a few suspicions, but the doctor made it clear that he had no more to say. In the end, there was nothing we could do. We simply had to carry on, which is what we eventually did. We never found out precisely what had robbed us of Father. Whatever ailment cost him his life remains a mystery, even today.

Mother. (c.1949)

Uncle Charlie

Chapter Three

Dangerous Liasons

Minutes after my father died, Mother and I left the hospital. We were both in a state of disbelief and despair. Instead of going directly home, I made my way to my church, where I knelt in tears before the altar. Some of my grief came from knowing that my father and I would never really know each other. Even though over time I had gradually detached myself from him, I'd always cherished a hope, deep in my heart, that eventually he and I would be close. That possibility was gone forever. I also felt a heavy weight on my shoulders, realizing that I would have to take my father's place as the man of the family. After a time of kneeling and weeping, I felt God dry my tears. Somewhere in my heart, I sensed His reassurance that He understood my grief and loss. I remember explaining to God that my father was gone.

"I need *You* to be my Father now," I told Him.

Mother had walked to and from the hospital, which was about a mile from our house, while I had gone on my bicycle.

She and I now arrived home about the same moment. She was in a state of shock, repeating, "I can't believe it!" over and over. Despite all her anger, my father had been her childhood sweetheart. Like me, Mother had always clung to the hope that life with him would get better. She had long cherished the dream that romance would return to her marriage.

She and I clung to one another. We wept together. "I don't know what to do now! What are we going to do?" she asked me.

"I don't know," I tried to comfort her, "but somehow we'll make it." What I didn't express was an idea that had suddenly awakened in my mind: *I may be only fourteen years old, but I can do a better job of running the family than Father did.* I quickly banished that treasonous thought. Still, I knew I could take care of my mother. I silently vowed to make her life easier.

I don't know how word got around town, but within an hour, people were knocking on our front door. One of them was Pastor Connors. "I'm so sorry!" he said, echoing the others. Neither my mother nor I had any idea how to respond appropriately. She simply kept repeating, "I can't believe it. I just can't believe it!"

As the hours passed, reality began to sink in. When Mrs. Hughes appeared, I suddenly was relieved and grateful. I felt protected and secure in her arms. She was so important to me now, and I knew she would guide me in my new role. Like everyone else, she tried to encourage me by saying, "You're the man of the house now." At that moment, she and Pastor Connors were my two anchors in life. But while I felt comfortable and safe with Mrs. Hughes, I was already a little bit afraid of Pastor Connors.

Mother and I had no idea how to organize a funeral. Thankfully, Pastor Connors made the necessary arrangements for us. On the day of the service, a wide mix of people showed up, some from my church, several of Father's drinking buddies, and a host of relatives, including a few I had never met.

Will and his friends attended and I was so glad to see them. After the funeral however, Will never mentioned my loss; he was his usual aloof, self-contained self. I was drawn to his strength of personality, but wounded by it as well. In some ways, however, I think he was a role model for me during this difficult time. Will never discussed his own father, and my mother and I often wondered what had happened to him. Later, we heard that Will's father was in prison. When Will would drop out of sight now and then, he and his mother had been visiting his father.

Following the funeral, I watched as Father's casket was lowered into the freshly-dug soil. It was more than my emotions could take. People tossed flowers on top of it, then walked away. They paid their respects, disappeared, and some of them were gone for good. I was so shattered that I didn't want to face anyone. Nonetheless, Mother and I spent the entire afternoon and evening hosting everyone who came to our house.

While she and I were trying to deal with our sorrows and uncertainties about the future, our relatives were ransacking our house, determined to acquire something as a "remembrance" of my father. His brother took my father's guns (I was rather glad to have them out of the house); others took his clothing; and several of the men congregated in the basement and divided his tools among themselves, never thinking that Mother and I might need them to repair our house. While they were down there, the men made a shocking discovery—they found a case of dynamite left over from Father's mining days. They promptly took it out to a field and detonated it.

I had seen that same case in the basement many times, but had mistaken it for a similar-looking case of flares my uncle had brought home from the railroad. From time to time, we kids had played with those flares, lighting them at night in the backyard. I can only imagine what might have happened if we had mistakenly lit one those sticks of dynamite instead! When I heard about the dynamite, it brought to my mind the many trips our family had made to the mine, with boxes of dynamite on the floorboards behind the driver's seat of Father's car. It frightened me then, and it frightens me even more thinking about it today!

Once everyone finally left—with most of Father's personal possessions in hand—I was able to reflect a little on what had happened and how I was feeling. Even then, I was aware of God's presence. And I do believe God answered my heartfelt prayer, asking Him to be my Father. I can truthfully say, to this day, that He has never forsaken me. Even when I've made very bad choices and have eagerly pursued my own plans, He has saved me again and again. In the darkest hours of my life, I have always known that I have a Father who loves me.

Still, Mother and I had no idea what to do once the funeral was over and our friends and family had all gone back to their daily lives. Who would support us? Mother still had her Avon job, but it was only a small percentage of what we needed to keep us going. During those difficult days, Pastor Connors was amazingly helpful. He came to our house several times; he hugged me and told me how sorry he was about the death of my father. He seemed so loving. I remember wishing my father had been like that.

Meanwhile, we had legal issues to deal with, and Mrs. Hughes knew just what to do. She suggested that we see her brother-in-law, a lawyer, and he proved to be indispensable. He determined that Father's employer had provided a life insurance policy for all their employees. He also found that Social Security would send a check every month if there were an underage child in the family. Since I was fourteen, I quali-fied. It wasn't much money, but every little bit helped.

In a few weeks, the insurance settlement check arrived. For a short time, Mother and I felt happy and wonderfully cared for. Then came a giant let-down. One day in the mail, Mother received notice that an outstanding loan had to be paid in full. Neither of us could understand why or when this loan had been taken out; Mother knew nothing about it. We visited the loan company and they showed us the original papers, which were signed with my mother's name. She was dumbfounded. "I never signed that paper!" she whispered to me. I was quite familiar with my mother's signature. This was not it.

We both knew the loan was precariously close to the amount of the insurance check. We told the clerk that we would be back; right then we didn't have enough money to clear the loan. This was a serious dilemma for my mother. Should she refuse to pay off the loan because it wasn't her signature? She knew this would make my father a criminal in the eyes of the community. Or, should she quietly pay it off, and leave us without the support the insurance check would have brought?

Judging by the date of the loan, it seemed to have been a leftover from Father's disastrous mining days. "I thought we were finished with all that!" Mother exclaimed. Our lawyer quietly informed her that she was probably responsible anyway, since husband and wife share liability for any family debts. In a bitter finish to a troubled marriage, Mother paid off the loan. As for me, I was enraged. This was the final straw. How could my father leave us so vulnerable and unprotected?

"What should we do now?" The question became more urgent. Our short time of feeling secure was over. After paying off the loan, we didn't have enough to live on. One morning, Mother proposed the only solution she could think of. "We'll have to lease the house to somebody and go live with your grandmother."

I didn't object. I had recently been to Los Angeles to visit my father's mother, and I liked the area she lived in. But then Mother went on to say, "You'll have to go down there right away so your school year won't be interrupted. I'll come down and join you once I get the house ready to rent and have finished up all the legal paperwork."

I was half-man, half-child. Before leaving, I tried to help my mother, but I did more harm than good, creating unnecessary problems for her. For example, in earlier years I had ripped up the front stairs and they had been poorly repaired. Now I tried to replace them, but after removing the steps, I had no idea how to put them back, and Mother had to enter and exit by the back stairway. After I left, she hired a carpenter to finish the job, but the repairs were costly and depleted what little money we had.

Grandmother lived in Lynwood, California, a Los Angeles suburb that lay at the crossroads of two transportation corridors, about half way between LA and Long Beach. From my perspective, Grandmother's house was ideally located. The bus to Long Beach and the amusement zone known as the "Pike" was just around the corner, and out in front was the light-rail line that ran into downtown Los Angeles. Unfortunately, Grandmother had her own ideas about where I would spend my time, and her plans didn't include either destination.

It wasn't long after my arrival that I began feeling depressed and very much alone. I missed Mrs. Hughes, the young people at church, Mother—and most of all—Will. I wrote to Will almost every day and waited in vain to receive his responses by return mail. Later on, I discovered that he had passed my letters around, mocking me and making fun of my heartfelt words. My homesickness seemed to have given Will and his buddies a good laugh.

Meanwhile, I was quickly learning that Grandmother didn't approve of the way my mother had raised me. She thought I was a spoiled brat. Noting that I was very self-sufficient and able to travel on my own, she decided to take me down a notch or two. I don't know if my father had confided in her about my years of destructive behavior, but for some reason she decided that I needed very strong discipline. This took various forms, which only served to make my life even more unbearable.

I didn't know anyone at my new school, but to my relief one boy took a liking to me. I liked him as well, and we were soon on our way to becoming friends. I was delighted when he asked me to spend the night at his home, which I wanted to do for two reasons. The good reason was that I very much needed a friend. I had no one to talk to or share things with and he was an excellent candidate. The bad reason was I had secret hopes that something sexual might happen if this boy and I shared a bed together.

I don't know how she could have read my mind, but Grandmother must have been thinking about the second reason when I asked her if I could stay overnight at the boy's house. She said, "No!" and her answer was both emphatic and final. The next day, when I told him I couldn't accept his invitation, the boy must have felt rejected. From that day on, he was no longer interested in being my friend. There wasn't much I could do—I simply had to obey my grandmother.

I had to ask her permission for everything I wanted to do, and almost invariably, the answer was, "No!" Seeing myself as the brave adventurer who often traveled alone from San Jose to San Francisco, I wanted to explore greater Los Angeles as well. Grandmother wouldn't even let me go to the corner store. She was determined to shape me up. I was determined to ship out as soon as possible.

I spent two months with my grandmother, and then my mother arrived. I confronted Mother with an ultimatum, "I don't care where we go; I am not living with Grandmother! Get me out of here!"

At first, my mother rejected my complaints, pointing out that we had no money. But before long, under my grandmother's iron rule, things weren't much better for Mother. Soon she was being disciplined, just as I was. My grandmother pointed out that she wanted Mother to know how "proper folks" lived.

Before long, Mother and I became co-conspirators. She would say, "I'll distract your grandmother while I'm helping her with her chores. You slip out and do whatever you want to do." Sometimes this worked. Either Grandmother didn't notice I was gone, or she needed my mother's help and kept her complaints to herself. Other times she did notice, and we both got a tongue-lashing. Mother and I now found that we had something in common: a mutual hatred of Grandmother.

The control increased until Mother and I couldn't even talk to each other in the house. Grandmother was always listening and—just to let us know she hadn't missed a thing—she would sometimes comment on our private conversations. We had to sneak off to a corner coffee shop to talk. We agreed that we would leave Grandmother when my school term was up, but where could we go? One day, I picked up a California map and we sat in the coffee shop dreaming and plotting a new course for our future. Mother and I both recalled how much we had enjoyed our beach vacations in Capitola, so we decided to head in that general direction and see what we could find.

June finally arrived, the school year ended, and as quickly as possible, we said goodbye to Grandmother and took the train to Santa Cruz. We arrived with no idea where we would live. All we knew for sure was that we had no money, so our accommodations had to be cheap. We were relieved to find a cottage just a block from the beach and the boardwalk. I was also delighted to be hired for my first job, working at a miniature motor-car race track. All I had to do was strap little kids into the cars, whip the rope that started the engine, give them a push, and off they went. I felt even more like a grown-up when I received my Social Security card.

Most of all I loved being away from Grandmother. But once again, in Santa Cruz I had to face a new school. In an all-too-familiar scene, I walked into the school yard the first day of class, not knowing a soul. It didn't take long for me to learn that the Santa Cruz kids were decidedly unfriendly. It was a small town and they had grown up together—no newcomer was welcome in their clique. After all I'd been through, this intimidating scene raised serious questions in my mind about how I would survive as a complete outsider.

Jeff was my answer.

Although he was one of my classmates and in the same grade as I, Jeff looked like a full-grown man; he was about six feet tall and weighed over two hundred pounds. I never knew why he was still in middle school. But Jeff befriended me, protected me, and defended me. I was soon to find out that he was the drug lord of Santa Cruz, but I really didn't care. When I was confronted by bullies, Jeff stood in front of me and fended off my attackers. I began to follow him around after school. I confidently marched with Jeff into the local pool hall, and sometimes tagged along with him to one of the seedy bars off of Santa Cruz's main drag.

As it turned out, Mother and I weren't long for Santa Cruz. We had a huge problem with our tenant in San Jose. She had signed a lease agreeing to pay us fifty dollars a month, and we desperately needed those fifty dollars—our rent in Santa Cruz was ten dollars more than that. But it was wartime. Rentals were controlled by a government rental board, and our tenant had successfully made an appeal to have her rent reduced. They cut the rent in half—to twenty-five dollars a month—leaving us financially high and dry. We could no longer afford our beach cottage. Mother had good reason to announce to me one afternoon, "Frank, we're going back to San Jose—and I don't want to hear any objections from you!"

Still, I have always believed that her real reason for fleeing Santa Cruz was to get me away from Jeff, my drug-lord friend. Sometime later, when I heard that he had been shot and killed, I felt sorrow because he had been a real friend to me. And a friend is all Jeff ever was. I never thought of him sexually, nor did I fall in love with him. I just genuinely appreciated his companionship and the protection he gave me.

Our return to San Jose was anything but easy. To begin with, our tenant refused to move. Once again, we had to contact our lawyer and wait months to get the dispute on the court calendar. Meanwhile, our Santa Cruz landlady wanted us off her property because the high-rent summer season was coming. Once again, we had no place to go. Finally, reluctantly, she extended our time.

When our day in court arrived at last, we won the case, but our tenant was given several months to vacate. Eventually we moved back in, but by then our tenant had vandalized the house. Before leaving, Mother had arranged a storage room in the attic where she kept many of our personal belongings. We discovered that the lock had been ripped off and the storage room was bare. Every keepsake and photo, and all of our personal papers—were gone. What I missed the most was my photo album. I had been given a camera when I was around five and had taken many pictures since that time. Not a scrap of those photographs remained. [1]

It didn't take long for Pastor Connors to express his delight in seeing me again. He was quick to tell me that Mrs. Hughes was retiring and that he wanted me to take her position as church organist. I knew very well that Mrs. Hughes wasn't retiring at all—she was being fired and there was nothing I could do about it. When I talked it over with her, she sadly acknowledged that it probably was time to leave the church anyway, and that she was glad I was the one who would be taking her place. "Frank, I can't teach you anymore than what you already know," she went on to say. "You need an organ teacher who is more advanced than I am. Maybe you can find someone in San Francisco."

---

[1] The two or three early photos included in this book were from my grandmother's belongings.

I made up my mind to do exactly that.

In a week or so, Pastor Connors tracked me down again, offering yet another new opportunity. "What is your financial situation?" he asked.

I told him Mother was going to go back to Avon but that I needed to look for work. He was quick to inform me that there was about to be a second retirement in our church. It seemed that the church janitor was leaving, too. I had always loved this old man and didn't want to take his job. I talked to him privately and asked if he was retiring. "No," he said. "Nobody's said anything to me about retiring!" Like Mrs. Hughes, however, he resigned himself to the news, conceding that he was getting tired of the job anyway, and that perhaps his departure was meant to be.

"We old folks don't fit into Pastor's plans," he explained. "So don't worry; I'm not sorry to go."

I couldn't believe the amount of money I was about to receive; it was the same salary my father had earned. If I saved my money, I could buy a car. More to the point, Mother and I would not have to worry about paying the bills.

I felt enormously glad to be back, but many of the kids I'd known before had left the church. Only a few remained and I soon became aware that this was no longer the happy, close-knit youth group we had once enjoyed. Those who remained were very critical of Pastor Connor. There were no more parties, barbeques, or special projects. This was not because Pastor Connor didn't suggest them and try to make them happen, but because the remaining kids held resentments against him and wouldn't cooperate. No one would say why, but I knew that some of them had been exposed to Pastor's sex talks. It was hard to imagine that they didn't know about the pants-dropping incidents, too.

Of course, now that we were back in San Jose, I went to see Will as soon as I could. I found him at home when I walked to his house one evening. I was puzzled because he acted like I had never been away. As I was leaving after that first visit, I asked him when we could get together again. "I'm pretty busy these days," he replied coolly. "I can't promise anything." Will remained indifferent to me until I told him I was saving up money to buy a car. After that, he suddenly became a close friend once again.

I probably was not the best janitor in the world. But Pastor Connors gently let me know when I didn't do my work up to his standards or forgot some corner of the church. What I really didn't like was cleaning up the women's restroom. I hated emptying the wastebaskets, which were stuffed with smelly sanitary napkins. I also disliked cleaning wash basins that were smeared with gooey make-up. I guess I must have had a low view of women in those days. At first, the church ladies complained that I was avoiding their area, but eventually I got over my disgust, did the cleaning properly, and the complaining stopped.

Before Mother and I had left San Jose after Father's death, my friends at church, along with Will and Uncle Charlie, had provided me with a social life that met my relational needs. Now Uncle Charlie was in another town, and my church friends were either scattered or too unhappy with Pastor Connors to be any fun. Will was around when he wanted to be, but in my view, not often enough. Once again, I began the search for a man who would give me affirmation and attention. It was difficult to get away since I had such a heavy schedule, but at times I managed to cut high school and go to San Francisco. There, I searched the museums and parks for men who would befriend me. I did make a few contacts, but they weren't what I was looking for.

I had never thought of Pastor Connor in a sexual way. He was my surrogate father, my employer, and God's man in my life. One day while working at church, he called me into his office. "Frank," he began, "I have something very important to talk to you about."

A worry flashed through my mind. *I am either a bad janitor or a bad organist. Which is it going to be?*

But that's not what Pastor Connors wanted to talk to me about. "Sit down and listen very carefully. What I have to say is about your life and your future." The pastor paused dramatically and fixed his eyes on me with an intense look on his face. "Frank, you are a homosexual."

A what? I had no idea what he was talking about.

"I don't know what that is, Pastor,"

"Frank, a homosexual is a man who loves other men."

I was seized with panic. *Oh God, he's seen me staring at boys!* Yet I couldn't remember doing that in his presence, so what was he talking about? Another possibility came into my mind. *Maybe he knows about Will, and how much I love him. But how could he know? I don't think he's ever met Will. Maybe someone told him…!* Yet another possibility occurred to me. *Does he know that I sometimes go to San Francisco looking for men? He is seeing through me as if I'm clear glass. Does God tell him these things?*

It was surprising that I had never heard the word "homosexual," not even when Uncle Charlie was in trouble. Mostly I just heard the word "queer." So, was Pastor Connors saying he thought I was queer? I knew I had crushes on boys, but I'd always assumed I would outgrow my crushes and become interested in girls.

Now it seemed that Pastor Connors was telling me that I would never like girls, that I was going to be this way for the rest of my life. *I've had so much bad news lately,* I thought, *I don't think I can handle one more negative thing.* I wanted to ask him why he thought so, but I guess I didn't want to hear the answer. Anyway, I was in shock and I said nothing. He could see that I wasn't taking this news very well. I could feel my body shrinking in shame. For some reason, at that moment, I didn't make the connection that his behavior with the church's young boys was homosexual behavior.

Instead, a different question popped into my head. *What is it I really want from the men I've been looking for? Is it sex?* I hadn't thought of that before. I knew I wanted touch. I wanted somebody to hold me—not Pastor Connors, however! I wanted a man to embrace me, to cuddle me. I didn't know what sex was like with a man, so I was unable to envision it. All I knew was that I wanted a man to love me.

Sitting there in complete misery, I assumed that the next thing Pastor Connors would say was that he didn't want me around the church anymore. Since I'd taken the janitorial job, he had sometimes walked over to me and given me a hug. Now I wondered if he would ever hug me again. I had to admit that I liked his embraces, even though I was also somewhat afraid of him. But never once had I entertained sexual thoughts about him.

"Frank, it's not a bad thing," I heard him saying with a smile. "No...much to the contrary! Homosexuality is a beautiful gift from God! God made you this way, Frank. He designed you. He knew you were going to be homosexual."

I couldn't help but think of poor Uncle Charlie, who had gone to jail for that very thing, before he was run out of town. *I'm not sure it's such a good thing,* I told myself. But I didn't argue.

Pastor Connors was far from finished. "When two men are in love with each other they are called lovers. Remember the Bible story of David and Jonathan, Frank? They were lovers, they loved each other. Ruth and Naomi were lovers, and even Jesus and John were lovers. And if Jesus had a lover, obviously you can see that it can't be a bad thing, but a blessing from God. Haven't you figured out that I am also homosexual? Yes, I have a wife and three kids, but you know I love men."

Then it hit me. He didn't love men at all. He loved *boys*, just like Uncle Charlie.

I couldn't help but wonder what my father would say about this situation. He had hated queers, that much I knew. But still, I comforted myself, *Pastor isn't upset with me. He thinks I am just like him.* In a way, it felt good to me that Pastor Connors understood me, or at least had some idea about what I was going through. But in the process, he was extinguishing my dream of someday being attracted to girls.

I'll listen to him, I thought, *but I'm never going to give up the hope of becoming normal.*

Because we shared the same secret, for a while after that conversation Pastor Connors and I became very close. What I know today, but didn't know then, is how perfectly I embodied the "pre-homosexual." I was fatherless. Not only was my father dead, but I had never been affirmed in my masculine identity by him. I was also a loner, not by choice, but because I'd been taunted and rejected by my peers. I was shy, I hated sports because I was uncoordinated, and I was fond of music and art. Small wonder this pastor came to the conclusion that I was homosexual. Today, however, I strongly believe that he could just as easily have directed me toward a heterosexual life and I would have gladly followed his lead. But he had other ideas.

Today I console myself with yet another possibility. In the grand scheme of things, maybe there was an unexpected benefit in my following a homosexual pathway for a while. Perhaps it made me able, later in life, to point out to others—others who also struggle with same-sex attraction—the way out of such a destructive lifestyle.

Life was certainly different those days. I remember a particularly dark spring afternoon, the skies pouring down drenching rain, when we heard that President Franklin Delano Roosevelt had died. It was April 12, 1945, and it seemed like the end of the world. Since Roosevelt had served three full terms and was embarking on his fourth, his presidency had amounted to almost my entire life span; I had never known any other President. We were still at war and the whole country seemed in a state of alarm.

Roosevelt had been a father figure to the nation. He frequently spoke on the radio, providing the nation with detailed reports on the war and other issues. In my youthful eyes, the whole country loved and trusted our President. And because he was such a larger-than-life character, few knew anything about the Vice President who would be taking his place. "What's going to happen now?" was on every tongue. The nation was blessed to have a powerful replacement, Harry Truman, who was not afraid to make hard choices. We were in the best of hands, but few realized it at first. Soon the war would be over and the nation would be swept up in an economic upsurge that would create wealth for almost anyone who was willing to work.

As for me, I was close to my sixteenth birthday when Pastor Connors once again called me into his office. He wanted to see if I was adjusting to my new identity. I never admitted that I was fighting this whole idea of being homosexual. I went along with him because I loved and needed him. I convinced him I was doing well, and he seemed satisfied.

In reality, I was conflicted. On the one hand, I simply could not get over the feeling that homosexuality was wrong. On the other hand, I continued to make my clandestine trips into San Francisco. I told myself that my search for a man didn't affirm my homosexuality, but only indicated that I was lonely and wanted male touch and attention.

Occasionally, some man or another would talk to me and, of course, I enjoyed that tremendously. Now and then, I attended organ concerts and afterward would make my way to the front to speak with the organist. Because I had been sent so often to the library during gym class, I had gained a good knowledge of art and sculpture. Now in museums, I would sometimes talk to men about the art we were viewing. I knew that Rodin had produced ten Thinker sculptures during his lifetime (a dozen or more were cast after his death), and where they were in the world. I knew much about various artists' lives, and other information that surprised nearly everyone I talked to.

At the same time, although I was aware of my increasing sexual desire, I'd had no opportunity to view pornography so I had no mental pictures of sex, with either men or women. By this time, I was open to having a sexual experience with a man, but I kept telling myself that, deep in my heart, what I was seeking was not sex, but attention.

Those were good days for me financially and it wasn't long before I had enough money to buy a car. I found a '29 Ford Coupe for $200. Everyone liked it, but Will seemed especially enthusiastic. He and I shared the same interest in railroading that I had inherited from my Uncle Charlie. We both loved trains and railroads and now, with a car, Will and I could follow along various rail lines and take photographs. We could also ride trains we'd never ridden before.

Exciting as these new opportunities were, they were difficult to fit into my hectic schedule. I went to high school full-time, worked a 40-hour week as church janitor, and played for Sunday services. Pastor Connor seemed to realize that I needed time away from all my responsibilities, and he allowed me to change my schedule as necessary, as long as I put in my 40 hours. Looking back I can see that it's quite possible he was a bit afraid of me since I had personal knowledge of his sexual orientation and his behavior with the boys of the church. This, however never crossed my mind at the time. I was just grateful that he was willing to indulge my wanderlust.

One thing that hindered my car trips, was that gasoline was still rationed. I learned from some guys at school that my car would run on cleaning solvent, which was not rationed and was available at most service stations. It was actually cheaper than gasoline. This opened the door to some glorious adventures. One summer Will and I took off for Los Angeles, checking out all the interesting sights along the way. One goal of mine was to photograph every California Mission. Will was not interested, but it was my car, so we saw all the historic missions along the way.

One particular day, because I was driving us somewhere Will did not want to go, he grabbed the car's ashtray and threw it out the window. I was seriously annoyed, not the least because the dashboard looked bad with an empty hole in it. So I stopped the car and we searched for hours before finding the ashtray. Over the next few years, we went up and down California's Central Valley, north to Eureka, and to Nevada. There were many times when we were stranded along the highway—cleaning solvent burned hotter than gasoline and it melted the head gaskets. Before long, though, I learned how to replace the ruined gaskets so we could be on our way again.

Will and I often slept together in the same bed during those trips. Will never made advances toward me or even talked much about sexual matters. And I didn't allow myself to think of Will in a sexual way. I didn't want to lose his friendship. Still, I very much wanted touch and affirmation from him— something I never got.

Sometimes after Will was asleep, I would cuddle up to him and hold him in my arms. I tried not to go to sleep when we were lying together; I didn't want to miss a moment of such great pleasure. I felt that this was everything I needed or wanted. Being close to Will was the most precious experience of my life. The next morning Will never mentioned my embraces and I certainly didn't bring it up. I was very afraid that he would tell me to back off. Now, I wonder how he could have not known? Beneath his cold exterior, did he need intimacy as badly as I did?

Before long, Pastor Connors summoned me once again to his office. "Frank," he announced, "you need someone to take care of you, someone who will see that you get your college education, who will help get you started in business. I have just the person for you!" He smiled expansively as he went on to tell me that one of our church members, a man in his late thirties, was also a homosexual.

Pastor Connors instructed me to "be nice to this gentlemen," and to "not resist him." Then, looking very intensely into my eyes, he said, "Don't hold back your love." I knew what he was saying. But there was no way on earth that I wanted to leave home and go live with this (from my perspective) fat old man. Even if I had wanted to, I knew my mother would see through this situation instantly and I did not want a war between my mother and my pastor. She was already very suspicious that things were not quite right, and I sometimes had to lie to her to throw her off the track.

"I can't do that!" I blurted out.

For the first time, Pastor Connors got angry with me. "I have *promised* you to this man! You have to do this! Please don't make it difficult. Just do what I say!"

I got out of there as quickly as I could. For the next couple of days, Pastor came looking for me, demanding a different answer. "Well, have you changed your mind?"

"Pastor, I can't leave my mother. She needs me!"

"Stop hanging on your mother's apron strings! You're a man now, so make your own decisions. Don't be such a baby!"

He tried one more time, again calling me into his office. "Look Frank, what's wrong with you. Don't you want sex?" That was about as plain as it could get. "Have you ever even had complete, adult sex?" he asked in a rather mocking tone. Of course, he knew I hadn't. In fact, I didn't even know precisely what he meant. Naturally, I wanted some kind of sexual release but I wanted it to be with someone of my own choosing. Most of all, I desperately wanted intimacy.

"Yes, I do want someone in my life," I tried to explain.

"But since I accepted Jesus, I've been trying my best to be good and resist my sexual urges. Also, I find this man very unattractive. Anyway, you know that my mother would have a fit if I left her. Can't you see why I can't do this?"

Pastor Connors was frustrated and angry. Finally, he returned to a now-familiar theme. "So what do you think David was doing with Jonathan, or Jesus with John? If they had sex, what makes you think it is so wrong?" Then he stopped talking, and after a few minutes of silence, he asked me to leave his office. From that time on, he cut me out of his life. The only time he would talk to me was to criticize my work. Repeatedly I thought he was going to fire me, but for some reason he didn't.

As I was working around the church, I became aware of a tall, handsome young man in a Navy uniform who seemed to be there every day. I noticed that he attended our youth group, and I learned his name was Larry. I asked one of the girls in the group about him and she seemed to have more worldly knowledge than I. "Larry is Pastor Connor's *special friend*. He was in the Navy, but now he has been discharged. They like each other a lot and lately Pastor is spending all his time with Larry." She rolled her eyes so I wouldn't miss the innuendo. I didn't.

I was practicing the organ one day after school when Larry appeared and leaned against the organ. "Will you play for me?" He smiled, "I want to make a recording."

"Sure, just bring me the music and I'll be happy to play for you."

Larry brought the music and day after day, I played while he sang. From what I know now, Larry's recording was going nowhere, but it brought us into frequent contact.

Of course, Pastor Connors took notice. "Stay away from Larry!" he warned me, an angry look flashing in his eyes.

I would have stayed away, but Larry continued to seek me out; he wanted to have lunch with me or to go somewhere with me at the end of my work day. Pastor Connors had to head home to his wife and kids, so Larry and I saw each other almost every night.

One evening, Larry told me why he was no longer in the Navy. He and some other guys had been caught having group sex. Larry was given a dishonorable discharge and sent home. Even though the war was now over, the draft was still in effect, and Larry couldn't find a job because all his prospective employers asked the same question: "Why aren't you in the service?" When he disclosed the dishonorable discharge, everyone refused to hire him, because it would be unpatriotic to hire someone who had let the country down.

As the weeks went by, Larry also told me more about his relationship with Pastor Connors, but he never revealed what kind of hold the pastor had over him. He said instead that he hated Pastor's advances, that he found him disgusting. Larry also confided that he liked girls, too, and wasn't completely homosexual. Yet, despite all this, Larry was at Pastor's beck and call, and obeyed whatever was asked of him. It was strange; I have never found the reason for his complete acquiescence to Pastor Connors.

Will had discovered girls and was now spending less time with me, although he was always available for trips. In the meantime, I found I was loving Will less, and Larry more and more. Even though Pastor never saw Larry with me, he knew we were spending a lot of time together. One day he confronted me angrily, "You know I told you to stay away from Larry, and you have been disobeying me! I am counseling Larry and I don't want any interference from you. If you continue to see him, there will be consequences!"

Ironically, I wasn't the only one who liked Larry. The girls at church were all over him. Every Sunday after church, they all wanted their pictures taken on the church steps with Larry. Larry graciously obliged his admirers, but then brushed them off. Then, away he went with me.

When we were together, people thought I was Larry's younger brother. By now, I had gained a few pounds and my looks had improved somewhat. Larry was not as afraid of sports as I was; he was always throwing a football around or playing volleyball. He decided to help me out by teaching me how to play these games. He would gather up a bunch of girls and we would go off and play volleyball. We often played catch with a football and he even tried to get me to play basketball, but that was beyond my capabilities. I guess a good word to describe Larry would be "dashing." He had longish black hair, a great tan, and was a little over six feet tall. He wasn't as muscular as Will, but still had a well-defined body and he spent as much time as possible on the beach. The good thing was that he was almost always around. And while Will was always tearing me down, Larry never stopped encouraging me.

As time went by and I spent more time with Larry, I made a startling discovery. Despite all his worldliness and sexual escapades, Larry knew Jesus. In his more reflective moments, I saw in him the same kind of excitement about Jesus that my organ teacher, Mrs. Hughes, had demonstrated. Larry really loved Jesus. I had been slipping away from the Lord since Pastor Connors had come along. Pastor seldom mentioned Him, except to remind me that Jesus and John were lovers, and his sermons had become increasingly psychological in nature.

My mother had been baptized with me, but she never took much interest in spiritual things; life was too hard for her to have the luxury of time with God, or so she thought. Will didn't respond at all when I tried to talk with him about Jesus. As it turned out, Larry was my only spiritual connection. We developed a pattern: first, we would have a beer or two at a local bar, Larry would play a few pinball machines, then we would take a bus out to the Santa Clara Mission to pray at the altar. There

was never anyone else around; we had the chapel all to ourselves. We had become two lost sheep without a shepherd.

By that time, I would have liked to have had a sexual relationship with Larry. Yet in all sincerity, I wanted Larry to know
and serve Jesus far more than I wanted anything else. Others,
including Pastor Connors, might have been guilty of leading
him astray, but there was no way I wanted to do that. Pastor
had told Larry that I was homosexual, but Larry knew I was
fighting same-sex attractions the best I could. Although he did-
n't mention it, I think that like me, he also wanted a normal life.
One time, alone in my room, I lay on the floor, asking God to
either change me or take me home because I was so tired of this
battle. He did neither at the time. Only later did I learn that His
timing and our timing are quite different.

In any case, at that moment I was very much aware that I
was losing the battle. My sexual fantasies were increasing and I
was trying to come to grips with what I'd been told—that I
would always be like this, destined to be different. Still, I
believed I could hang on as long as I had Larry to lean on. I
clung to the bond between Larry, Jesus, and me, just the three of
us facing life. And I think Larry genuinely loved me. Even
though I saw myself as skinny and not good-looking, Larry
assured me that one day I would fill out and become handsome.
I really liked hearing that from him. At least part of his prophecy
did come true: I did fill out. I'm still hoping for the rest!

There were times when Larry had to go away with Pastor
for several weeks. Pastor always took him to seminars and
conventions. I felt like Cinderella, left behind to sweep the
floors—I was, after all, the janitor. Those were lonely times
without Larry. I tried to connect with Will, but he was only
interested in car trips, not in daily interaction or any kind of
personal connection. To make matters worse, he was now ridiculing me to others more than ever. He had become less a
friend than an enemy.

Whenever Larry returned from his journeys with Pastor Connors, he would tell me how repulsive the man was to him. Yet, it was clear he never refused to do anything Pastor asked of him. We didn't discuss the whys and wherefores. We just happily returned to our usual routine, including visits to the old mission where we thanked God that we were together again.

By now, my graduation from high school was coming up. Ever since buying my car, I had fantasized about driving to New York City. It seemed this summer might be my only chance. A few months before graduation, I quit my janitor job and left Pastor Connor. I began to look for an automobile that could survive the distance from California to New York and back. I'd always had Will in mind as my traveling companion. We had talked and planned the trip throughout the year, but now that the time was rapidly approaching, Will backed out. "I can't afford the time or the money," he told me. I tried to get him to change his mind, but to no avail. I even asked Larry if he would come with me, but he said Pastor Connors never would agree to that. I was sad, but determined. Alone or not, I was going to New York.

Graduation day came and all my relatives gathered for the big event. It was a first—no one in our family had ever graduated from high school. I was issued a cap and gown, and went through rehearsal without incident. That night, the auditorium was filled with five hundred or more people. The school officials and all my teachers were standing on the stage. As I surveyed the scene, rage unexpectedly began to surge inside me. I hated each and every one of those people! And one of them in particular, a math teacher who also had taught my mother, I hated most of all. My mother thought she was wonderful, but I most certainly did not. She had abusively ridiculed and humiliated me when I couldn't answer her questions. I'd had enough of her!

This woman had been selected to hand out the diplomas—and lo and behold, there was my gym teacher standing beside her. I hated him almost equally. These people had made my life miserable. They had never tried to understand me. Mostly, they ignored my pain while they allowed the other students to harass me constantly. This was emancipation night! I would be free from their control, and from all the others I had come to loathe so intensely.

Since my last name started with "w," I was one of the last to walk across the stage. My family was proud of me—at least, for the moment. With a fake smile, the math teacher presented me with my diploma. Once I had it in hand, in a burst of anger I yanked the graduation cap off my head, ripped off the tassel and threw it at the feet of my mother's beloved teacher. The auditorium fell silent. Someone awkwardly quickly picked up the tassel and carried it off the stage.

My family was stunned. My mother couldn't believe I would behave this way. My aunt whispered, "What's wrong with Frank? Why would he do such a thing?" My mother had no answer. She had never realized the extent of my torment at school; maybe I'd never told her. But considering the amount of vandalism I had done in our home, you would think by now, she would have grasped the depth of my rage. Apparently, she never really did.

As soon as possible, I headed for New York. My late-model used car served me well. The trip took about six weeks. In 1947, there were no freeways, just two-lane roads crisscrossing the United States. I have always been thankful I took my journey then, while I could still see the country-side without being boxed in by cement sound walls. It was exciting to visit Salt Lake City and the Mormon Tabernacle, then the Continental Divide. Predictably, Kansas was bor-ing—the highway followed the property lines, so every mile or so there would be a sharp right or left turn. It seemed like I was making no progress, but eventually I found myself crossing the Mississippi River. For the first time in my life, I was in the eastern part of the U.S.A.

I had saved money for this trip throughout the past year, and one of my obsessions had been to stay at the Waldorf-Astoria Hotel in New York City. I arrived there late one night. With a great sense of accomplishment and aplomb, I strolled into the opulent lobby and checked in at the reception desk. The guest room itself was a disappointment, nowhere near as glamorous as I had hoped. Still, I'd made it that far. I was in New York, staying at the Waldorf-Astoria Hotel! I had somehow made one of my favorite dreams come true.

From New York, I traveled to Atlantic City and from there, I began the long drive home. Somewhere in Pennsylvania, I picked up a hitchhiker. Kirk was about two years older than I was. He was friendly and made a good traveling companion. He was headed for Denver, Colorado, to visit friends. Before leaving California, I had purchased a series of travel books, one for each state. These books gave the mileage between points of interest, and a description and history of each site. Kirk was happy to read aloud as I drove. I don't think we missed anything of interest between New York and Denver.

I enjoyed my time with Kirk. Several nights I had cuddled against him while he slept, just as I had done with Will. The results had been the same—the next morning he said nothing.

Eight days after picking him up, and about three miles outside the Denver city limits, I had a flat tire. Throughout the trip, this was the first problem I'd had with the car. It was very dark and I asked Kirk to hold the flashlight while I changed the flat. For some reason, there were two tire irons in the trunk. As I was loosening the lug bolts with one of them, I saw Kirk pick up the other. I watched him raise it over my head. Fear gripped me as I understood his likely intention—Kirk was about to kill me. Perhaps he hoped to steal my car; perhaps he had other reasons.

Without looking at him, I lifted my hand, took the tire iron from his grip and said, "Thanks, I need that iron. This one isn't working."

"Yeah, this one's better," he muttered, and got back into the car.

Not a word passed between us until I dropped Kirk off at his friend's house. Our hasty goodbye left me with a great sense of relief. I realized full well that I'd had a narrow escape. I might just as easily have been a body found in a ditch somewhere alongside the road. Instead, Jesus had saved me. It was clear that God had a plan and purpose for my life.

As yet, however, I had no idea what He had in mind.

Frank at 15.

Frank at 19. (1948)

Frank's 1929 Model A Ford Coupe.

Pastor Connor's church.

*Frank poses at the Continental Divide
on his way to New York. (1947)*

Chapter Four

Life in the Big City

Kirk and the immediate danger he had posed were soon in my rearview mirror, but as the adrenaline began to subside, I was overwhelmed with feelings of horror and isolation. My long-awaited, grand adventure had ended badly, and I wanted nothing more than to be home. But home was miles away, and I was exhausted and emotionally drained. Once I found a cheap motel, I immediately drifted off to sleep. In the morning, I arose early with two resolutions in my mind. One was to make the trip all the way from Denver to San Jose that same day. The other was never to tell anyone about the physical assault that had nearly happened.

As I drove, I thought about the consequences I would face if I told my mother about my encounter with Kirk. I knew all too well that she would never let it die. Every time I would set out to go somewhere, she would surely bombard me with warnings about picking up hitchhikers, and all the other dangers she could imagine. Telling Will about it would be no better, because he would immediately spread the tale of how dumb I had been. I didn't even want Larry to know—he'd be filled with regret that he hadn't been along to protect me.

My drive was no longer pleasant. The trip had taken a dark turn, and I could no longer enjoy the scenery. I was now only concerned with progress, and as the miles sped by, I contemplated my future. I made up my mind to pack up my things and head for San Francisco as soon as I got back. I needed a job, and I already knew there were none to be found in San Jose. Then, as always, my thoughts turned to Larry. A warm possibility drifted into my imagination. Was it possible that he would want to leave San Jose, too?

Mother was glad to see me. She seemed uncharacteristically delighted as I presented her with all the mementos I had chosen for her along the way. One was a little metal replica of the Empire State Building which she kept on the mantel until the day she died. Satisfied that I was safe and sound under her roof, she enthusiastically took charge of my dirty laundry and began to clean out my car. Once she was distracted, I left her to her tasks and went to see Larry.

I found him in a rather morose mood. He hugged me and, without further detail, simply said, "I have to get away from Pastor Connors, Frank. I need to leave *right now.*"

My heart skipped a beat or two. I could hardly believe my good fortune. Clearly, I didn't have to convince Larry of anything. Whatever had happened, he was more than ready to leave town—to leave it all behind. I didn't ask him why, and he didn't offer any further explanations. I had long been aware of the strange control Pastor had over Larry, although I wasn't sure what it was. But now, weary as I was after my coast-to-coast adventure, a sense of excitement rushed over me.

"Can you be ready to leave tomorrow morning?" I asked.

"I'll be ready!" Larry exclaimed. His face lit up with relief.

It was the fall of 1947. The war was over and the whole country was alive with excitement and expectation. Those were days of euphoric optimism and everyone seemed to agree that better days were just around the corner. I, too, was filled with hope for the future and earnestly began trying to implant that same hope in Larry.

The next day, as the early morning train pulled out of the station, I felt like celebrating. It was a heady moment. It seemed that Pastor Connors was out of our lives forever, and Larry was free from bondage to him. I was glad to leave Will in the dust, too, because he had become more and more hostile to me. I left my car at home for Mother to sell, as I couldn't leave it on the street in San Francisco, and garage fees would have taken a major part of my earnings.

When Larry and I disembarked at the San Francisco train depot, in order to get downtown, we had to transfer our heavy luggage and my foot locker onto a waiting streetcar. It wasn't an easy operation, but no matter how heavy the load I was carrying, my heart was as light as a feather. I couldn't believe that I was living such a dream-come-true. Larry and I dragged everything up the steps of the Y.M.C.A. and booked ourselves into a room for $17.50 a week. After we split the bill, the clerk gave us our keys and pointed out the elevator.

Our new home was on the fourth floor overlooking the entrance to the building. We had a back-side view of a giant globe that was suspended over the front door. The room had two single beds. If I'd thought the Waldorf was shabby, this was beyond dilapidated. The wallpaper was peeling off and there were cockroaches in the drawers and all around the windows. But Larry and I saw it through the eyes of love, and to us it was beautiful—it marked a new beginning.

Once we'd stowed our luggage, we wandered around San Francisco for the rest of the day. I couldn't wait to introduce Larry to the out-of-the-way places I'd discovered on previous trips. We talked excitedly about finding jobs, my plans to attend college, and Larry's ambition to be a singer. Toward evening, we returned to the "Y." After a game of handball, we went for a swim and a shower. That night as we went to our separate beds, we reviewed just how extraordinary the day had been. I lay alone in my bed, and although sex didn't cross my mind, I remember wishing Larry were lying next to me, holding me close. Above all else, I was happy—so very happy.

The next day we set out to look for work. I registered at the employment office and combed the newspapers. By the end of the second day, I'd had one interview and had lined up several other possible job opportunities. As for Larry, whatever he did that day brought him back to the "Y" feeling a little depressed. "It's going to be hard for me to find work," he complained. I knew it was the same old story—his dishonorable discharge from the Navy continued to limit his options. Still, I assured him that I had found many job openings and that he would find something too, sooner or later.

Money was short—my savings account was long-gone, thanks to my New York trip. Larry and I went to eat a nearby cafeteria where we dined on the cheapest of fare. On the way back, Larry bought some candy bars, to save on lunch money.

A few months before my New York trip, I had wandered into San Francisco's Grace Cathedral and heard the men's choir practicing with organ accompaniment. I was swept away with the beauty of the whole scene. Sunlight was filtering through the elaborate stained-glass windows, casting colorful designs on the marble floor, while heavenly music emanated from the front altar. That day I had patiently waited until practice was over and then, in a state of near awe, approached the organ chancel.

There, I had introduced myself to Richard Purvis, the church organist. He was a rotund little man who was very gracious to me. He'd asked me where I was from and whether I had an interest in music. I told him that I'd had about six years of piano and organ study and that I needed a more advanced teacher. Hesitantly I had asked, "Do you have any openings in your teaching schedule?" Mr. Purvis had then made an appointment for me, and in a few days I had auditioned for him on the giant cathedral organ. He decided that I was sufficiently advanced to warrant his time and energy. Now, when this warm, friendly man heard that Larry and I had just moved to San Francisco, he was effusive. "I want to have the two of you to lunch on your first day here," he told me. And so it was, that on our first day in town, Larry and I visited his home and enjoyed a delicious meal. It was to be our last experience with good food for some time.

Meanwhile, I had noticed a chapel on the grounds of Grace Cathedral, which was open 24 hours a day. I decided this chapel would serve as our private worship center, as the mission had done when we'd visited it in San Jose. Our second night in San Francisco, Larry and I walked into the cathedral's chapel and prayed together, kneeling at the altar rail.

On day three, I had a great interview at the Army Exchange Service, the agency that stocked the Army PXs (Post Exchanges), convenience stores located in military posts. A woman in the employment office told me it was almost a sure thing that I would be hired. She confided that I could safely cancel my other job interviews and just wait for her call. That set me free to explore more of San Francisco with Larry, who was trying to build up his courage before attempting to re-enter the job market.

A day or two later, Larry unexpectedly informed me that he needed to return to San Jose to see his family. He was gone for four days—a lonely time for me. I faithfully went to the chapel to pray every evening, which took me up Powell Street past Union Square and the St. Francis Hotel. The walk exhilarated me. I was captivated by the city's atmosphere, the clanging of the cable cars and the liveliness of the crowded streets. But I was also puzzled. Strangers approached me with, "What are you doing tonight?" One man smiled at me; another wanted to know, "Where are you going? Need some company?"

Are these guys propositioning me, I asked myself, *or are they just lonely, too?*

Once Larry returned, my loneliness diminished. He still didn't have a job, but I soon got that phone call, advising me to report for work the following Monday morning. The way the government payroll was handled, it would be nearly four weeks before I got my first check. I wondered how I could stretch my money that far, but I was glad to be employed. When I arrived at work that first Monday, I found myself in the heart of the city on lower Market Street, and discovered that I was the proud possessor of a nice, clean desk, surrounded by half a dozen pleasant female co-workers. One of them even bought me lunch. I was in Accounts Payable and the work was easy— most of it entailed running long tapes on the adding machine.

While my work situation flourished, I could see that Larry was sinking lower and lower into a funk. I had no idea if he was seriously looking or not, but he didn't find any work. He grew more quiet and preoccupied. One Tuesday night, we had had our meager dinner together, played a few games at the "Y," and went to bed early.

I was completely unprepared for what followed.

How could I have known that Larry was hungering for sex? But now he told me everything. He explained that he and Pastor Connors were frequent sexual partners, and now he felt deprived. For several hours, all he could talk about was sex. He described every relationship he'd had since he was a young boy, and there had been many. He had experienced a varied and active sex-life, all with boys or men. In full detail, he described some wild episodes in the Navy, and I found myself thinking, *No wonder they dishonorably discharged you!*

Of course, the point of all this was that Larry wanted me to get out of my bed and into his; nothing could have been clearer. I was both excited and afraid. My emotions were at the breaking point. I had long fantasized about an encounter just like this one, yet here it was and I was profoundly conflicted. I wanted to give myself to Larry, to comfort him and feel his love. Yet at the same time I didn't.

In those confusing moments, I didn't want to defile Larry any more than he had already been defiled. I didn't want to be like Pastor Connors. I was still hoping that this season of my life would come to a close and I would be normal—heterosexual—like everyone else. I had never had sex with anyone—man or woman, and one fear that kept me in my own bed was that if I engaged in even one homosexual act, it would cement that pattern into my life forever. I finally fell asleep, and my dilemma was temporarily over.

The next morning, Larry was deeply ashamed of himself. As I was waking up, he had already packed his bags and was ready to go out the door. "Frank," he quietly said, "I have to go home; this isn't working for me." I could see the humiliation in his eyes. I knew he was leaving so that *he* wouldn't defile *me*. He didn't want to lead me into a homosexual way of life. Instead, he was returning to Pastor Connors, whom he could count on to meet his sexual cravings.

I was devastated.

Financially I could no longer afford the room at the "Y," so I moved to a rooming house where breakfast and dinner were included in the rent. I also moved because I couldn't emotionally cope with the room at the "Y." I couldn't bear to look at Larry's empty bed. But I didn't want to stay in the dark, small room at the boarding house, either. I was increasingly afraid that if I didn't keep myself busy, I would soon succumb to the men on the streets. I spent long hours in the cathedral chapel, praying in desperation that Larry would return. Nonetheless, I had seen the determination in his face when he left. Prayers or no prayers, I knew in my heart he was never coming back.

To distract myself from the pain, I threw myself whole-heartedly into my work. My employers were so pleased with me that they gave me a raise. My job description changed a little, too. I now had the added responsibility of serving as driver for a U.S. Army colonel. His secretary phoned me from time to time and said, "Be out front with the car in ten minutes."

I drove this officer to various army bases. Now that the war was over, he was in charge of dismantling the PXs, which entailed a lot of work. Sometimes the trips were quite long. I stayed in a hotel in Las Vegas for a week, while he went about his business. It was a particularly memorable journey, because on the way back we ran into a sandstorm so severe that, although it was daytime, we had to use our headlights. Later, we discovered the sand had blasted all the paint off one side of the car.

Back in San Francisco, I was lonely—intensely lonely. What had once been a magically colorful city was now shaded in gray. During my time with Larry, I had kept my sexual urges under control. The warmth of our friendship kept me from entertaining lustful thoughts, but now things were different. I was losing the will to resist temptation. In fact, I was in a severe depression, but unaware of it. It didn't help that I was attending a liberal church that thought homosexuality was a good thing. I had no one to whom I was spiritually accountable, and I was in a state of constant conflict. I still believed it was wrong to engage in homosexual behavior, but I also knew it was only a matter of time before I gave in to my longings.

Night after night, I walked to the top of Nob Hill and prayed that God would sustain me, that I would be strong and able to resist temptation. As I walked through the streets, men continued to proposition me. I now understood that they were more than simply lonely; they wanted sex. I always said "no," but if they had been a little more persistent, I surely would have gone with them. So deep was my inner conflict that when I didn't think I wanted them, there they were...yet on weekends, as

I hiked through the parks and hung out in museums hoping someone would notice me, I seemed to be invisible. Even at church, no one said so much as "good morning" to me.

There was no one in my life. How could there be? I was still grieving. I needed Larry, and only Larry, and I decided I simply had to talk to him. I took the train back to San Jose and went to his family's house, but they told me he had moved to a seaside town about eighty miles away. It was dusk when the bus I was on pulled into that beach town; I had spent all day searching for him.

I found the house and, with my heart pounding, I rang the bell. Larry came to the door but he offered me no warm greeting. Clearly, he was not happy to see me. I asked him to come back to San Francisco. After some hesitation, during which Larry seemed to be weighing some idea or other, he said that if I would stay overnight somewhere in town, we could talk about it in the morning.

He had found a job at the local YMCA, and the next day I found him there. Once again he was cold and detached. He seemed as conflicted as I was. "Frank, I'm trying to build a new life," he explained. "I don't want Pastor in my life, and I want to break every connection to my past. Sorry, Frank, but that includes you. You're part of that old life, so I don't want to see you anymore."

I stared at him, speechless and sorrowful. Then he continued, "But I do have one request to make of you, for old time's sake. Please do this one thing for me—just because we used to mean so much to each other."

I didn't know what to expect, but had nothing to lose. "I'll do anything for you, Larry," I responded, "...*anything.*"

"Frank, I want you to take my cousin, Alice, back to San Francisco with you. She has never been out of this small town and I know it would be good for her. Will you take her back with you?"

What was he trying to do, kill me? Take a girl back to San Francisco with me? What was I going to do with her? Didn't he know by now I couldn't relate to girls? This was nothing but sheer cruelty. Still, I didn't refuse—I couldn't. A little later, during Larry's break from work, he and I walked on the beach. As we started back, Alice, his cousin, came to find us. It seemed he'd already told her I would be taking her back with me to San Francisco.

The first thing I noticed as she drew near was that she was wearing Larry's clothes—clothes that I knew so well.

Soon Larry was gone, and I was left alone with Alice. As we walked around town and talked, Alice wanted to know all about San Francisco. She eagerly grabbed my hand. She talked and acted like Larry. She even looked a little like him. In fact, if she had been a boy, she would have been handsomer, more beautiful than he was. As we talked, I learned that she and I were only months apart in age, and we seemed to have a lot in common.

One hard question kept repeating in my mind. *If I let her come with me, what do I do with her?* Then I looked at the clothes she was wearing—Larry's clothes—and my heart softened. *Well, at least I'll still have something around as a reminder of Larry,* I told myself.

After we had looked at whatever that little town had to offer, Alice took me for a hike in the surrounding hills. Again I encouraged myself, *I guess having her around will be better than nothing—which is what I unfortunately have now.* Alice was happy and carefree, like Larry once had been. Finally, I decided I liked her.

I didn't know what I might feel for her if she changed clothes. Still, I had to admit that she was very beautiful and anywhere we went, I could be proud to be with her. Her long auburn hair reached to the small of her back; she was about five foot seven, slender, and her eyes were green. She certainly was lovely to look at. She posed on a rail fence and I took her picture. *Yes,* I decided, *I am going to do this. I'm taking her to San Francisco with me.* I asked her when the next bus would leave.

"In an hour," she smiled, "and I'm already packed."

What a strange day!

We arrived at my boarding house late that night. Fortunately, Mrs. Murray was still awake and delighted to have another guest. The house was arranged so that the men lived on the top floors with the women downstairs. Alice got a basement room, but she was so excited about being in San Francisco she didn't mind. The next day, she loved having breakfast with so many people. "It's just like having a great big family," she told me, beaming with pleasure. That idea had never occurred to me. I had not tried to befriend anyone at the boarding house, although I did say "good morning" to a few acquaintances there.

Naturally, everyone thought Alice was my girlfriend. They made a fuss over her and let me know that she definitely met with their approval. Like Larry, Alice didn't seem overly anxious to find a job; perhaps her family had sent her off with a sizable amount of money. In any case, before looking for work, she wanted to see San Francisco—every corner of the city. Day after day she went exploring, and when it was time for me to get off from work, she was often waiting for me at the entrance to my office building. My co-workers immediately took notice. The men said, "Lucky guy," or, "How did you get a girl like that?" The women said nicer things, "She's very pretty," and, "What a lovely girl, Frank."

Alice was always excited about something. In those days she wanted to show me everything she found. Tired as I was after a day's work, I never failed to follow her wherever she wanted to go. After dinner at the boarding house, we'd start out again, walking the streets, hand in hand. Soon she knew all my favorite places. For example, I had always loved the stairways going to the top of Telegraph Hill. There were beautiful gardens, some hanging over cliffs, and small Victorian cottages. I particularly remember a very large, formal roof-garden atop an old warehouse on a street below.

Alice was quite a trophy, and I was particularly conscious of that when we walked through some of the rougher neighborhoods. I often wondered if I would be able to defend her if necessary. I tried to imagine what would happen if I faced a showdown with another man. There was no question that I was becoming very attached to her. As much as I enjoyed her companionship, however, I would have been more comfortable if she'd seemed a bit more stable. Larry had walked out on me. I was very much afraid that Alice might do the same.

We both liked art and enjoyed visiting museums. During my high school years I had often been banished to the library during gym class. In the process, I had read every art book I could get my hands on. I was especially interested in the Impressionists. When Alice and I came across a painting I'd read about, I told her whatever I knew of the artist—but I soon found that Alice was also quite well informed. We both enjoyed those conversations, and I loved being with her. I wondered if I loved her.

After a few weeks we decided that we both needed to check in at our homes. One weekend, she went back to her seaside town, while I went to visit my mother. I frequently talked to Mother on the phone, but didn't often see her. For one thing, San Jose made me sad; so many negative things had happened there. This time, Mother had some particularly disturbing news. Our house was located two blocks from San Jose State College. She had just received a notice that the State of California was about to appropriate all the property in a four-block area, through eminent domain, to expand the college. Our house was located right in the middle of their newly-designed campus.

Mother was depressed, and I couldn't blame her. We had just made the last payment on our house. We finally owned it free and clear. "Where are we going to find another house where we don't have to make house payments?" she asked me more than once. Adding insult to injury, we soon learned that the amount of money the State was offering us would never purchase another house. By the end of the day, Mother had made up her mind—she wanted to come to San Francisco to be close to me.

The next day at work, I happened to mention all this to the woman whose desk was next to mine. She looked at me hopefully and said, "Oh, Frank—that's such great news. I need a live-in baby sitter! Do you think your mother would consider coming to live in my house?" I called Mother and she thought it was a great idea. She was promised a small salary, and would have a place to live and even food to eat. Once again she had to sell all our furniture, but at least she didn't have to tidy up the house this time. It was about to be demolished.

In a few months, Mother arrived in San Francisco, and for a while, she was content with her new situation. She enjoyed being in the city, and we saw each other more frequently. Mother was, of course, very suspicious of Alice. She wasn't at all sure that Alice was good for me, but then I don't think Mother ever believed anyone was good enough for me. She did seem happy that I was away from Will. Mother had always suspected that there was something sexual between Will and me, even though Will had invariably remained aloof and distant.

By now, Alice was making more frequent trips to see her family. When we were apart for a little while, I kept thinking about her. How I enjoyed seeing her pretty, smiling face waiting outside my office! My workmates kept repeating, "Frank, you're in love with that girl!" One thing I knew for sure—when I didn't see her I missed her very much. Maybe this really was love!

Everyone assumed Alice and I were living together because we shared the same address. They enjoyed talking about this "young love" relationship, and sometimes even said things about Alice getting pregnant. Even though I told them otherwise, they were eager for a juicy scandal, so they refused to believe we were only friends. All this certainly made me feel proud. Meanwhile, the two of us were inseparable. We spent almost every evening together, went to coffee houses (although I didn't drink coffee!), and talked about everything—except Larry. I assumed that Larry had asked her not to mention him to me.

One evening, Alice was not waiting for me at the bottom of the office stairs, and although I didn't think too much about it, I longed to see her. I assumed we would meet up later that night for dinner at the boarding house. Dinner came and went, and Alice never appeared. Later, I sat in the lobby waiting for her. After several hours, I felt humiliated and didn't want the other boarders to start asking awkward questions, such as, "So you're waiting up for Alice! Where is she anyway?"

I went to bed, but I couldn't sleep. *Was she all right? Had she met with foul play? Had she found someone else? Why didn't she tell me she was going out?*

Then a new and radical thought came into my mind, *"Maybe Alice is upset that I've never talked to her about marriage."* I mulled this over. True, she had never mentioned marriage to me, but perhaps even though she didn't talk about it, she secretly wanted to be married. The next morning, Alice was at breakfast and I tried to be casual. I asked her what she'd done the night before. She replied offhandedly, "Oh, I went out with my roommates. They took me to some bars. It was fun…"

I immediately realized I didn't want Alice going out without me. Instantly, I knew I loved her. Then, just as suddenly, I recalled Pastor Connors' words, that I would always be homosexual; I could never be normal. *Hey, Pastor Connors*, I thought to myself, *you were wrong! I am in love with a woman, I am normal! I've made the change from men to women. I may have been late in doing it, but now I've arrived.*

I asked Alice to go out with me to dinner that night, and she said okay. It was so good to find her waiting for me once again after work! I took her to an expensive restaurant, and noticed that she was wearing a skirt and blouse. I was going to ask her what had happened to Larry's clothes, but thought better of it.

When we were finally seated in a dark corner of the restaurant, I really didn't know what to say. Other times, we had talked about anything and everything—my job, her city adventures, art, whatever. We had never been at a loss for words. But that night was different. Alice was quiet too. I think she must have known what was on my mind and was already preparing her response.

Finally, I said, "Alice I love you, and…" I was going to go on, but she anticipated what was coming next.

"I'm never going to get married!" she abruptly announced. "I don't want to be married! My roommates and I are going to go live on a farm. I don't love you; I could never love a man! I can only love horses…and other women."

We both fell silent again. I had no idea how to respond. I certainly knew about homosexual men and their emotional dynamics, but it had never crossed my mind that a woman could be homosexual. (We didn't use the term gay or lesbian, back then.) I paid the check. We went home on the streetcar and said goodnight. The next morning, I learned that Alice had checked out of the guesthouse. I never saw her again.

Now emptiness flooded me, nearly drowning me in pain. I could not face the loneliness again. I needed comfort; I needed advice. The one person I'd always been able to turn to was Pastor Connors.

As much as I had wanted to get away from him, he had long been a father figure for me. Besides, he was the only person I knew who could answer my questions. First of all, I wanted to know if women really could love other women the way men love other men. Was that true, or had Alice lied to me? Had she made that story up because she was trying to escape me? I was in a state of utter bewilderment, and could not figure all this out on my own. I didn't have the strength. I needed someone to hug me, to promise that things were going to be all right. Who but Pastor Connors could do that?

I found him and poured out my heart to him. By then, he and Larry were apart again. "I need somebody," I explained. "I'm lonely and very confused. I didn't know women could be homosexual. Is that true? How could this happen?"

He hugged me and assured me that he understood. "Now that Larry's gone again, my life is empty, too," he confessed. He said he held nothing against me, and seemed to have forgiven me. "Larry makes his own choices," he shrugged, "and neither one of us is responsible for what Larry chooses to do."

We were both quiet for a long moment. "So, how are you doing at the church?" I asked, changing the subject as gently as possible.

"Things are going very well," he smiled. "The youth group is growing fast and the elders of the church are finally seeing the fruit of all the hard work I've done. They've come to realize that the changes I made in the church were necessary."

To show their appreciation, Pastor Connors went on to say, the elders had presented him with a brand new car.

He reported that his wife and three children were fine, too. I couldn't help but wonder if his wife knew about his behavior with the boys of the church. I hoped not, as she was a plain and pleasant woman and I had always liked her. In fact, I had prayed that she would not be hurt by his actions.

Then Pastor got very serious with me. "Frank, you must be nineteen by now, right?"

"Yes, I'm nineteen."

"And you still haven't had sex with anyone?"

"No…"

"Frank, you are denying the gift God has given you! Homosexuality is God's special gift to you, and you are refusing it. All through history," he said, "those who accepted this gift became successful artists, musicians, even kings. You are turning your back on God. Be what you are! Grasp it! Make it work for you!"

We stared at each other for a moment before I dropped my eyes.

"Look Frank," Pastor Connors continued, "I love you, but you have been a fool and have caused yourself a whole lot of grief. If you deny what you are, well, of course you are going to be lonely and depressed! That's the penalty for rejecting what God has made you to be."

"I have always known what you are," he insisted, his tone growing harder and colder. "I even tried three years ago to bring you happiness by finding a very special man for you, but you turned him down. You thought you could do better. You wanted Larry, didn't you? But look where you are now! I hate to say it, Frank, but you deserve the loneliness you are now feeling."

"But Pastor!" I tried to explain, "You don't understand! I loved Alice. I wanted to marry Alice! I was normal. I had finally made the change from loving men, to loving a woman. You said I would always be homosexual, that there was no hope for a normal life, but I have *been* normal. I had normal feelings for a woman! And now I am so confused. I don't know what to think or do."

Pastor sighed, shook his head sadly, and then declared, "Frank, you were *not* normal. Don't you understand? You weren't in love with a woman; you were in love with *the man inside a woman.*"

"What? What are you saying?"

"Alice was manlike. And you saw her as a man, not as a woman. You already admitted that you liked her in Larry's clothes, right?"

"Well, yes, but I don't understand how Alice could be a man inside, and a woman outside. Are you saying that I didn't love the outside, only the inside?"

"Frank, stop resisting! Just stop it! Develop and blossom. Be the person God created you to be and you will be happy. You won't be lonely and confused. Find the man God made for you and live a blessed life. Remember, God has given you a special awareness, a love for men, just like Jesus loved men. So, go and use this gift from God!"

Once the conversation ended, I stood up and said goodbye. As difficult as the conversation had been, I felt somehow relieved that Pastor Connors had found a way to comfort me. But what now? I replayed his words again and again in my mind, and began to draw some conclusions. Certainly "normal" hadn't work for me—instead, it had caused me terrible pain. Furthermore, I didn't want to be out of God's will. I wanted to experience whatever He had planned for me.

I paused on the church steps and cried out to God, *Lord, he's Your man, and You heard what he said. Haven't I been troubled and tormented enough? As far as I'm concerned this is settled. I'm going to be what he says I am, and what You seem to have made me to be. I can't go on any longer in this state of confusion.*

I was still alone, but somehow I was beginning to feel surges of hope. Maybe a new life really was awaiting me! I prayed that, as Pastor had predicted, I would be blessed with a wonderful, successful future.

Then I made a promise to myself, *I'm going to find a man who loves me—someone I can love in return. This time I won't blow it. I'll learn to be more aggressive. I will dedicate myself to finding a lover. I'll go wherever I have to go—bars, clubs, bathhouses, and all the other places I've avoided.*

On the train back to San Francisco, I tried to remember where I had seen bars that especially catered to homosexuals. I was excited, determined to find not just one new hangout, but many. It was a huge relief to have the same-sex issue settled at last. It seemed in those moments, that a bright new world was opening up before me, a world no longer darkened by shadowy questions about what was right and what was wrong.

Frank at 20. (1949)

The Wayside Shrine of St. Francis Grace Cathedral,
San Francisco.

Chapter Five

My Brave
New World

As I self-consciously opened the door of the Hyde/Cal Club, I found myself staring into a surging, energized, all-male crowd bathed in atmospheric blue light. Just at that moment, the jukebox was playing "Blue Moon," and I will never forget seeing dozens of men dancing together and looking so happy. Eyes turned toward me as I rather shyly made my way in, and before long a number of eligible males were smiling, sidling up to me and making small talk. I could have gone home with any number of these men, but despite my determination earlier that day to start a new life, I was still afraid.

Yes, I was driven by relentless longings, yet, at least on the conscious level, I really wasn't looking for sex. I was looking for a relationship. And it was clear to me, naive though I was, that sex was the only thing those flirtatious young guys had in mind.

My life had been so marred with trauma and rejection, I didn't want to go from bad to worse by getting involved in shallow, one-night stands. I knew I needed someone to talk to. I wanted to find out more about the homosexual life, not engage in quick, anonymous sex. I needed a friend more than a sex partner. It didn't take long to figure out that wasn't an option in this place. The guys who populated the Hyde/Cal Club were into having fun, they were not interested in having a serious talk with a curious kid. It dawned on me as I looked around and listened, that above all else, I was looking for a Larry-replacement. San Francisco was, however, the "big city," not a small town, where relationships might be easier to form.

Still, that first night on the town wasn't wasted. I managed to learn from casual conversation where the other homosexual bars were located in San Francisco. I even got warnings about which bars refused to pay off the authorities, and were therefore subject to frequent raids. It seemed that this new life might be stimulating, but it could also be dangerous.

I was soon spending at least four nights a week in bars or cruising homosexual areas. One day I gave myself a lecture. *This isn't good*, I told myself. *This is going nowhere! You need to go to college.* Almost all of my friends from high school and church had enrolled in San Jose State College. After high school, I had wanted my freedom and an escape from the abuse I'd suffered. However, I now saw that even freedom had its own set of problems. I was adrift, and my lack of direction frightened me. Perhaps there were more stable people going to college than going to bars. I imagined meeting someone special there.

Nearly every day I walked past the University of California's San Francisco Extension campus. Now, I opened the door, sat down, and talked with one of their counselors. He helped me develop a plan for my education. I discovered that the school had a great musical department, so I enrolled in Music Theory, Organ, and Choir Directing.

I also signed up for French, which wasn't such a great idea. The first day of class, the teacher said, "This is the last time I will be talking to you in English. From now on, I will speak only in French." That might have sounded good theoretically, but as she rattled on and on, I could not understand one word she said. After a couple of classes, I gave up. The other French students were so far beyond me, I knew I would never catch up. Still, I loved my music-related classes and did well in them. And having homework to complete made me cut down on my bar-cruising time.

My landlady, Mrs. Murray, and I became friends. I learned that she, too, came from San Jose and in fact, had lived just a block from my grandmother and uncle. We reminisced about San Jose and all the changes taking place there. She was a widow who had done very well in the real estate market. After her husband's death, she had moved to San Francisco and bought a duplex. From there she had traded up to a four-plex, then to a small apartment building. Now she owned a twenty-six unit building, as well as the boarding house. She was even considering moving up again.

"Buy something, Frank," she urged. "Buy anything! Today's bad buy is tomorrow's wise investment. We are in a rising market."

Mrs. Murray's story inspired me and in subsequent years, I followed in her footsteps. But at the time, I was renting a room with two beds, and only rarely was the other bed occupied. One night as I returned from class, Mrs. Murray hurriedly called me aside. "Frank, I've rented the other bed in your room to a merchant seaman." She explained, "He rents from me whenever he's in town. But don't worry—he'll only be around for a few days." I shrugged and headed for my room.

I wasn't prepared for what I saw when I opened the door. A very masculine, muscular, nude man was lying on the bed, fully exposed. Assuming he was heterosexual, I thought, *Wow! I'll bet he gets every woman he goes after!* As I sat at my desk trying to write a letter to a friend, this stranger proved to be a formidable distraction. I was drawn to his body like a magnet. At first, he was lying on his stomach, but then he rolled over on his back and my level of distraction increased dramatically.

I kept hoping he would wake up so I could talk to him, but it was now past eleven, so I gave up and went to sleep. In the morning he was gone. All day I visualized him in my imagination. He wasn't at dinner, and I had to leave for class, but I very much hoped he would be there when I arrived home. I was not disappointed. Once again, upon opening the door, I again saw his perfect body sound asleep. I felt guilty staring at him, feeling I was taking advantage of him in some way. But still I stared.

The third night, when I walked into my room, he was awake.

"Hi there," he said with a smile. "My name's Carl, who are you?" We talked for a while and in the process, I learned a few things about being a merchant-marine seaman and working on a ship at sea. *Maybe that's what I ought to do,* I mused, as he spoke. The pay was three times what I was making and I thought it might be fun.

After an hour or so, Carl said, "Hey, listen; I have a motor-cycle, and I'm going to tool around the city for a while. You want to come along?"

Yes, I certainly did. Even though I had to get up early to go to work, I was eager to hang out with Carl. I assumed he was straight, and I was a little afraid of him, but at the same time, I was delighted that a straight man wanted to spend time with me. I remember thinking, *I'd better be careful not to sound like I'm coming on to him. I don't want to lose any teeth tonight!*

What a night it was. We rode along the beach, then to the top of Twin Peaks, where we stopped and looked at the city lights. It was very romantic. As we took off again, Carl asked me to put my hands in his pockets so I could hang on more securely. Looking back, I can see that this was an invitation to fondle him in some way, but at the time, I didn't get it. "I'm okay," I told him. "I won't fall off."

It wasn't long before he dropped me at our front steps. "See you, kiddo. I got things I got to do."

The next night, as we sat talking in the room, Carl took out some pictures from his dresser drawer and tossed them across the bed. "You might like to have a look at these," he said with a sly grin. I found myself staring at two naked men in strange positions. As I studied the photographs, I noticed that one of the men was Carl. What were they doing? Then I realized that the pictures had been taken in our room, and that some of my things were in sight, which meant the photographs had been taken in the last couple of days. Now I knew what Carl did while I was at work.

"I don't understand what you guys are doing," I remarked, feeling puzzled and slightly embarrassed.

A disgusted look crossed Carl's face." You dumb little s—!" he growled, and stormed out the door. The next morning when I awoke, Carl was gone, presumably back to his ship. Meanwhile, I felt like a fool. *I really need to know more about the lifestyle I'm supposed to be part of,* I told myself.

After that humiliating scene, I was determined to be in control of any future relationships that might come along. So far, potential friends and lovers still kept walking out of my life and leaving me lonely and depressed. I moved out of the boarding house and rented a three-bedroom apartment. I had no furniture, so I went to a second-hand store and bought a double bed and a few other pieces for my own room. Then I put an ad in the classified section of the San Francisco Examiner, hoping to find roommates for the other two bedrooms.

The very next day, a man responded to my ad. "I can move in tonight!" he excitedly informed me.

"Okay, but the room is unfurnished," I cautioned him.

"That's okay. I can just bunk with you until I find some furniture. Can I come over now?"

Len arrived within the hour. He was about six years older than I and seemed like a nice enough guy. "I think we're going to get along very well," he winked at me. "I'm going to go get my things. I'll be back in an hour."

Len didn't have much to move, just a few clothes and one suitcase. We talked for a while, and then decided to call it a day. Once we were in bed, Len moved on me aggressively. I knew that nineteen years of innocence was about to end, and by then I was tired of the struggle. I needed someone—anyone—desperately, and perhaps this enthusiastic stranger was the person I'd been waiting for.

Len was anything but gentle in bed. It was obvious that he was interested only in his own gratification. I begged him to stop, thinking my body could not bear any more. Still he persisted, not caring in the least about my feelings.

Truthfully, I really didn't know what I was feeling. My pain was intense, but the warmth of his body somehow eclipsed my discomfort. This wasn't the kind of love I had dreamed about, but in my loneliness, it seemed better than being on my own. The next day, Len realized that I was not happy with his forceful behavior. He approached me again, but his time our encounter wasn't so rushed, and he made a point of satisfying my sexual desires, too.

In the days that followed, Len was pleasant and gentle in the mornings but uncaring and rough at night. Two weeks later, he said we needed to talk. "I've found someone else," he informed me, "so I'll be moving out today. But I like you Frank, and I still want to be friends with you."

I was quite ready to see the last of Len as a lover, but we did manage to maintain a sort of friendship in the years that followed.

That evening, Len's new lover, Bernie, came to help him

pack. "Len hasn't been completely truthful with you," Bernie confided. "He's always had his own apartment. He just moved in with you for the sex. Now he's going back to his own place again. We don't live together because Len likes his freedom. Right now, I need a place to live. Can I move in?"

Bernie had his own furniture and since he was Len's lover, I figured he wouldn't be sleeping in my bed. In the meantime, Len was still around at night, only now he was sleeping in Bernie's room. I wondered how I was going to feel about that, but I actually felt relieved, freed from that abusive and brief relationship. On the nights Len didn't show up, Bernie slept with me. He was sweet and gentle, and I found I liked him, but I wasn't in love with him.

Soon I had rented both rooms, with two in a room, except for mine. My tenants seemed to have lots of friends who needed a place to live. By keeping the house full, I was able to live rent-free and even save a little money each month.

Meanwhile, Mother wasn't doing so well at her baby-sitting job. My colleague was complaining about Mother's work, and my mother was complaining about the number of extra duties that had been piled on her—things that hadn't been included in the original agreement. Now she had to wash windows, do piles of laundry, prepare food for the family, and all the while continue to watch the children.

With the cash I had saved and the little bit of money left from the sale of our San Jose home, Mother and I decided we could buy a house of our own. I found just the right place in the Sunset District of San Francisco, near the zoo. It only required a thousand dollars down. We bought it. I left the apartment to the guys living there, and moved in with Mother.

I quickly developed part of the house into another rental apartment. So once again, I was living without either rent or house payments. My tenants' payments covered all our expenses.

By now, I had several gay friends and was meeting more and more of them at parties. I got to know a banker who was interested in me. He offered to finance any real estate I bought, so I borrowed money from his bank. I was careful to make my payments on time and managed to build up a solid credit rating. Now and then, one of my new friends waited for me at the bottom of the stairs when I got off work. My office mates wondered what had happened. First, there had been a beautiful girl waiting. Now there were men and some of them were obviously homosexual.

Most of my office mates were women, but there was one male employee, Rich, who befriended me. He was perhaps four years older than I, and married with two children. One Friday night, he invited me to dinner at his house. The minute I walked through the door, I could sense that his wife resented me. She complained throughout dinner. Afterwards, Rich announced that he and I were going out for the evening. She said something like, "Go ahead! Who cares?"

We got in Rich's car and headed for the nearby town of Vallejo. He parked in an alley. "Come with me," he said conspiratorially.

"Where are we going?"

"Are you a virgin?" he responded.

I didn't know how to answer. *Well, maybe half a virgin now*, I thought to myself.

He looked me up and down and proclaimed, "You need a woman!"

I was quite sure that *wasn't* what I needed, but obviously Rich was trying to help me be heterosexual. I told him to go ahead and do whatever he wanted. "I'll wait in the car for you."

Rich wasn't happy. "I'm doing this for you!" he grumbled as he climbed a fire escape and disappeared into a window. When he got back he said, "You should have gone with me. It was great!" He went on to explain, "You know my wife is pregnant again, and I don't have sex with her while she's pregnant."

"I see," I said quietly. I was thinking, *Not only is he "doing this" for me, but he also thinks he's being considerate of his wife. I wonder what she would say about his way of being supportive?*

"I'm taking you out again next Sunday night, and next time you're going in with me!"

I really liked Rich and didn't want to disappoint him. On some level, I recognized that I needed his heterosexual friendship. So the next Sunday, I went over to his house, although this time not for dinner. His wife met me at the door with a scowl; her dislike was more obvious than ever. Rich pushed past her and we were off. This time, we went to downtown San Francisco, to the Tenderloin district. I knew I would lose Rich's friendship if I didn't go with him, so we went up a back stairway, and knocked on a door which was answered by an older woman. "Get in here quickly!" she said hoarsely, ushering us into an inside waiting room. The place looked like a movie set with red flocked wallpaper, red velvet chairs and couches, beaded curtains hanging in doorways, and very soft, low lights.

A dark-eyed girl walked up to Rich and said, "Okay, let's go!" They disappeared through the beaded curtains. I waited on the couch for awhile, until a red-haired girl came over to me. "Hey there, I'm Sandy. I'm Rich's favorite girl here, but he gave me to you tonight, so...let's go!"

I was trembling with fear. "I think I'll just wait here for Rich," I told her, "but thanks anyway."

Sandy went to find the madam who marched over and glared at me. "Look kid, you pay either way. We don't care what you do—wait here or go with Sandy. But either way, you gotta pay. Sandy gets eleven dollars an hour, so pay up!"

It was an eleven dollars I was glad to give up, in order to escape an awkward situation. I just hoped Rich would hurry, so another eleven dollars wouldn't be due for the next hour.

Sandy had a few choice words for me, beginning with, "You little *queer...!*"

Finally, Rich emerged, looking satisfied. Of course, he thought I'd been with Sandy. "How was it buddy?" he grinned.

"Fine," I mumbled, and quickly changed the subject. I am not sure if Rich ever found out precisely what did or didn't happen that night. He never mentioned it, but he never asked me to go with him again, either.

In the days that followed, I pondered the situation. Why hadn't I gone with Sandy? I finally concluded that I'd been afraid I couldn't perform. I had no idea what to do with a woman, and I assumed that Sandy would have expectations I couldn't meet. At the end of my self-analysis, I came to the realization that I would always be a relationship-person, not wanting sex-on-demand with either a man or a woman. But I felt bad about letting Rich down. Sadly for me, our friendship faded after that.

By then, I'd had about two years of training with Richard Purvis, playing the Grace Cathedral organ, and I was also studying organ in college. Richard thought it was time I earned some money playing the organ professionally, so he listed me as a substitute organist to fill in around town when other organists went on vacation or had to be away. I quickly found myself busy every Sunday, playing all over the Bay Area. One Episcopal Church in the East Bay hired me for a month. I was surprised that after church, the congregation went to the social hall, where I was introduced to what they claimed was "the longest bar in California." Everyone gathered around and enjoyed mixed drinks. *So church really can be fun!* I smiled to myself. I had to be careful however—it was a long drive home and I didn't want a DUI.

Finally, a church in a ghetto area of San Francisco hired me permanently. The congregation was a mix of many races. I was supposed to be both organist and choir director. I couldn't do much directing, however, since the choir answered to the pastor's wife who, in turn, directed me about how to direct the choir. It wasn't a pleasant situation. One day she announced, "I want you to be youth director, also. From now on that will be part of your job here, too!"

I actually thought that might be fun. The adjoining social hall had once been a youth center, and a few broken and dilapidated games were still there. I used my own money to refurbish the pool table and other games. Loving the outdoors, I led the group on Saturday adventures, including hikes to the beach and to Fisherman's Wharf. Most of the kids were teenagers and very uncooperative, but I enjoyed myself anyway.

During an outing, a man propositioned one of the teen-age boys. I was enraged. I called the police, but they said, "Hey, this happens all the time. Nothing we can do." That night at home, I reflected on this event and vowed never to be a predator.

Meanwhile, I was deeply affected by what I'd heard during Sunday services at the various churches I attended. Now and then, the message came through loud and clear that homosexuals are not God's elect. They are lost, and cannot be saved. This disturbed me greatly. I knew I was saved, but I also knew that all my desires were homosexual. A conflict was growing inside me that would come to a head a year or so later.

Mrs. Silverman, the pastor's wife, was very critical of me. I have no idea if she suspected I was gay, but she seemed to take an instant dislike to me. In her distinct accent—I never could figure out her nationality—she criticized my playing.

"Enough of this!" she decided. "You direct the choir. *I* will play the organ." Actually, she was quite an accomplished musician and I wasn't very good at directing the choir, so I decided it was time to leave.

Meanwhile, my gay friends were an increasingly bad influence on me. Most of them were cynical about my desire for a loving relationship, having abandoned such a hope for their own lives. Even Bernie, who had taken Len away from me said, "I know Len isn't faithful to me. I know he has sex every chance he gets. I'm not as promiscuous as he is, but believe me, I play around when I get the opportunity."

My own behavior had quieted down considerably now that I was living with Mother, but I still kept an active social life. This, of course, greatly interfered with my studies. I skipped classes and began the process of flunking out of college. Just then, one of my friends confided, "I go to Lake Merritt Park in Oakland. There are some great guys there who will go home with you. You should try it."

I decided to see if he was right. One night around 11 P.M., I parked alongside the lake and wandered into a dark, forested area. It wasn't very long before three Air Force men in uniform approached me. "Give me your wallet and you won't get hurt," one of them ordered. I surrendered; they cleaned the money out and threw the wallet into the shrubbery. I thought it was over, but as they were leaving, one of them knocked me down. They all started kicking me, and then beat me brutally. It took weeks for my injuries to heal.

During my recovery I thought wistfully of Pastor Connors' promise that I was about to enter a beautiful life. I began to long for his spiritual counsel, and I was more than happy to hear that he was coming to San Francisco soon. In the meantime, I tried to read my Bible. I started at the beginning and read to the point where the Israelites tricked a group of men into being circumcised, then slaughtered them while they were weak and in pain. Their foul play sickened me, and I didn't want to read another word.

Meanwhile, life with Mother wasn't easy. When she heard Pastor Connors was coming, she expressed herself freely, as always. "He's been a very bad influence on you and I don't want you seeing him! Tell him you have other things to do and can't meet with him!"

Naturally, in order to see him, I had to lie.

Mother seemed to know that Pastor Connors was gay even though the subject had never come up. She probably recognized in him some of the same characteristics she'd seen in her gay brother. I didn't really care what she thought. I needed my old father figure now more than ever. My life was going down the drain, and I craved his encouragement.

Pastor Connors' first words to me were, "Let's go somewhere we can talk." For good reason, he was uncomfortable with my mother. We drove to a local coffee house and before long he said, "I'm writing a book on homosexuality and I need to experience a little of this lifestyle for myself. I want you to take me to some homosexual bars."

I was still hoping for a serious conversation, but off we went. Along the way, I tried to tell him how unrewarding the gay life really was; and that I was now drinking more than I ever had before; and that I was into casual sex, something I never thought I would be doing. I tried to explain that I wasn't doing so well in college, either, and why there were so many interferences.

Pastor Connors gently placed his hand on me. "You've abandoned your ideals and settled for promiscuity," he told me quietly. "Right now you could be living in a fine home, doing well in college, and being prepared for a successful life. But Frank, you turned down the man I selected for you. What you need to do is return to your original desire. You know very well that you need to find the right man and settle down."

Pastor was not his usual animated self that night. He seemed rather depressed, and disclosed to me that things were not going so well in his church. He was no longer appreciated there, and his family life was also troubled. This was the first time he had ever shared with me any details about his personal life.

Still, as our conversation continued, his attention seemed to be drawn relentlessly to the shirtless bartender serving us.

The Black Cat Bar was a very unusual place, populated by a wild mix of homosexuals and bohemians. It was part art gallery and part gay bar, a tourist attraction, and a San Francisco institution. I suppose I was relieved when the night ended without incident. Pastor Connors returned to San Jose, and I went home to Mother.

While Pastor's advice wasn't particularly spiritual, it did motivate me to change my ways. I determined to start searching again, and to not go to bed with anyone who couldn't become my life partner. I dropped the bar scene, stopped going to the nude beach, and only went to gay parties for the purpose of finding Mr. Right.

About that time I met Jay. He was a rail enthusiast, and I didn't know whether he was gay or not. I wasn't planning to be sexually involved with him; I just enjoyed his company and wanted to know him better. Of course in the back of my mind, I hoped he was gay and that something might develop. It was unlikely that he would become my lover, since he valued his settled life in Los Angeles and I didn't want to leave San Francisco. Nonetheless, I invited him to come spend a week with me.

Jay and I shared many common interests. During the week we visited museums, art galleries, and the usual tourist attractions. As days went by, I hoped more and more that those who said Jay was homosexual turned out to be right. Sure enough, before long, our closeness led to sexual activity—at home in my bedroom.

I was careless about hiding what had happened, and left telltale signs behind. My mother discovered the evidence, and rightly assumed that Jay and I had been sexually active. I had just said goodbye to Jay when she stormed toward me, got in my face and shouted, "You're queer aren't you? Get out of my house!"

At first I tried to deny it, but Mother confronted me with

the evidence. Finally, I shouted back, "You want me out? Okay, I'm out!"

I had been smarting under her control anyway, and this was an opportunity to regain my freedom. I went back to my former apartment and lived there for about a year. During that time, I didn't see my mother at all. I phoned her only when I had to discuss financial matters, and when we talked, her tone was icy. Once, I caught a glimpse of her on the street and it broke my heart to see her so down and depressed.

Then, during a gay bash, I met Hal. He was six years older than I, had an excellent job, and seemed very stable. As we got acquainted, I learned he had a dream of being a real estate developer. I told him about the house I had divided into two units. "That's the very thing I want to do!" he exclaimed.

From my perspective, it was refreshing to hear another gay man talking about something besides sex. I was sick of that kind of talk. Hal and I began to see each other more and more. Soon we were lovers, although there was no real spark or much activity in that area. It was our common interest in real estate that bonded us together.

After a few months, Hal and I visited a real estate office together, hoping to find an investment property we could share. The realtor directed us to a four-bedroom house in the Castro District of San Francisco, and helped us find a way to purchase it with no down payment. The asking price was $9,500. "Make an offer for $10,000," he advised, "and I am sure they will take it." They did.

Hal and I immediately began to remodel it into rental units. I learned how to do plumbing, even laying sewer lines. Our two units rented quickly and Hal converted the basement into an apartment for himself. "Why should I be paying rent?" he stated.

Later, he encouraged me to sell the house my mother and I owned in order to buy a three-unit building with a great view, on Twin Peaks. By this time, Mother had reluctantly reconciled with me and she was more than ready to move. Mother moved into the back apartment of the Castro District house Hal and I had first bought, and with the proceeds from the sale of her house, we were able to purchase the Twin Peaks triplex. We immediately rented out all three units of the triplex, and Mother was happy in her own new apartment in our Castro district house. She loved having more windows, a back garden, and shops nearby.

Curiously, Mother liked Hal. As far as I know, he was the only friend of mine she ever thoroughly enjoyed. Hal paid a lot of attention to her, buying her things, and he listened to her talk, something I tried not to do. Hal considered me his lover and all his friends considered us a couple, even though there was practically no sex between us. Even without that, however, I was happy, and I felt willing to forgo sex for a stable relationship.

Hal and I had just purchased our third property, a beautiful four-story Victorian with a panoramic view of the city, when Pastor Connors called again. "I'm stuck in my book on homosexuality," he explained. "I need to gather more information. First, I need to interview you, but I also want to spend a little more time in gay bars..." There was a pause in the conversation. "I'll be there tonight," he added.

I was immediately uneasy. I hadn't told Hal about Pastor Connors. Now that Hal and I had found each other I wasn't so needy, and I guess I'd been hoping Pastor had forgotten about me. But he clearly hadn't. And, although Hal and I didn't spend nights away from each other, I wanted to have this night free.

"My pastor is coming up from San Jose tonight and he wants me to take him to a couple of gay bars."

Hal was incredulous. "Your *pastor* wants to go to gay bars?" He stared at me in disbelief. "What kind of pastor is that? Pastors don't go to gay bars!"

I had no choice. I had to tell him more. I explained that it was Pastor Connor's advice about finding a life partner I'd been following, when he and I had met. I told him about the book on homosexuality Pastor was writing. Still, Hal was skeptical. Like my mother, he was very suspicious of the whole picture.

Hal and I were just moving into the top flat of our new building. Things had never been better between us. Hal had helped me find a job that paid double what I'd been making. He had also arranged for his own place of employment to hire Mother on a part-time basis and now she, too, was earning more than she'd ever made in her life, and loving her work as well. By now, Hal and I had also shared several wonderful holidays together. We had toured London, stopping off in New York on the way, and we were now planning a trip to Hawaii. Life was good. Then the doorbell rang.

Hal greeted my Pastor rather coldly. He said to me, in front of him, that he had work to do. He pointedly asked if I could please come home early to help him.

Pastor Connors and I first went to a coffee house, where he quizzed me about my personal preferences: What type of men did I like? What did I look for in a man? Did I have any fetishes? What kinds of sex had I had and what kinds did I reject? Then we went to a gay bar, where nothing much was going on. "I think I have enough information," he told me. "Let's go to my hotel room and you can help me put what I've learned into categories."

That wasn't all he had in mind. In his room, for the first time, Pastor became sexually aggressive. He kissed me, and then lightly wrestled with me. I didn't want to get involved with him so I shook him off. "I can't have sex with you," I told him. "You're a married man and we would be in an adulterous relationship."

"My wife knows all about me and she wants me to be happy. There's no problem. It's okay with her."

"But I'm in a committed love relationship," I protested. "I did what you suggested. I found the man I want to spend my life with, and I can't cheat on him."

Pastor Connors wasn't impressed with my arguments. "You've known me for about ten years now, Frank. Your loyalty should be with me, not with someone you just met a year ago." His voice hardened a little. "You owe it to me, Frank. Year after year I've spent my time on you freely…"

With those words, he pushed me down on the bed. I had never imagined he could be so physically strong. He tore his clothes off and eagerly began to undress me. "I *have* to have you," he insisted as he fumbled with my buttons. "All these years I've fantasized about you! I've wanted you since the first day I saw you. You owe me, you know." In a flash of guilt, I remembered taking Larry away from him. Maybe I did owe him.

There was no time for further discussion. A thousand different feelings rushed through me, as he took me as his own. I knew I was hungry for sex, but I'd never thought of cheating on Hal. Hal was a rock to me. He had brought maturity into my life. In some ways, he was more of a father figure than Pastor Connors. But it was too late to think about that, or anything else.

When the passion subsided, Pastor held me in his arms for a long time. Although that was comforting to me in one sense, I also felt dirty and defiled. Above all else, how was I going to face Hal?

I had no intention of telling Hal what had happened, but I guessed he might figure it out anyway. I was right. Pastor dropped me off at the house and Hal met me at the front door. He sized up my rather rumpled condition and knew instantly that I'd been intimate with Pastor Connors.

Hal was more than angry. He was crushed. I also was devastated by what had happened. Trying to salvage the situation, I lied outright, adamantly denying that I'd had sex with Pastor Connors. Hal knew very well that I was trying to deceive him.

In those terrible moments, his heart was broken. Our relationship was shattered. Although our business connection continued and we remained housemates for many years, our pleasant and secure life together would never be the same.

Chapter Six

Triumphs, Troubles, and Turning Points

Despite our broken personal relationship, Hal and I continued as business partners, and for a time it seemed that everything we touched turned to gold. We found ourselves making thousands of dollars marketing garden ornaments, plants, and other decorative imports. As our business grew, we traded one piece of property for another and ended up with a large retail building near the San Francisco Civic Center. This site had a huge basement that accommodated our garden-ornament factory, and around 10,000 square feet of retail space on the main floor. At first, we rented out concession space; soon, however, we made hurried trips to Japan, Hong Kong, and Taiwan where we quickly bought enough merchandise to fill several 40-foot shipping containers to stock our new store.

It wasn't long before we were operating a lucrative import department-store featuring jewelry, clothing, pillows and bed sheets, piñatas, all kinds of furniture, rugs, kitchen items, and even food. Our vast array of merchandise enticed the new generation of "flower children," and we had a great location where they loved to browse. All we lacked was a name. One morning while shaving, the words "Black Market" flashed across my mind. When I told Hal, he agreed with my inspiration. We immediately adopted it as our company name. It was a perfect fit.

Soon we had a second store in San Rafael, then a third in Carmel, and a fourth in the Union Square area of downtown San Francisco. We owned two of our locations and business was booming. Hal and I bought a vacation house in Carmel, along with another commercial building. Many adult toys followed—a Corvette, a 40-foot boat, and a house in San Rafael with a dock.

On the downside, with the various real estate properties and the four store locations, our lives were frantic. I could see that Hal was working off his grief with busyness and possessions. He spent his entire days and evenings in his office paying bills, collecting rents, doing paperwork, and being totally consumed by our holdings. In the eyes of what few-remaining gay friends we had, we had become tycoons. However, trouble was just around the corner.

By now it was late 1963. The stores had done well all year, and we had every reason to think our enterprise would continue to thrive. Earlier in the year, we had stocked up for the Christmas season, which required us to allow six months for delivery from our many overseas suppliers. This holiday season promised to be the best we'd ever had, so we did what we had been doing all along—we took a huge risk. We ordered hundreds of thousands of dollars worth of merchandise, assuming we'd make more than enough holiday profits to pay it all off.

Hal and I were at our main store's counter ringing up sales on November 22, 1963, when a man burst through the door shouting, "The President's been shot!" All the customers looked up and stared at him.

We all asked the same question: "The President? What are you talking about?"

"I'm talking about President Kennedy! He was shot just a couple of minutes ago in Dallas!"

Everybody started talking at once, asking questions he couldn't answer: "What's President Kennedy doing in Dallas?" "Who shot him?" "How bad is it?" "Are you sure this is true?" and, "Who told you?"

At the same time, our downstairs employees had been listening to the radio while working in the garden-ornament factory. Now, they rushed upstairs with the same terrible news. About twenty of us gathered around the radio and waited for further reports. Of course, the news went from bad—to the worst possible outcome.

John F. Kennedy was a beloved president and we all mourned his passing. The whole country began to grieve, just as it had done when President Roosevelt had died years before. Almost immediately, our business dropped off by nearly 100 percent. It did not take us long to realize that there was to be no Christmas in 1963. As the days went by, it was also clear that there would be insufficient sales to pay our staggering bills. As an emergency measure, we quickly sold an eight-unit building in downtown San Francisco that we had recently acquired, but it hardly made a dent in what we owed.

Just before Christmas, Hal and I talked late into the night, trying to strategize a way to save ourselves from bankruptcy. What should go and what could we save? When January arrived, it was time for inventory, and I decided to do the work myself at all four stores—I didn't want any employees guessing rather than counting. Unfortunately, the more I counted, the more I realized that something was wrong, terribly wrong. Our inventory was short not by a few dollars, but by around a hundred-thousand dollars. Now we were really in trouble, because we could not borrow against our inventory.

I began to visit the three stores in the San Francisco area every day and our Carmel store once a week. I carried along my camera and took pictures of every aisle and fixture. The employees assumed it was for insurance purposes and paid no attention to what I was doing. As days went by, I became aware that certain large, expensive items had disappeared. After closing, I would check the cash register tapes to see if anything had been sold in that price category. Sometimes I found the transaction, but more often than not, there were no sales reflecting the disappearing merchandise.

Hal quizzed the manager of our Union Square store, but he didn't seem to know anything. It seemed to me, however, that there was more merchandise missing from his store than any of the others. He began to take his own inventory and checked it every morning before opening for business. One day he confided, "I just don't know what's happening! I know very well that no one on my staff sold these things, yet they are missing."

Our San Rafael store also had unaccounted-for items, but not as many as the downtown San Francisco store. When I called the San Rafael store manager, he said, "Oh, yeah, that's because I loaned a few things to different people. Some charities wanted props for skits and fashion shows, and I let them have them. Don't worry, they promised to bring them back in a few days. Also, some of our customers wanted to try some things out, to see if they would look good at home. I let them do that, too. It will all be returned or be sold, so don't worry about it."

Since I had been taking pictures, I knew which items were missing and I was keeping track of them. One morning our Union Square manager called saying, "You know that big brass tray you left here yesterday? This morning it's missing! I hope you don't think I'm stealing from you!" I assured him that we trusted him—but the truth was, by that time I didn't trust anybody.

Then Hal suggested a new plan. "I'm going to hide in the Union Square store all night," he said. "Let's see what happens."

The idea of staking out one of our stores made me a little uneasy, but I agreed that we had to find out was going on. Hal arranged some furniture, hung drapes over a false window, and hid himself behind the drapes.

About three in the morning, he heard the key turn in the front door lock. Someone entered and turned on the lights. Hal waited a few more minutes, listening carefully. He heard footsteps and the sound of a ladder. At last he revealed himself. Standing before him, holding a stack of bedspreads in his arms, was our San Rafael manager. Outside, a truck was parked with its back gate open; he was about to load it up with our stock.

"David, what are you doing?" Hal asked calmly.

"Oh, Hal, how nice to see you!" David replied innocently. "Some of my customers want to try these things out in their homes. My store has sold out of them but I knew this store had them."

"Where did you get a key?" Hal inquired.

"Frank left his keys with me when I had to make a delivery," David explained, "and I didn't think anyone would mind if I had a copy made."

David drove off without any merchandise. We changed the locks the next morning. Meanwhile, Hal talked to the San Rafael police department and they suggested we hire a private detective to find the stolen merchandise. We did, and within days, he discovered that David had a warehouse filled with our missing merchandise. Hal filed charges against David, but when the case came to court, the judge would not allow the evidence because the investigator had not obtained a search warrant. The judge allowed David to plead no-contest.

That was the end of the line for us; we couldn't recover any of our wares. David left town, and we thought we had seen the last of him. Instead of pursuing him, it was time for Hal and me to see a bankruptcy lawyer.

The lawyer immediately filed Chapter 11 for us. Part of the agreement was that four of our buildings would be sold at public auction on the Court House steps. This was one of the saddest days in our young lives. In addition, our Carmel store, our Union Square store, and our main store near the San Francisco Civic Center were closed down. We took all the merchandise to our San Rafael store, since it was our strongest and most profitable location.

My mother was living in one of the sold properties, so I had to figure out what to do with her. At the same time, our San Rafael building now went up for auction, and we were given thirty days to move. Half a block down the street was a large building that had once been an auto dealership. We needed something that size to hold all the remaining merchandise from the four stores. At first, we didn't realize this building was in San Anselmo, not San Rafael. The building we leased was on Greenfield Avenue, a sleepy frontage road, but highly visible from the main roadway. The downtown San Anselmo merchants did not want to see Greenfield Avenue developed into a competing business district. To their dismay, we were the first of many businesses to move there. Thankfully, both areas prospered.

We didn't intend to open for business until we'd found appropriate fixtures and could organize our stock, but even as we were carrying merchandise into the building, customers flooded in through the open doors, and were soon digging through all our boxes. It turned into an insane rummage sale—and the traffic never stopped. We couldn't do anything except answer questions like, "What is this? And how much do you want for it?" Because we had also lost the building where we lived, some of our personal possessions were in boxes along with everything else. I noticed one woman digging through a box of clothing—and realized it was my dirty laundry.

On the day we received the keys to the building, with only a small portion of our merchandise moved in, we went home with a full bag of money. We finally did get organized. Within a few years, we even had to rent the building next door because business was so brisk. By that time, we had paid off all our obligations and were debt-free, although now we owned far less real estate. We were even able to buy my mother a one-bedroom house in Mill Valley, where she lived until she died.

Hal no longer had to spend long hours on the books, and was adjusting to a new way of life. Because we had far fewer holdings, both of us had more free time. One day, I saw airline tickets on Hal's desk—two tickets to Maui.

"Are we going to Hawaii?" I asked him.

"Well, *I* am going to Hawaii, but you're not invited!" he said rather coldly. "I've found someone I like, and we'll be gone for two weeks. I'm sure you can take care of everything while I'm gone."

It was a lonely two weeks. Even though I was extremely busy, I couldn't help wondering about Hal's new friend. Was this going to be a permanent relationship, or was it just a one-time getaway? When they returned, Hal certainly seemed to be in love with this twenty-something young man.

I wasn't sure what I was feeling, but my feelings didn't make much difference anyway. As it turned out, Hal's new relationship lasted for the next ten years, until the young man found a woman and married her. At that point, Hal vowed never again to have another love relationship. From that time on, he became increasingly reclusive, and true to his word, until the last day of his life he never had another same-sex relationship.

As for me, sometime around my thirtieth birthday, I finally began to fill out physically. I had always been very thin, but now I was gaining weight. For the next ten years, I felt good and looked great. By the time I turned thirty-three, however, I had grown weary of short-term sexual encounters and wanted a special person in my life.

One night driving home from work, I talked to God for the first time in a decade, "Lord, I am hurting! I'm so lonely, and I need someone to love me. Please help me."

Some people have since told me I shouldn't have spoken to the Lord audibly about such a thing; there are Christians who believe Satan can intercept what we say aloud, giving him the opportunity to come up with his own plan. I rather doubt that, but I do believe it was wrong for me to ask God for someone to engage in a sinful relationship with.

As it turned out, my prayer was soon answered, although I'm not prepared to say that God was the one who answered it. In any case, the very next day, a friend stopped by to tell me about a young man who wanted to meet me. Later on, he brought Joe to my store and introduced us. We immediately liked each other, although we had little in common. Joe was around twenty years old, and he was enamored with cars.

Joe and I hadn't been together long, when he told me he needed money for a carburetor. Soon, he needed money for a series of other automotive things he couldn't live without. On and on it went. My relationship with Joe was a long-lasting one, but the most costly I ever experienced. It was not just financially costly, but emotionally and spiritually draining, as well.

From day one, Joe made it clear that he intended to have other people in his life. "Don't expect me to be faithful to you, because I can't, and I won't," he warned me. Since having Joe was a take-it-or-leave-it proposition, I agreed to an open relationship. He liked to travel and we took short trips together, but before long, he wanted to go farther and longer. I couldn't leave the store since Hal was now taking more time off with his new friend.

Then, Joe disappeared for about two months. I assumed he was taking one of those long trips he wanted so much. I was right. One night he phoned from the East Coast, "Hey Frank, I have no money to come home! Can you send me a few hundred dollars?"

How did I feel about this? At first I enjoyed Joe and was happy with the relationship, such as it was. I don't think I was ever really in love with him, but for a while, he filled the void in my heart. Meanwhile, I had sufficient finances to make him happy, so I always did what he asked me to do. In this instance (and many to come), I knew if I wanted him back, I had to send money. He'd come home for a few months and we would have a fairly good relationship, then he'd do the same thing again. This was to be our pattern for eleven years. As it turned out, while Joe was away, I spent most of my time dreaming of finding someone else to love.

That's when I met Jerry. We had a lot in common, and for two months we saw a lot of each other. I was feeling very attached to Jerry and was planning to move in with him. I even told Hal that I might be moving out. Hal simply said, "Better think it through, Frank. It's a big step!"

I thought it through, and decided Jerry was the man for me. One afternoon I was about to tell him that I cared for him and wanted to live with him, when he spoke first.

"Frank," Jerry began with an uncomfortable look on his face, "there's something I have to tell you..."

I had a sinking feeling inside. "What is it, Jerry?"

"I can't see you anymore!"

"Jerry, why not?" I asked, my heart pounding.

His answer felt like a bucketful of ice water in my face. "To be honest, Frank...it's because you aren't handsome enough for me."

That was a turning point for me. I realized at that moment what a shallow world I was living in. It had to sink in, of course. In the midst of that humiliating scene, though, I could not envision any way out. Change, in fact, was coming, but so were some very difficult circumstances.

Through our network of friends, Hal and I learned that David, our former store manager, was in trouble again. After getting off without any legal repercussions, he had gone on to swindle someone else. Apparently, the next victim was more fortunate than we had been—David was serving a six-year prison sentence. What we didn't know was, David was already planning his next heist, and Hal and I were once again his target.

By then, another Christmas had arrived, and on the last Sunday before the big holiday, our store was jammed with people buying anything and everything. Our shelves were practically bare. We had taken in tens of thousands of dollars, and could not deposit the money until Monday morning. This situation, involving a lot of cash-on-hand on weekends, was something that David knew about all too well. About 2 P.M. that Sunday afternoon, Hal got a phone call. A terrified look crossed his face as he listened to the anonymous caller's words:

"You don't know me, but I know who you are. Don't ask my name, but listen to me. David just got out of prison, and he and two of his cellmates plan to rob you tonight."

Hal instantly called the San Anselmo Police Department. "Sorry, there's nothing we can do," they informed him, "until an actual robbery takes place. Just call us if anything develops."

Alone later that night, as I was closing things down, I saw a car parked across the street with three men inside. Quite obviously, they were watching the store. I called the police, and they were again entirely unhelpful. "If the car follows you," the officer on the phone advised me, "call us." This was many years before cell phones, and calling the police would mean pulling off the road and finding a telephone. It was about 8 P.M. when I finally headed home. In my rearview mirror, I saw the suspicious car make a U-turn and follow me.

I've got to call the police, I told myself. *Maybe if I stop to buy groceries, it will look natural and I can phone from the store.* I parked at a nearby market, grabbed a few items, and then asked the clerk to let me use the phone. "It's an emergency," I said as calmly as I could.

The kid behind the counter looked bored. "Um, I'll have to ask my boss...." Time was slipping by and my hands were shaking. The kid strolled off, then finally wandered back in my direction. "Okay," he shrugged. "If you'll pay for the call, you can use the phone."

I could see the men in the car were watching my every move, so I had to hide behind the counter to make the call. The police advised me, "Let them follow you. We'll phone ahead to the Mill Valley police and alert them. Don't worry! Police will be hiding around your house. Just let them go through with the robbery."

Their car had very distinctive headlights, so I knew they were on my tail all the way home. I parked in the driveway, unlocked the door, and told Hal what was happening. He called the Mill Valley police. "Yes," the voice said, "San Anselmo called, and we have two cars hidden by your house. Just let them go through with the robbery."

I was in the house about ten minutes when we heard a knock at the door. Hal said, "You answer. I'll hide in the bedroom and surprise them if anything happens."

I wasn't thrilled with this arrangement. All I could think was that I sure hoped the police were out there somewhere!

I cautiously opened the door and found myself facing three men in black stocking masks. I couldn't tell which one was David. Our house was on a hill, so the front door was at street level and there were two floors downstairs. The men burst in, knocked me down the stairs, and started beating me with the butts of their pistols.

"Where's the money?" they demanded repeatedly, between blows.

"I don't have it!" I insisted. It was true. Since David knew I always took the money home on Sunday nights, I had locked it in the safe at the store, instead.

"Search the house!" one of them ordered. "It's here some-where!" They tore everything apart, room by room. One of them entered the back bedroom where Hal was lying in wait. We had just received a shipment of Indonesian knives and Hal had brought them home to price them. As the intruder walked through the doorway, Hal plunged a knife into his chest. While the man writhed in pain, Hal escaped through the laundry-room door and ran up to the carport to see if he could find the police.

The man staggered after him, the knife still in his chest. Hal tripped and fell. The man now towered over him, brandishing a pistol. "This is it!" he declared. Just as he was about to pull the trigger, the intruder fell over backward and blacked out.

Seconds later, one of the others—who had made a break for the car—now drove up and somehow got the bleeding, unconscious man into the back seat. He took off, probably in search of a hospital. This left only one man, who had a gun pressed firmly against my back. "Start walking," he snarled.

It was a dark night and rain was pouring. As we walked down the street, he kept shoving the gun more tightly into my spine. A neighbor saw what was happening and called the police. The police said they knew about the robbery—and were on their way. When we got to the street corner, the man ran off into the bushes, still giving me orders. "Stay right there and don't move! I can see you!"

Suddenly, the police appeared and asked me if I was all right. One police car pursued the getaway car, while the other officers searched the bushes and found the gunman. They took him away, and everything was quiet again for the moment.

An hour later, a police car drove up again. "We chased the car," they said. "It overturned and we found a dead man in the back seat, with a knife in his heart. Who did that?" Hal admitted that he had stabbed the intruder.

"Sorry," the officer told him, "but we have to take you in."

Hal was booked on a murder charge, and spent the night in jail.

The next morning our attorney was able to get Hal released, pending a trial. A week later, the District Attorney dropped all charges against Hal. That was the good news. The bad news was that Hal and I would have to testify at the trial of the two surviving men. As it turned out, David had escaped when the car flipped over, so the trial only involved one man— the thug who had held a gun to my back.

During the trial, we were shocked to learn that this man had previously killed two other people. He was quite a wicked character, and he vowed to get revenge on Hal and me when he got out of prison again. We hoped he would never get out. Later on, we learned he killed a third person, his cellmate, so we concluded the chances were slim that we would have to face him again.

David, however, was another story. He was still on the loose, and to be on the safe side, the police advised us to sell our house, and not reveal where we moved. We later discovered that David would have every reason to seek revenge: Hal had killed David's nineteen-year-old lover. We both felt sad that this young man's life had ended so quickly and foolishly.

Years flew by after these incidents, and I soon reached forty. My years of looking good were now behind me. To make matters worse, a strange thing was happening—some of the gay bars and baths were now checking IDs at the door, and if you were forty or over, you were denied entrance.

Sometimes I studied myself in the mirror. I couldn't see any big changes, but others could clearly see I was aging. Younger gays were beginning to ridicule me. All too often I heard, "Get lost, old man." During this difficult period, my relationship with Joe became more important to me, and predictably, Joe was upping the ante. His tastes were becoming far more expensive than before, and his trips longer. At the same time, our store continually needed more merchandise, requiring me to make lengthy trips also.

We were able to obtain an exclusive line of rattan furniture, some of it manufactured in China, some in Hong Kong. It was beautiful furniture, but it did not fit U.S. needs. A number of customers were returning items, saying their TVs and stereos didn't fit properly. I knew I had to redesign the line for American tastes. I moved to Hong Kong for a while and worked in the factory, laying out the precise changes we needed in order to sell the products.

The manufacturers were delighted to have this information, and later, we found out why. Meanwhile, we developed a line of nearly four hundred items, which arrived at our store in shipping containers, sometimes several at a time. These items were a smash hit. Our only problem was the factory could not keep up with our orders. Later, we learned the factory owners were strategically planning to start their own business in the U.S., once they had the right products. Hedging their bets, they had been withholding merchandise from us in order to stockpile it in Los Angeles for the grand opening of their own U.S. outlet.

Nonetheless, our customers would show up the day the containers arrived and literally grab their favorite items out of our hands as we unloaded them. Our store was out-performing large corporate chains. Hal and I had more disposable income than ever, and I bought everything I could possibly want for myself. However, those were not happy years for me. I was lonely, and I was gradually becoming embittered. My relationship with Joe was unrewarding, like a thorn in my side. I really had no one to turn to.

By then, we had a trustworthy store manager who made it possible for both Hal and me to be away for extended periods. I had to spend time in Belgium, where we had a contract with a factory making faux-oriental rugs. The sixties generation was buying our rugs as fast as we could get them in, not only putting them on their floors, but also using them to decorate walls and ceilings.

During one of my trips, our manager, Bob, hired an eighteen-year-old kid who looked like a hippie. I saw this boy working in our stockroom one day, and I didn't like his appearance. "I don't want him out on the retail floor," I told Bob. "I don't want the customers to see him."

Bob defended the young man, whose name was Mike. "He really is a good boy, Frank. He's smart, and I need his help." I agreed that Bob could employ Mike as long as no one had to look at him. Apart from the kid's appearance, I was relieved that Bob had found someone reliable to help him.

After another trip abroad, I returned to hear that Mike was in the hospital in very serious condition. As I thought about this young man in such difficult circumstances, tears flooded my eyes. I remembered the wonders of being young, and thought how sad it was that Mike might die in his youth. It had been about ten years since I had last talked to God, and the results of that self-serving prayer had not played out well. But now, I went off where I could be alone and prayed for Mike.

This was another turning point for me, and it was a big one. Looking back now, I can see this was my first step in reconnecting with God. He was right there, waiting for me to invite Him back into my life.

As I prayed for Mike, I thought about my relationship with God and the excitement I had once felt when I used to pray with Larry. I even prayed that Mike would come to know Jesus, as I had once known Him. I couldn't have imagined the impact this prayer would have on Mike. Even more, I couldn't have imagined the impact Mike would soon have on me.

Months later, I came home from a trip to North Africa and Europe to find a handsome young man running the cash register. "Bob, who is that?" I asked. "He looks kind of familiar." "Don't you recognize Mike?" Bob asked with a smile.

I could not believe my eyes. Could this be the same hippie boy who'd once upset me with his long, stringy hair and tattered clothes?

"That's *Mike*?" I was dumbfounded. After closing time, I decided to talk to him. He didn't seem in a hurry to go, so I asked, "Mike, what in the world happened to you? You look so different! I didn't even recognize you!"

Mike told me his story. He had been hospitalized with cancer, and one of his testicles had been surgically removed. A pastor from a local "Jesus People" church had gone to the hospital to visit him and pray with him. In the course of their conversation, Mike had prayed to receive the Lord. Now healed from his cancer, Mike was living in the pastor's house, and had become a worship leader in the church.

I had always played it straight, and assumed that only other homosexuals realized I was gay. I was ever the perfect businessman, well-dressed and careful to play the part properly. Needless to say, I was shocked when Mike told me he had his whole church praying for his gay boss. The Jesus Movement produced some strange and wonderful people. Little did I know that I soon would become a "Jesus Freak," too.

Mike already wanted to do some negotiating with me. He was very offended that we carried occult items at our store. "If I buy every occult item in stock, would you agree not to stock them again?" he asked me. This was a hard choice. The "flower children" in the area were buying up everything I ordered; not stocking our magical merchandise would disappoint my customers, and other sales would probably drop as well. But as I saw Mike's sincerity, and recognized the purity that now seemed to radiate from him, I could not refuse.

For the next year, I watched Mike very carefully. Strangely enough, although he was extraordinarily handsome, I was never attracted to him. I respected his belief in Jesus and the way he conducted his life. I never wanted to dishonor him by thinking of him in that way. Meanwhile, my twelve other employees thought he was slightly crazy and constantly made fun of him. They were especially amused when he bought such items as "crystal" gazing balls, took them out behind the building, and smashed them with a hammer.

As for me, I became more and more aware of the contrast between the purity of Mike's life and the degradation of mine. Every time I saw Mike, I thought of my early years, the excitement of being young, and the relationship I had once enjoyed with God. I was so happy Mike was experiencing what I had once felt. Sometimes, however, a profound sadness would overshadow me, when I imagined that I could never return to those days of purity and wonder. I grieved the losses I had experienced over the years and, most of all, I mourned the loss of my own integrity, purity, innocence, and healthy relationships.

It now had been about twenty years since I had seen Pastor Connors. During our last encounter, he had seduced me with his words, "Frank, I have to have you!" I could not have predicted how many times in my life I would hear those words from innumerable men. By the time Mike came along, I had learned that "I have to have you!" was nothing more than a throwaway line, opening the door to a one-time encounter. Gay or straight, after making a sexual conquest, more often than not the predator has no further interest in the prey.

As for Pastor Connors, I had long been grateful that he'd never appeared again to interfere in my relationships. Now, as my depression deepened, I began to think that maybe I needed him in my life after all. I found myself wondering what he would look like after so many years. Inquiring around at my home church in San Jose, I learned he was no longer there—he had been asked to leave. I heard he had started a new career in real estate and was living in Monterey, so I drove down there. Looking through the phonebook, I saw his wife's name, but not his. I located his wife in a real estate office, and she told me that Pastor Connors had died at age 43. He'd been gone for years.

I returned home more depressed than ever, feeling that the only person who had ever really understood me was dead. For me, all hope was gone. The more I thought about Pastor Connors, the more I missed the closeness I'd once had with him. It didn't help that I now was 43, the same age he had been when he died. My material possessions no longer brought me pleasure. My lover, Joe, was hitting me up for more and more money, and spending less and less time with me. I was washed up in the gay life, and my business was increasingly demanding and unsatisfying.

I was beginning to question my very existence. I had traveled to so many places in the world, but there was no place I really wanted to live. Maybe I didn't want to live at all…! I had no goals, no vision, and seemingly—no future. I was having frequent panic attacks. I crossed the Golden Gate Bridge at least twice a day, and had done so for years. Now, I found myself obsessing about an altogether new thought: *One of these days, I'll just stop the car mid-span, and I'll jump. Then, maybe I'll have some peace!*

Frank at 30. (1959)

Black Market Imports.

Hal and Frank. (c. 1960)

... and at age 40. (1969)

*Frank while on a buying trip
in Hong Kong. (c. 1970)*

Chapter Seven

Destiny Bridge

Once again, I was crossing the Golden Gate Bridge. Once again, I was thinking about the emptiness and futility of my life, pondering my destiny. Every time I had driven across the bridge's picturesque span in recent days, I'd grown more convinced that it would be remarkably easy and sensible to end it all right there. Then on one particular day, as if out of nowhere, a completely contradictory thought entered my mind:

If you are willing to take your life, are you willing to give it to Me?

When I asked myself, *Where did that come from?* the unexpected words repeated themselves in my mind:

If you are willing to take your life, are you willing to give it to Me?

Was that God? I wondered, my heart pounding. I was stunned by this new perspective. However, it didn't take me long to find problems with the idea. *Of course, I'm willing to give my life to God,* I thought bitterly, *but what good will it do?* I knew I couldn't have a relationship with God while I continued to live in homosexual sin. Anyway, I had asked Him to change me when I was sixteen and He hadn't done it, so what was the difference now?

For the next two weeks, I could think of little else beyond the great debate raging inside me. Once I'd had a great relationship with God, but the gay life had ruined it. *Lord,* I prayed one day, *You and I both lost this battle many years ago. Now, what's the use of going back to all that conflict and trauma?*

Immediately, I flashed back to age 23, when my gay-life-vs.-God conflict had come to a head. I had been in such turmoil, I had honestly been afraid of losing my sanity. I remember taking an afternoon off work and driving through Golden Gate Park. I was so frustrated with God. *Lord,* I had told him, *our relationship is over! You won't change me, and I can't serve You the way I am. This conflict will kill me, so it's goodbye!*

In those days, I was playing the organ in churches all over the Bay Area. Occasionally the issue of homosexuality would come up during a sermon, and the words from the pulpit were always very condemning. "Those people can't be saved!" one preacher or another would rant. "Don't waste your time on homosexuals!" Sometimes a fired-up minister would say the worst word of all, "*Abomination!* Of all the sins, homosexuality is the worst. It is an *abomination!*" Sometimes the word "dog" was even used to describe gays.

That day in the park, I had decided I would no longer play the organ or even enter a church. *Never again,* I had promised myself, and I had now kept that vow for 21 years. From that day on, whenever I'd heard church or the Christian life mentioned, I had always felt the same negative emotions.

At first, I was sure God had spoken to me on the Golden Gate Bridge, but before long I started to talk myself out of it, trying very hard to deny it. *It couldn't have been God. What would He want with me?* I kept asking myself. After a couple of weeks, I had pretty well convinced myself that it had just been a random thought, and that I'd better put it out of my mind or I would have to face that insane turmoil again.

Now it was May 25, 1973. The store was running well and I had a free afternoon. I had spent a troubled night, tossing and turning, thinking about the emptiness of my life. I'd gained everything I had ever wanted, except the one thing I wanted most—a loving, meaningful relationship. I also admitted that, along with feelings of hopelessness, my futile search for sex was interfering with my effectiveness as a businessman.

I had been getting no enjoyment from work, and as thoughts of suicide came and went, I had found myself wrestling with two opposing thoughts. One was that perhaps if I would spend more time on my search, somewhere just around the corner I would find the fulfilling relationship I was seeking. The second thought was that I had tried everything I could think of, but nothing had worked out, and the search was useless.

From time to time, when I had decided to try again, I would take a week off from work, go to another city, and spend my time in bars and gay cruising grounds. After a few days, I would be thoroughly disgusted with myself. Those binges had never brought me any peace or resolution; they only brought self-condemnation. I felt driven by a wicked force that was destroying me, yet I was helpless to gain mastery over it. In fact, it was gaining more ground on me with every passing day.

That particular May morning, I had decided to try one more time. One of my friends had told me about a new gay bathhouse that had just opened. I no longer went to the baths because I could not face the rejection. But my friend had assured me that this establishment was different from the others—there were no lights, and it was impossible to see anyone. *Darkness like that makes me think of hell!* I had thought at first. *Anyway, I'm not that hard-up.* Now, I changed my mind. *Yes, I am that hard-up!*

That day, I left my office with every intention of visiting the new bathhouse, but something happened to me that words simply cannot describe. There was no bright shaft of light, but suddenly I had another flash-back. I was fourteen again, kneeling at the altar, asking God to be my Father. I had just watched my own father take his last breath and I was feeling so completely alone, so lost. I had wanted to die that day, too. I realized I was experiencing those same lost, hopeless, abandoned feelings once again.

Now, as I walked down the long corridor outside my office, I heard an audible voice speak to me, "I want you back!"

This was no still, small voice; it was a shout. It was not a voice I could associate with any of my employees or, for that matter, anyone I'd ever known. I was frightened out of my wits. *I may have been saved all these years,* I thought, feeling panicked, *but my salvation is over today!*

In that moment, although I was feeling tremendous remorse for my evil lifestyle, a different and profound truth broke through: God had indeed fulfilled His role as Father in my life. He had saved me from numerous life-threatening situations. I had been beaten and robbed several times, yet I had always survived. In my travels, I had once been within blocks of a deadly bombing, and I'd had several harrowing experiences while flying. Now, in an instant, I could clearly see how, time and again, He had protected me. I knew beyond the shadow of a doubt that He was still my Father.

My next thought was that I had to find Mike. I desperately needed to talk to him.

I rushed to the stock room and found Mike in a conversation with one of our suppliers. I broke into their conversation and said quietly to Mike, "Sorry, but I have got to talk with you right now! Please drop everything and come with me."

Mike excused himself and took my arm and led me to a quiet corner. "Okay, Frank. Calm down and tell me what's happening."

"Mike! God spoke to me!"

Mike smiled and shrugged, "Frank, God speaks to me every day."

"No!" I protested. "You don't understand!"

"Frank, this seems to be very important to you. Look, I have the keys to my church. Let's go there and talk.

We drove to Stewart Chapel at the San Francisco Theological Seminary in San Anselmo, where Mike's congregation—Agape Fellowship—met. It was a glorious day in May, but I didn't notice that as we entered the chapel. We sat on the front pew and I explained the sequence of events, quoting God's words to me, "I want you back!"

"Frank, that means God wants you to rededicate your life to Him," Mike, explained. "To do that, you need to pray a 'sinner's prayer.'"

"How do I do that?"

"I'll lead you, and you just repeat what I say. But you have to mean it!"

The prayer started something like this, "Lord, I have sinned against You; I have misused the life You have given me. I'm sorry I have been away from You for so many years. Forgive me for grieving Your Spirit. I renounce Satan and his hold upon my life. Come into my life Lord Jesus…"

Mike went on for twenty minutes. He covered everything he thought I might have done in the gay lifestyle. Since Mike was never gay, he was a bit inaccurate, but I confessed to it all, anyway. If God had something for me, I wanted it, and I wanted it badly. Tears were rolling down my face. On the one hand, I felt somewhat embarrassed because I was Mike's boss. On the other hand, I knew something very significant was happening to me and that it was going to be life-changing. And it was—as we left the chapel, I physically felt as if a huge burden had been lifted off my shoulders. I felt wonderful!

As we walked outside, I saw the world around me as if for the first time. Suddenly, I was aware of trees in bloom and the remarkably beautiful day. For the first time in years, I felt real hope surging through my body. I had no idea what would happen next, but Mike assured me that God had everything in His trustworthy hands.

It wasn't long before a serious problem occurred to me. What was I going to do about Joe? We had been seeing each other for eleven years. Would I have to tell him our relationship was over? When I asked Mike what to do, he said, "You owe it to Joe to tell him what happened. Maybe he will be saved, too."

It was Friday and I was planning to spend the weekend with Joe. About three in the afternoon, he called me. "I'll be there at six as usual."

"Okay, see you then," I said. Then I added, "I have something to tell you."

I asked Mike to stay with me after closing. I didn't trust myself and was afraid I would not say the things I needed to say. I could easily imagine myself going off to spend the weekend with Joe instead.

Six o'clock came, all the employees left, and I locked the door. Mike and I waited for Joe. Mike agreed to stay out of sight, and appear only if I needed him to explain something. "In that case," he said, "just come find me."

Hours passed, and by nine o'clock, Joe still had not appeared. Mike and I decided to go to our respective homes, but I was anxious. I knew at some point I would have to face Joe, and without Mike's support, I didn't know if I could say what I needed to say. I fully expected Joe to appear the next day, Saturday, but he didn't.

Sunday arrived and Mike was expecting me to attend a worship service with him. It had been years since I'd darkened the door of a church. I dreaded it, but decided to go anyway. I had made a deal with God and I was determined to keep my part of the bargain. I had exchanged my sinful, depressing life for a new life in Him. I was now His property, not my own; I would do whatever He asked of me. Besides, I was feeling exhilarated for the first time in decades.

Mike picked me up for church. When we walked inside, I saw about a hundred noisy people hugging each other and being completely informal, as if we'd walked in on some sort of a celebration. Then, I noticed everyone was looking at me, and all at once I got it. They were staring at Mike's gay boss—the one they'd been praying for. Later some of them told me they'd never expected their prayers to be answered; they had never heard of any gay person leaving the homosexual lifestyle.

I was already a little disoriented. Then, all at once the service began—with a blast of rock music. If there was anything that I, a former organist, hated, it was rock music. Even after I learned we were listening to *Christian* rock, it took me a while to get used to it. That wasn't all. I was further astonished to see men get out of their seats and gather in the aisle, where they found another man and danced to the music. I remembered the first time I had seen men dancing together—in a gay bar. *What kind of church is this?* I wondered.

As more people drifted in, I saw various worshippers whispering to the newcomers and pointing at me. I could almost hear them say, "Can you believe it? That's Mike's gay boss!" During the service, a few people spoke out in tongues, something I had neither heard, nor heard of, before. *What is this?* I asked myself more than once. *What have I gotten myself into?*

Once the time of praise and worship finally ended, the pastor got up to preach. Mike whispered, "That's Pastor Leonard, who visited me in the hospital and brought me to the Lord." This preacher spoke with a pleasant look on his face, but his message was direct and clear: "Get your act together, and do it now!" Later that morning he shook my hand and said how happy he was to have me in his church.

I didn't understand at the time that a new spiritual wind was sweeping across the country. It was called the "Jesus Movement," and Mike's church was one of hundreds of informal fellowships that had sprung up. Seemingly from out of nowhere, a new hero had emerged from the midst of the counter-culture: Jesus Christ. This was not a fragile, limp Christ on the cross, but a robust, revolutionary Christ, a Christ of power.

Like the community of Christians described in the book of Acts, many converted hippies lived in communes where everything was shared. Of course this was controversial—some conservative church members didn't see it as a return to first-century Christianity, but as a form of communism. Meanwhile, in churches and communes alike, there were excesses, errors, and extremes. The Jesus movement was not only untamed, but was also greatly misunderstood and mis-represented by the mainline churches. Today, my personal belief remains that it was indeed a genuine work of the Holy Spirit—the third Person of the Trinity.

After church that Sunday, I went back to work at my store. Although these new experiences seemed very bizarre, I noticed I was feeling happy for the first time in years. One of the songs I'd heard that morning had said something about the joy of the Lord. *Maybe that's what I'm feeling,* I thought with a smile.

That afternoon, Pastor Leonard and a woman from the church came to visit me at the store. I ushered them upstairs to my office. After they were seated, Pastor revealed the reason for the visit. "Well, now that you have a changed life," he informed me, "you should be married. This is a good woman," he gestured toward the uncomfortable-looking lady seated next to him. "She will make you a good wife."

Hey! Wait a minute! I thought. *I've only been out of the gay lifestyle since Friday!* I was at a loss for words, but somehow I managed to say "no."

Meanwhile the poor woman shrank into a corner, praying desperately in tongues. We never said a word to each other.

Pastor Leonard was disappointed in my refusal to consider marrying this stranger, so he left rather abruptly. I was beginning to have second thoughts about this "new life." It really was a bit too strange for my taste.

Just as all this was running through my head, more visitors arrived to see me—a trio of men from Mike's church. By this time, I didn't know what to expect; I was rather apprehensive. Since I had turned down the potential bride, I was afraid they were going to tell me they didn't want any gay people in the church. As it turned out, that was not their purpose at all.

As these men talked, I learned that one was single and the other two were married. The married guys were making regular, secret trips to San Francisco's gay bathhouses, and the single guy had same-sex partners there in Marin County. These men all wanted me to help them, even though it had been only three days since my rededication!

I didn't know what to say, but the Lord gave me a single word for them. That word was, "Surrender." I explained how my gay life had grown so empty and depressing that I had not wanted to go on living. "I was contemplating suicide, but God asked for my life," I said, "and I've given it to Him as completely as I know how. In other words, I've surrendered everything to God."

In talking together, we found that none of us knew why we were attracted to men, and we had no idea how to change our orientation. From that point on, the four of us would get together from time to time, and whatever lessons I had learned, I would share with them. We were all trying to live one day of surrender at a time.

I no longer carried the heavy burden of suicidal thoughts and depression, and I was grateful that I had Mike to talk with. Every day after work, he would give me a short time of Bible study. Before long, he insisted I go to the church's Wednesday night Bible study group. I thought to myself, *Do I really need this?*

Things seemed pretty good. I was not yet struggling with sexual temptation and for the time being I wasn't even thinking about sex. It was a great relief but I didn't know how long that would last. I decided I'd better do what Mike was asking, since I fully believed God had given me Mike as a guide for my new life.

Mike repeatedly admonished me to keep reading the Bible. "Frank, God is carrying you right now while you get firmly grounded in His Word. But," he cautioned, "sooner or later, He will set you down and expect you to handle things on your own. He wants you to be able to take authority over the enemy in His name. There will be tough times ahead, so prepare yourself now!"

My first week was surprising. Many attractive young men crossed my path, yet I remained uninterested. By the second week, however, some of my joyous victory had begun to slip away. Another battle had started raging in my mind. Everything I had heard or felt those last two weeks was challenged. *Is it real*, I kept asking myself, *or are Mike and the rest of them deluded?* I struggled with doubt, skepticism, and a deep longing for sexual relief. In the meantime, I had heard so much talk about Satan, demons, and deliverance (exorcism), that I felt like I was on an extended Halloween adventure.

During this process, I was learning not only about myself, but also about the spiritual strengths and weaknesses of my new Christian community. I was beginning to see that God, indeed, was real, but not everything I was hearing was the absolute truth. Mixed into my friends' sincerity and faith, there were very human elements of exaggeration, enthusiasm, and a superstitious belief that speaking something aloud would make it come true. I was quickly learning not to doubt God, but to question some of the things His people were saying and doing.

With Mike's encouragement, I decided to take a week off, go to my house in Carmel, and read the Bible, cover to cover. It was summer and the weather was beautiful. Every day, sitting on my deck overlooking a forest of pine trees, I read for hours. I managed to get beyond the place where the Israelites killed all the unsuspecting circumcised men, and although there were a few more atrocities to wade through, I found many interesting and illuminating stories.

Reading the whole Bible in one week turned out to be an overly optimistic goal; it took a little over two weeks to get to Revelation. In the process, though, I gained a better understanding of what was happening to me. I realized God was going to make me whole in all aspects of my life, not merely in the homosexual part. That spiritual retreat was one of the most pleasant times I had ever enjoyed.

Back home, I found Mike wasn't finished with me. Now, he added an early-morning Bible study group to my schedule, in addition to the one on Wednesday nights. I did my best, but I am not a morning person and didn't always make these meetings. However, I worked in the store seven days a week, and the Agape Fellowship faithful stopped by every day to see how I was doing. At the time, I was unaware that this is called "accountability." Today, I realize that it was one of the main reasons I never returned to the gay lifestyle.

Still, it was not easy. At times—especially alone at night—I struggled with the past, and with feelings of longing and lust. Then, one particularly tormented night, the peace of God flooded my soul and the most intense part of the battle was over. That blessed release led to some very strange experiences.

As far as I was concerned, my recent encounter with God qualified as spiritual "deliverance," but Mike did not agree. One day he said, "Frank, I feel you need a *genuine* deliverance."

"Mike," I told him, "I'm doing just fine, but thanks…"

Mike was persistent. In explaining deliverance Mike said, "It's an exorcism—and you need an exorcist!"

The whole idea sounded spooky, but by now I was getting used to spooky things. If you don't believe the things that happened next, I don't blame you. Sometimes it's even hard for me to believe they all really happened—but I know they did.

I do believe there is such a thing as spiritual deliverance. It has, however, been ignorantly used as a cure-all for almost everything, often doing more harm than good. On several occasions a close friend of mine, who suffers from cerebral palsy, has been pulled from her wheelchair and commanded to walk by someone rebuking a "spirit of sickness." People who struggle with same-sex attractions have often been in similar situations. Someone decides to "lay hands" on them, while the so-called demon of homosexuality is rebuked. Despite pronouncements of deliverance, effective results are usually lacking.

I personally do not believe there is a "demon of homosexuality," so I'm not sure what happened to me that night. I was wearing a T-shirt, and as Mike began to pray for me, I felt a crawling sensation around my navel. As it seemed to move up toward my neck, a buzzing sound became louder and louder. Suddenly, a huge black fly emerged from the neck of my shirt and flew out of the room.

Mike didn't seem particularly shocked. He said, "That was Beelzebub, the Lord of the Flies; he is also the ruler of demons."

I was amazed. I'd had my T-shirt tucked in, so the huge insect could not have simply crawled in at the bottom. How in the world did it get there? I still don't know—but from that time on, I had increasing peace and contentment. Now Mike began to teach me how to do spiritual warfare. "There is power in the name of Jesus," he told me. "You can rebuke the devil in His name. You don't have to be a victim of Satan's deceptions and attacks. He is limited in what he can do to you; he can do only what God allows. You have power over him."

This was all very confusing to me and I wasn't sure I believed in this spiritual, otherworldly stuff. A few weeks later, though, I had the chance to use Mike's instructions. I woke up one night, feeling something was wrong. Opening my eyes, I saw black figures hovering around me, but surprisingly, I wasn't frightened. Instantly and spontaneously, I rebuked these figures in the authority of Jesus' name. Immediately they vanished. I thought to myself, *Wow, this really works!* Then, I remembered Mike saying that after deliverance, evil spirits try to return. I didn't really understand it, and perhaps never will, but one thing was—and is—abundantly clear to me. There is a very real battle going on between good and evil. We need to understand our authority and our arsenal of weapons.

One evening I had worked late, and around midnight as I was locking the door, I saw a young man running toward the bus stop. I knew the last bus had already departed. He noticed me leaving the store and came over to ask if I would give him a ride. I was a little uneasy about picking up a hitchhiker at night, but he looked like a good kid and he clearly needed help.

Once we were in the car, he asked my name, and then mentioned he was going to a bar downtown, which I knew to be a gay hangout. He went on, "But I would rather go home with you." Then, this good-looking young man grabbed my hand and urged, "Please?"

I had a fleeting thought, *Where were you when I was available?* I rebuked it. Thanks to Mike's tutelage, I recognized this as a test. Still, I hesitated, weighing my own desires. I was grateful that I could honestly answer my own question, *No, I have no desire to go to bed with this young man.*

"I was gay myself," I told him, "but I'm not anymore. Jesus changed my life. He can change your life, too, if you will let Him."

"You can let me off at the next corner," he quickly answered. "Just park, so I can get out!"

I stopped the car, but instead of opening the door and leaving, he began to talk about his life, which, as it turned out, had been very similar to mine. He was raised in the church, seduced by his priest, rejected by his peer group, and labeled "gay." He'd left the Catholic Church, and then attended a fundamentalist fellowship. However, when he had confided in someone about his struggles with same-sex attraction, the leadership had asked him to leave.

We were quietly talking, when suddenly, he seemed to be seized by some alternate personality. He threw his head in my lap and made every effort to arouse me. Of course it took me off guard, but I was even more shocked by my reaction, because I felt no sexual response. As he lifted his head from my lap, he asked, "What's wrong with you? Don't you have any desire?"

"I am dead in Christ," I tried to explain. "I was a man of desire, but I died in Christ. I offered you the hand of Christian fellowship, but you abused what I was offering." At this, he opened the car door, got out, and walked away into the darkness.

After he got out, I felt very surprised at myself. He was a handsome young man and I had turned him down. *Wow, things have changed!* I told myself, and I thanked God for making it possible. I also prayed that this young man would seek and find a changed life in Jesus.

The next day when I related this story to Mike he said, "Frank, that's all well and good, but you won't always be temptation-free." Then he repeated his previous caution. "God is giving you a period of grace so you can get grounded in His Word. He wants you to keep building up your resistance to temptation. Use this time wisely, learn all you can, and read Scripture every day, so when temptation returns, you'll be able to stand."

Mike then added a couple of more church events he wanted me to attend. One was a Thursday night worship service and the other was a series of Renewal Movement events on Saturdays, which were usually concerts by popular Christian vocalists. Occasionally the popular faith healer, Katherine

Kuhlman, came to town and when she did, thousands of people gathered.

I first saw her at the Oakland Auditorium. A huge crowd was waiting for the doors to open. It turned into a mob scene, with excited people pushing and shoving their way in. I remember thinking, *I hope she really does know how to heal, because there are going to be some injuries in this crowd!*

Katherine Kuhlman was amazing. I know she was a controversial figure, but to me the healings seemed quite genuine. I later learned that Pastor Leonard had come to the Lord through Katherine Kuhlman's ministry—she had healed his mother during her final days in a terrible terminal illness. Five years later, Pastor Leonard's mother was still in good health, and that particular problem never returned.

Through the Word of God, and through seeing prayers answered in my life and in the lives of others, my faith continued to grow. Soon, it was time for me to attend the fall Gift Show in Los Angeles. For decades, I had attended this trade show twice a year. For me, it had always been a week of sin as well as business. This time, I feared it would be a dull, tedious trip, devoid of any excitement. I could not have been more wrong.

I had never noticed before, but there were displays of Christian merchandise in the convention area, and I had a great time talking with several merchants who were believers. In addition, before I had left, Pastor Leonard's mother had insisted the first thing I should do in the LA area was attend the Church on the Way, to hear Pastor Jack Hayford preach.

I called the church and they invited me to a Tuesday night prayer meeting. As I approached the church, I had no idea that I was about to face another choice between light and darkness. I needed to use a restroom, but did not want to ask for the bathroom the minute I walked into the church. So instead, I decided to buy gas at the station across the street and use their facilities. When I opened the restroom door, I was completely shocked to see half a dozen men participating in a sexual orgy. I instantly shut the door, got into my car as fast as I could, and drove over to the church parking lot. I was shaken by the experience, which both tempted and taunted me. I believe Satan was trying to keep me from a divine appointment.

I am convinced that God hovers protectively over new Christians and those returning to Him from a destructive lifestyle. During the church service, Pastor Hayford asked us to pray for the person on our right. A young man was sitting next to me. "Oh, please pray for me!" he implored, and began to describe his life of homosexual involvement. "I have done things so bad," he told me quietly, "they couldn't even be discussed in the dark of night." How well I understood. After I briefly shared my own story, he said, "I know in my heart that God has brought us together!"

Until then, I had never prayed aloud for anyone. I did not want to disappoint this boy, though, so I took his hands in mine and began to pray. I was astonished that the Holy Spirit brought forth words from my lips that were intended for both of us. This young man re-connected with the Lord that night, and I continued to pray for him for many months afterward. I returned home from Los Angeles on a spiritual high. Without a doubt, it was the best Gift Show trip to Los Angeles I'd ever had.

All this time, I had come to rely on Mike not only for spiritual guidance but also for business advice, so I decided to promote him to Assistant Store Manager. He asked if he could hire church members whenever we had employee openings, and I agreed. We had about twelve employees and within a few months, over half of them were Christians. Before the store opened each day, we began with prayer. Soon, even my store manager became a Christian.

In those days, cassette tapes were new and quite popular. Churches recorded weekly sermons and Christian bands were all making their own tapes. One day Mike said, "Frank, you're having so many great experiences with God, I think it would be a good idea for you to record these things on cassettes. Someday, you won't be able to remember everything God has done, and the tapes will encourage you when things get tough."

Since the store was well-managed, I had free time to work on a tape. Stewart Chapel was surrounded by beautifully landscaped grounds. I found a place under a huge oak tree and started to record my adventures. When I got back to the office, however, the tape was blank. This happened several times. At first, I thought I didn't know how to use the recorder correctly, but each time I checked it was obvious that I'd been doing it right. Finally, I successfully recorded my testimony and began to add more every day. However, after several weeks of work, when I tried to play the tape back, once again it was blank.

Mike declared this was spiritual warfare, and I believe he was right. It took me many months to get a completed tape. Then Mike gave me a new challenge. "Don't you feel obligated," he asked, "to reach back into the gay community and help others find their way out?"

This had never occurred to me, primarily because all my homosexual friends were so thoroughly disgusted with me. They felt I had deserted them and they often ridiculed me. On the other hand, Pastor Leonard required every member of our church to have a ministry, or take part in an existing ministry. I had previously talked to God about this, saying, *Lord, I don't know a thing I could do for You. If there is something I'm missing, please tell me.*

Now I wondered if the Lord was speaking to me through Mike, but I said "no" anyway. "I don't know how I would do that Mike," I countered.

"All you'd have to do is to advertise your taped testimony!" he eagerly suggested.

I groaned inwardly. *Do I really want the whole world knowing I was gay?* I still had family members who would be quite shocked. I gave Mike the same answer he always gave me. "Okay, I'll pray about that."

I wanted to be free from homosexuality. I never wanted to have to think about it again, so why would I want to obligate myself to a homosexual ministry? My mind was crying out, *Oh, say it isn't so!* but my heart knew I had given myself to God. I was hoping He would ask me to do something else, but at the same time, I knew He had enormous compassion for all gay people.

By the time I walked away from it, I had been in the homosexual lifestyle for about 25 years, and I could speak about it with some authority. I still did not understand the root causes of same-sex attraction. The only path I knew out of homosexuality was the path of total surrender, allowing God to do anything He wanted with my life. That was the best advice I could offer, and I decided I was willing to share it with others.

Since yet another recorded tape had turned out blank, I decided that instead of recounting my own experiences, I would direct my next tape toward those needing help. Mike advised me to have it professionally copied, so I took it in and ordered ten copies. Back at the office, I received a call from the studio saying the front side of the tape was good, but there was nothing on the back. Mike and I looked at each and shook our heads, "Not again!" This time, though, I had a transcript of what I had said on side B, so it was easy to re-record it.

The next step was to advertise.

Mike and I called all the local papers, but when they learned the tape was not promoting homosexuality, they gave us an emphatic, "No!"

In the gay lifestyle I had occasionally purchased *The Berkeley Barb*. It was a New Age paper, used mostly for finding sexual contacts. Rather desperately, I called their office. I asked the woman on the phone if she would take an advertisement of a Christian nature.

"Honey," she laughed, "we will take any ad, no matter how bizarre."

The first ad ran in November, 1973. It read, "Let Jesus break the chains of homosexuality. Have you hit bottom and need a way out? Brother Frank tells how Jesus changed his life. Send for the tape on free loan…"

Once, one of the articles in the *Barb* was headlined, "Bombing for Jesus." When I saw that, I concluded they did acknowledge Christianity. But most of the articles weren't about such niceties. Quite often, there were nude photos of both women and men, and for months, the ad above mine was by a guy looking for someone with a toe fetish. Nevertheless, the response to my ad was immediate.

To keep local people from knowing about my ministry, I went to San Francisco to have additional tapes duplicated. I found a professional company that copied tapes four at a time. It seemed unlikely they would take an interest in my tape, but I was wrong. My worst fears were realized when I went to pick up my tapes and they began to question me about my ministry. I was embarrassed and decided to find a different place for the next batch.

Looking back, I have to admit that the "Brother Frank Tape" was rather odd. I gave a testimony of my life, described how I had changed, read innumerable Scriptures, and gave them an opportunity to accept Jesus into their life. Unusual or not, it reached those it was intended for: sexually addicted gays whose lives were out of control. Those who responded were desperate for help.

The first letter we received read, "It really surprised me when I read your ad in the *Barb*! About four months ago, I got completely fed up with myself. I'm now very close to Jesus and I know only He can help me. Pray for me."

Another letter said, "After twenty-five years of running and hell and torment, I have decided to put my trust in Jesus. I have no other way to travel as I have been to the pits of hell. The Lord reached out for me many times and I turned from Him. I know He is able to pull us out of the pits and help us defeat this power that has demanded so much of our lives. I really want Him to take over my life."

This man soon joined our budding ministry. As "Brother Arnold," he established our first live-in facility in his hometown of Colusa, California.

What a strange year I'd had! In my wildest fantasies, I never could have imagined all that had happened. I had gone from being an aging, depressed, washed-up gay person to a happy "Jesus freak." And always, loud and clear in my mind, were the words I'd heard on what I came to call my "Destiny Bridge": "If you are willing to take your life, are you willing to give it to Me?" I was so thankful I had said "yes" to God. It was the best deal I had ever made.

From what I had already experienced, I knew God was not offering me an easy life, but one filled with adventure and challenges. What I had so long wanted, I now had—a return of the close relationship with Him that I'd had when I was young. Now, though, I also had a mission in life that brought me even deeper meaning and purpose. I still wasn't sure where I was headed, but I knew I was well on the way. As you will see in the coming chapters, God would stretch me beyond what I thought I could bear. Thankfully, as He always does, God supplied the power I needed to do what He asked.

I was pondering all these things as I picked up the morning paper on my front porch. The headlines read, UNLIGHTED BATH BURNS, WITH LOSS OF LIFE.

Frank, in 1977, at Open Door Church.

Frank, at age 44, in front of Stewart Chapel.

Stewart Chapel, home of Agape Fellowship.

Chapter Eight

My Destiny Takes Shape

B y now, a flood of letters was pouring in and I realized that I had a legitimate ministry. I kept this to myself, however, and had no idea what to do next. In my longing to discern the Lord's will, I was fasting frequently and spent much time in prayer. In an early morning devotional meeting at the store, one of our employees suddenly began to tremble. I was alarmed, thinking he was going to faint. Then, he began to speak in an emphatic voice, "Frank I am pleased with you. Continue what you are doing in your ministry."

After this, he returned to normal. "I don't know what that was about," he said with a puzzled look. "You don't have a ministry."

I knew this was a word to me from God, that I was on the right track. I was so grateful. My tapes were now much in demand and, since some people did not return them, I needed to duplicate more. Mike heard that a local business called "The

Christian General Store" had a tape-duplication machine on which they reproduced Sunday sermons for Church of the Open Door. I was a bit apprehensive; I did not want someone only a block away from my store listening to my tape.

"It's okay, Frank," Mike assured me. "It's a fast duplicator that takes only two minutes to make a tape, and they do four at a time. There's no way anyone can listen in."

Somewhat convinced, I took the master in and met Betty Kenner, the store manager. She smiled warmly when I introduced myself. "I'd heard the owner of the Black Market Import store had become a Christian. I'm so happy to meet you!"

Just then, Kent Philpott, the Senior Pastor of Open Door church, walked in. His office was in the back of the building. Kent had also heard about my conversion, and was very cordial. I immediately liked them both.

I had discovered that there was much dissension between the local churches. Our Agape church members believed the leaders at Open Door were "sheep stealers"—that they had persuaded some of our members to transfer to their church, saying they would never be properly "fed" at Agape.

There were numerous outlandish stories and activities. For example, two mysterious men stood outside Agape Fellowship on Sunday mornings, cursing our church. They were from a fellowship called Grace Church, but I never found out why they thought it was their duty to condemn us. On the other hand, our members had passed along many tales about Grace Church. We heard they put diapers on adults and re-parented them—and those were just a couple of their dubious practices.

Meanwhile, I learned more about Kent Philpott. Along with several of his seminary classmates, Kent had started a Bible study group in the Haight/Ashbury area of San Francisco, which was in those days a haven for hippies. He also did street witnessing (evangelism), and had set up a drug-abuse center. In our local area, in addition to the bookstore, his church had established a series of "House Ministry" residences where people could live and learn about the Christian life. About the time of my rededication, Kent had merged his House Ministries with Church of the Open Door, which was pastored by several of his seminary friends. With the merger, Kent became Senior Pastor of Church of the Open Door.

By this time, I had been advertising my tape for three months, I was corresponding regularly with 30 men, and they all wanted to meet "Brother Frank." Since most of these men were in the East Bay, I rented a conference room at the Durant Hotel in Berkeley and on March 2, 1974, we gathered for the first time. About 35 men showed up, all sharing the same desire—to leave the gay lifestyle.

At our meeting, we agreed to get together regularly. Gradually, we grew into a committed group. Men came from all over the Bay Area, and even beyond. "Brother Arnold," from Colusa, attended as often as he could. It was an interesting fellowship. We had a baker, a schoolteacher, an accountant, several young men still in high school or college, a flamboyant cross-dresser, a retarded man, a construction worker, a house painter...and I can't remember the rest!

In January 1974, about eight months after my rededication to the Lord, temptation returned with a vengeance. It was a struggle for me to remain celibate, but I was determined. "Remember?" Mike nodded sagely, "I told you this would happen." He had instructed me to ground myself securely in the Word. I felt I had done so, but that did not change the reality of my struggle.

One night after the store had closed and all the employees had gone home, I was overwhelmed with the desire to go cruising in search of a sexual encounter. The primary thing that stopped me was that I did not want to ruin my record. I was afraid I would have to confess a failure to my church people, or disappoint the men in the group. I had often heard my church members say that Christians need to "stand on the Word." In my desperation to remain faithful, I placed a large Bible on the floor and literally stood on it. *Lord, I am going to stand on Your Word*, I told Him, *until this desire goes away.* It took nearly an hour for my fervor to pass, but once it was over, I knew I had won a victory.

Then, unexpectedly, Joe returned. I was working at the counter, helping customers, when I looked up and saw him standing there. I had thought about him daily since our phone conversation, on that day when I had returned to the Lord. I had prayed that he was safe and would someday come to know Jesus. Joe and I went into my office, where we could talk privately. "Where have you been?" I asked. He said he'd been on the East Coast, but didn't give me any details. "Why didn't you show up that night?" Joe's behavior remained an enigma to me.

"I know you told me to come by," Joe explained, "but your voice said something completely different. It said, 'I don't want to see you anymore.'"

"But Joe, you know I didn't say that!"

Joe smiled. "I know you didn't, but that was the impression I got."

I paused, and then tried to explain. "I did have something to tell you that night, and I knew it was going to affect our relationship. I found Jesus that day, Joe, and I wanted to tell you about it. Don't you think you need some changes in your life?"

Joe didn't hesitate. "Yeah, I know I do."

"So will you go to church with me this Sunday?"

"Sure, why not? For old time's sake, I'll go." This time Joe kept his appointment with me and for two months, he was in church with me every Sunday.

There was one young lady in church, named Judy, who had befriended me. She was a very attractive young woman and if I had been healed at that time, and a bit younger, I would have been interested in her. She took to Joe instantly and they often went out together. Judy tried her best to get Joe to accept Jesus, but sadly, he never did.

Joe no longer had a car. I don't know what had happened to his hot rod. Maybe he sold it when he needed money, or he might even have wrecked it; he never said. It wasn't long before he was borrowing Judy's car and using it every day. Later, when she started to get the feeling that Joe was taking advantage of her, she cut back his use of the car—but not soon enough.

Early one Sunday morning, Joe took Judy's car without asking first. Minutes later, he ended up in a three-car pile-up. Only then did we find that Judy carried no car insurance—not even minimum coverage. For some reason, both Joe and Judy thought it was up to me to resolve this problem. I paid thousands of dollars for repair of the other two cars in the accident, but I ran out of available cash before Judy's repairs were complete. When I did gather enough money to repair it, she'd had a change of heart and refused to let me help. By then, she and Joe had duct-taped it together so it was usable. Judy drove it that way for the next five years. Every time I saw her car, I felt guilty and sad—it had been a good-looking car. Judy never let this ruin our friendship, however. Right after this, Joe did one of his disappearing acts, and I would not see him again for many years.

In the meantime, inquiries to my ad were increasing and I needed more tapes. Betty at the bookstore was now a champion of my ministry. Responses varied to the tapes I mailed out. Some returned the tape without comment. Some did not return the tape or contact me. Others were excited about the possibility of new life and joined our group. Occasionally someone would send me pro-gay literature along with the tape.

These pro-gay Christian responses were my first introduction to "Gay Theology." Some letters said the Bible verses regarding homosexuality were added in later centuries by homophobes, and there was no need to be concerned with them. One letter, which really disturbed me, said that I was naive, and that we could never know what God really said. According to this person, the original Bible was lost, and all that remains are inaccurate copies, filled with contradictions. I asked Mike if that could be true.

Mike said, "Yes, the originals are gone." Then he launched into a lecture on "textual criticism" that left me confused and frightened. "Only the originals are inspired..." Mike said, going from bad to worse.

To me, this was not good news. If only the original texts were inspired and they were no longer available, where did that leave me? Had I been trusting a false message? For a week or so, I was very depressed. I knew that to determine the truth, I would have to study this textual criticism. Meanwhile, I was having a major crisis of faith. Had I given up my lifestyle for nothing? Was it okay to be gay? Did Jesus really say nothing about homosexuality?

While I was still confused and depressed over this new development, a second wave of despair hit me. I had gone to my house in Carmel to pray and study. One bright sunny morning, as I was driving along the beachfront listening to Christian radio, the voice of the venerable preacher, J. Vernon McGee, came on. This particular morning, he was speaking on the book of Leviticus, and focusing almost completely on chapter eighteen.

McGee read verse twenty-two: "You shall not lie with a man as with a woman, it is abomination." He spent most of his half-hour talking about the issue of homosexuality. "Don't waste your time trying to convert a homosexual," he scolded. "They can't be saved! They are not among the elect. Homosexuals are dogs and swine, so spend your time on people who can be saved."

This was the same message I'd heard twenty years before in the churches I had visited as a young organist. Would I never be free from these condemning words? These words of hopelessness had driven me away from God and caused me to throw myself wholeheartedly into the gay lifestyle. They were the source of much of my self-destructive behavior. Back then, I'd had the option of a wanton life, but now at my age that option was closed. I knew there was nothing waiting for me in the gay world. This time, these condemning words seemed they would have the power to destroy me, and all that I had accomplished thus far.

What am I doing? I asked myself. *Am I deceived? Am I really lost? Am I bringing a false message of hope to those who answer my ad?*

Once again, I considered taking my own life. For several days, I spent hours searching my soul. One question I asked myself was very much to the point. *So, if you have been involved in a hoax, do you now want to go back into the gay lifestyle?* I knew the answer to that question was "no." I had experienced almost a year of intense joy and happiness, something I had never known before. No, I did not want to go back. But where could I go?

"Lord," I prayed aloud, "I'm going to serve You, just as if I were saved. You may not want me, but I want *You*. So, even if I don't go to heaven, at least I will have a good life here." I hoped maybe God would change His mind about homosexuals, and I was going to try to help Him change it.

That issue was now settled, but I knew I still had to deal with the Bible. On returning home, I immediately went to the seminary library to learn about textual criticism. I began to study its key principles. First, I learned the earlier the copy, the more accurate it is deemed to be. Second, the greater the number of copies that agree, the more likely it is to have been copied accurately. In addition, when there is a debate about a particular Scripture, in almost all Bibles there is a footnote at the bottom of the page. The Scriptures regarding homosexuality have no such footnotes. And finally, Jesus said that none of His words would pass away. This might well also include the words of His apostles.

After absorbing these principles, I then carefully began to examine all the experiences I'd had. Certainly, God had intervened in my life many times. I didn't believe He would spend His energy on someone who could not be saved.

Gradually, I felt the comfort of God wash over me, reassuring me that I was saved, and that I was doing precisely what He wanted me to do. I could feel His arms embracing me. My depression and distress evaporated, but were replaced by anger. What if some of the men and women I had been working with heard the same broadcast? Were they now just as disillusioned as I had been?

I sat down at my desk and wrote out a reply to Mr. McGee. In it, I used the only ex-gay scripture I had found in the Bible, 1st Corinthians 6:11. In verses nine and ten, Paul is saying that those who engage in certain practices will not inherit the Kingdom of Heaven. Homosexuality is mentioned in this list of sins. In verse eleven he goes on to say, "...and that is what some of you were. But you were washed, you were sanctified, you were justified in the name of the Lord Jesus Christ and by the Spirit of our God." It was obvious that Paul knew people in the Corinthian church who had formerly been gay, but were no longer.

After I had written a couple of pages, I decided to call KFAX, the Christian radio station that had broadcast his sermon. I asked if I could have a half hour to counter what McGee had said. The station manager informed me that for $300, I could buy time for rebuttal directly after McGee's broadcast. I made a cassette tape and sent it to the radio station along with a check. I eagerly awaited the next Saturday morning broadcast, when I would hear myself on the radio for the first time. I didn't tell my friends at church, but later learned that almost all of them regularly listened to our only Christian radio station on Saturday mornings. Of course, they were quite surprised to hear my voice. Two men addicted to gay sex also were listening, and learned about our support group that day.

In April, 1974, I was looking forward to my anniversary—I had lived one year of purity. The Lord woke me up at three one morning and said to me, *Go see Kent Philpott and tell him about your ministry.*

"No way!" I murmured. My church was very suspicious of Kent's church because we had lost dozens of our members to Church of the Open Door. Up to this point, I had always done what the Lord told me. I guess I thought I now had an option, but I would soon reconsider. I could not go back to sleep. Instead, I kept thinking about the people in my church who had been so caring and attentive. How could I betray them?

At daybreak, I tried to get up, but found I was experiencing severe dizziness—an attack of vertigo so intense that I could not stand up. I had to lean against the walls to get to the bathroom, and then all I could do was return to bed. I couldn't even balance myself enough to get my clothes on. Thinking it might subside, I stayed in bed for an hour or two, but the vertigo remained unalleviated.

I had a busy day planned, and very much needed to get to work. Finally, realizing that this might be my penalty for saying "no" to God, I finally relented. *Okay, Lord, You win; I'll go see Kent.* Once again, I remembered I had given my life to the Lord and had promised to do whatever He asked. I now felt pangs of guilt that I had refused Someone who had loved and protected me all my life. At that point, my vertigo lifted and I was able to go about my usual morning business. I did briefly consider "forgetting" to do what I had promised, but now my fear of God was too great. I called the bookstore, and Betty answered.

"I would like an appointment with Kent today; is that possible?" I said, hoping it wasn't. By this time, I knew Kent was a "straight" man, married with three kids. I didn't know what his reaction would be to a ministry for homosexuals.

Betty apologized, "Kent's calendar is booked for several months. There is no chance you can see him today, or even any time soon."

Well, you did what you promised to do, I told myself, *so now you're off the hook.*

Just then, a voice in the background said, "Betty, Kent has a cancellation at three this afternoon!"

Oh, no! Now, I'll have to go through with this.

I arrived at the bookstore at three, and Betty escorted me to Kent's office. He greeted me warmly and said he remembered meeting me a few months earlier. I began, "Kent, I don't know why the Lord wanted me here in your office today, but it seems that He wants me to tell you about my ministry to homosexuals."

"I know exactly why you are here today," Kent replied. "Already this week, two homosexuals have come in wanting counseling, and now here you are talking about your ministry to homosexuals."

Kent went on to say that he had heard a few things about me, and I filled in what he didn't know. Then he said, "There's no Christian literature on homosexuality. Will you help me write a book on this subject?" Without waiting for a response, he took out a yellow scratch pad saying, "Let's make an outline of the chapters." The publisher would later give it the title, *The Third Sex.*

I overstayed my allotted hour while we made our plans. Kent invited me to use his office for my group meetings, and said he knew of some other gay people who could use a support group. I responded, "I'll gather up the people I'm working with and you can bring your people, and we'll meet together as soon as possible."

I was delighted to have such a knowledgeable partner in the ministry. On Thursday night, May 9, 1974, our first combined group meeting took place. Most of those who attended were from Kent's ministry, since the majority of my people lived in the East Bay or even farther. It would not be long, however, before they would learn to use the bridge and attend our meetings in San Rafael.

We were only a few minutes into our first meeting, when several announced that they did not like our name, "Brother Frank Tape Ministry." They demanded a name change. Both Kent and I agreed that we could search for a new name, but I wondered how this diverse group would ever be able to agree on anything. One man was claiming instant change; others didn't think change was possible; we were all in confusion about both the causes of homosexuality and the way out. I wasn't even claiming to be a heterosexual myself, right then. I might have thought so during my first eight months out of the lifestyle when I was temptation-free, but since then, I had been struggling. Fortunately, I was getting in touch with the idea that change was a process.

The next meeting we learned some members had been calling us "the gay Bible study." We all agreed that was not what we wanted, and continued to search for an appropriate name. A few weeks later, one of the three lesbians in the group suggested, "Love in Action." This phrase was taken from 1st John 3:18 in the Living Bible, "Dear children, let's not merely say that we love each other; let us show the truth by our actions." We unanimously agreed to adopt the name, "Love in Action." That name has now endured for more than 35 years.

The group was becoming comfortable with Kent, a straight man, in their midst. One or two were hostile to him, but most liked him and appreciated his interest in their problem. Kent soon brought up the idea for the book that he and I had outlined on our first meeting. The group wholeheartedly embraced the project and was willing to do whatever work was required.

We were not aware of any other book on homosexuality on the Christian market, so we believed that ours would be the first, and everyone seemed excited to be part of a pioneering effort. Over the next few weeks, several members allowed Kent to tape their testimonies. Each testimony would be a chapter in the book. Enthusiasm was running high and we couldn't wait for it to be published. Soon, the group grew too large for Kent's office. Jake, one of our members, offered his home as our meeting place.

Jake was loud, irritating, and extremely funny. People were always laughing around him, and partly, I think, at him. Jake certainly enjoyed entertaining people. We accepted his offer and began to meet in his cozy, Craftsman-style house. Jake spent all day before the meetings, preparing food for the pre-meeting social time. "This is great!" we all agreed aloud. But privately, I was having some second thoughts.

Since Jake now had a captive audience, he was becoming more riotous at each meeting. In the gay lifestyle, this is called "camping it up," or "holding court." Jake gave each of us a nickname; I was "Queen Victoria." I felt all this was unbecoming for a Christian group, and I noticed that many first-timers were not returning to the group the following week.

I called a meeting with Kent, Brother Bob, and Jake. We tried to be very loving because we all sensed that beneath the surface Jake was very fragile. We all had his best interests at heart, wanting him to grow and let go of his gay identity. I possibly aggravated him the most when I emphasized I did not want the group to become a gay social club. Not all gay people appreciate gay jokes and sexual innuendos. Gay people range from very conservative to wildly flamboyant. While all were welcome, we did not want to minister only to the flamboyant; we wanted to meet the needs of all our members.

Jake now had what he'd always wanted, a group of friends where he was the center of attention. He could not tolerate our advice or correction, and responded with an explosion of anger and hostility. Jake went off to seek support from the other members, telling them the elders had abused him. Almost everyone sided with Jake, believing we had unfairly attacked him.

Not long afterward, we heard about an additional weekly meeting. First, we heard the term, "Camp Meeting Time," and wondered what it meant. Then, we learned that Jake and Ted (who was from the original group) were holding these meetings at Ted's house. Gradually, our group attendance slipped to a handful of people. Jake soon let us know that our group was no longer welcome in his house, so, we returned to Kent's office.

Shortly thereafter, we heard that Dr. Ralph Blair would be speaking in San Francisco and that most of our group was going to hear him. Dr. Blair is director of Evangelicals Concerned, a ministry that proclaims, "We do not see homosexuality either as a sickness or a sin…" Soon, Ted started an Evangelicals Concerned chapter in the Bay Area and, thus, the XX-Gay (former ex-gay) movement began.

Possibly under pressure from Ted, several of our former group members—who had been so eager to have their testimonies recorded in *The Third Sex*—now recanted, claiming they had been victims of peer pressure and coercion. Nonetheless, once the book was completed and published, it brought in another flood of people seeking a way out of homosexuality.

Then, in the spring of 1975, I received a call from a distraught mother whose son had just left home to enter the gay lifestyle. This mother had gone to her local Logos Bookstore in Anaheim, California, to see what they had on the issue of homosexuality. She had bought a copy of our book, *The Third Sex*, and found my telephone number in the back of the book. Her name was Barbara Johnson.

Barbara's call came as I was ringing up sales at my store. She was crying, and trying to understand what had gone wrong. She had raised her son as a Christian and he had been active in her church, but now she felt betrayed. "Why would he do this to me?" she asked. It was difficult to explain the unfolding of homosexuality while conversing with customers. During the conversation, Barbara mentioned she had gone to her local ex-gay ministry for help, but they had rejected her. "We don't minister to parents," they declared, "only to gay people looking for change."

Barbara told me the name of the ministry was, "EXIT" (Ex-gay Intervention Team). Until that moment, I had thought Love in Action was the only ex-gay ministry in the world. I was very excited that another ministry existed. I told her, "If you will introduce me to the people running this ministry, I'll hop on a plane tomorrow!" Barbara was excited she would be able to meet and talk with me in person, so we agreed to have dinner together Friday night, and on Saturday she would take me to EXIT ministries.

My dinner meeting with Barbara became one of her most hilarious stories. Barbara's friend, Hilda, was worried about her meeting up with some strange man she had only talked to briefly on the telephone, and insisted on accompanying Barbara to dinner. Hilda had also cautioned, "If you're going to meet some stranger in Hollywood, you need to be prepared, you need some kind of defense." At this, she had reached into her purse and pulled out a long hatpin. "Take this, and if anything funny starts to happen, just pull this out of your purse and let him know you can defend yourself."

Barbara did not need to use the hatpin that night. Over dinner, I explained what her son had been feeling, and that he probably had been fighting these unwanted feelings for years. In her role as bodyguard, Hilda didn't say much, but she was pleasant and seemed interested in what I was saying. The evening ended with Barbara telling me, "If I ever get through this, I am going to have a ministry helping other parents find their way through these problems."

That declaration was prophetic. In a year's time, Barbara would launch Spatula Ministries, which became the largest parents' group in the world, supporting change for homosexuals. In a few years Barbara would write her first book, *Where Does A Mother Go To Resign?* This book, and her animated recounting of her personal story, would soon make Barbara Johnson a celebrity on the women's speaking circuit.

I spent the night in a motel and the next morning I met Barbara at Melodyland Christian Center in Anaheim, where she introduced me to EXIT's director, Jim Kaspar. Jim was a very personable twenty-something, well-educated and dedicated to helping people change. He led us through the offices where his staff was working. Jim and one of his staff members, Mike Bussee, would soon become good friends of mine. I was very impressed with their operation.

One thing that really impressed me was Jim's incredible organizational skills. Everything was color coded—the literature, the rooms, and even the furniture. We talked at length and it became apparent that Jim's approach to change was almost entirely psychological. Up to this point, my approach had been entirely spiritual. I'd had one class in psychology and could follow what he was saying to some degree, but I was eager to learn more. I asked Jim if we could meet together—his staff and my leaders—so we could learn from each other. He assured me that he would find time on his calendar to make this happen. It took Jim about a year to keep his promise, but when he did, it would prove to be well worth the wait.

As we talked, Jim asked about my method for helping people get out of homosexuality. I was embarrassed by the simplicity of my message. I was just learning for myself that change was a process, and I basically had three steps:

The first step was to be in agreement with God, that acting out homosexually was sin. The second step was to believe that God is able to change us. I now call this step "The Belief Principle." The third step was surrender, both to God and to those people God brings to help us out.

Jim seemed to be in agreement with what I was saying. As we all parted, I reminded them of their promise to meet with me next year to train my staff. I knew we could learn much from these bright young men.

Later, Barbara dropped me off at the airport and I had much to think about on the way home. It was becoming obvious that change was going to be a long and difficult process. As I thought about this, however, I realized the Christian life is also a long and perhaps difficult process. God's whole idea of change is to conform us all to the image and character of Christ.

I now feel sure this was what St. Paul was alluding to in 2nd Corinthians 1:10, when he said, "Who delivered us from so great a death, and does deliver us, in whom we trust that He will yet deliver us." While Paul was speaking of physical trials, I believe he was also speaking of the great change God was bringing about in his spiritual life. Like Paul, those of us who were formerly homosexual can say, "I was changed." We have been snatched from a life of rebellion and calamity. We can also say that God is in the process of changing us daily. And, because we have experienced God's faithfulness and trustworthiness, we can say, "God will change me." This means that God will complete the work He has started in us.

I had been observing the tragic consequences of rebellion in the lives of those coming to Love in Action. The gay lifestyle, which had seemed to offer everything they were longing for— connection, love, security, and identity—had betrayed them. Instead, they had been caught in the snare of addiction, helpless to help themselves.

Of course, some claimed to be very happy in the lifestyle, but I often wondered, are they in denial, or, is calamity just around the corner? I remembered my own feelings of happiness and excitement at first, but these were soon combined with emotional compromises, increased drinking, unrewarding casual sex, disillusionment, and eventually despair. I recalled the cynicism of so many, who had advised me to abandon my hopes for a committed, loving relationship. It seemed that in many cases, their proclaimed happiness was purely delusional.

I soberly pondered God's words in Isaiah 66:3-4. "Such people have chosen their own way and they delight in their abominations. I also will choose their delusions...their calamities and afflictions, and I will bring their fears upon them, because when I called, no one answered, when I spoke, they did not listen or obey, but they did what was evil in My sight, and chose that in which I did not delight."

I thanked God that Jesus came for just such people—as I had been—the broken ones, the deluded, those trapped in the prison of homosexual addictions. In John 10:10 Jesus proclaimed, "I came that they might have life, and have it more abundantly." This was now my new path of life and hope.

I returned home from Los Angeles, eager to learn more about the homosexual issue and eager to be of greater help to those God had brought my way.

The store was more prosperous than ever, which placed greater demands on my time and meant more trips overseas to purchase merchandise. I was struggling under my multiplied responsibilities. Then, an additional upheaval occurred that completely immobilized me.

One Sunday night, I arrived home from a trip and called my mother to tell her I was back. It was about 10 P.M., but there was no answer. I knew instantly something was wrong. When I told Hal, he said, "We need to get over there right away!" We immediately drove to Mother's house. We knocked on her door and there was no answer.

We kept knocking and ringing the doorbell, but still there was no response. Finally, Hal made a decision. "I'd better break a window and go in to see if she's there," he said.

Waiting out front, I heard the glass shatter. Then, in a few moments, Hal appeared at the front door. "Frank, she's dead," he told me. "I found her in bed...she's gone, Frank."

Like that broken window, my world suddenly shattered. In my devastation, I could not function. Thankfully, Hal took charge of everything, making all the arrangements for her burial. Looking back, I can see that a lot of my pain came from deep feelings of guilt. Mother had always been a complainer, and her phone calls tested my patience. In recent months, she had been calling me less frequently than before. Truthfully, I had felt happy not hearing from her.

But something even worse haunted me. During one of Mother's lengthy calls not so long before her death, I had put the phone down—while I washed the dishes. Occasionally I had picked up the receiver to grunt, "Uh-huh," to make her think I was listening. Then, once when I picked up the phone and said, "Yeah," she exclaimed, "Well! I thought so!"

"What?" I asked. "What did you say?"

"I said, 'I'll bet you wish I was dead!'"

I had tried to backtrack my way out of that one, but from then on, Mother continued to believe I really wanted her to die. She had even reminded me about it from time to time.

For that reason and many others, my mother's death affected me far more painfully than my father's. I grieved over not having treated her better—although most of the time, I believed I had done my best. I had taken her to New York City, where we'd had a room overlooking Times Square, and she had enjoyed seeing all the action from her hotel window. Also, I had taken her to Hawaii, a place she had always wanted to see. Now, however, those gestures seemed inadequate, my regrets were many, and I was overwhelmed with grief.

Nevertheless, I did feel the comfort of the Lord, as I had never experienced it before. I never will forget how closely He drew me to Himself during those difficult days. Deep within, I felt the joy of knowing Him and of being able to lean on His strong arms. I also realized how merciful He had been, for

Mother had been facing the amputation of both her legs. And, though I could not be sure whether she really knew the Lord, I had to trust that when Mother was baptized she really had accepted Christ into her heart. By God's grace, despite my shock and sadness, it was not long before He revived me.

In the meantime, our group had been thriving. One day, Pastor Ray Stedman of Peninsula Bible Church paid us a visit. He had given a lecture on homosexuality, which Ed, one of our group members had attended. We weren't sure what provoked Ed, but he had stood up, interrupted Ray, and opposed what he was saying. Afterwards, the two had talked, Ed had told him about our group, and Ray had decided to visit us.

We learned from Ray that there were many homosexuals in his church. One church leader had fallen in a homosexual encounter, but had later been restored to leadership. Ray wanted us to start a branch Love In Action ministry in Palo Alto, and offered to find us a place to meet. We agreed and were excited about reaching people in a new area. Ray said the restored elder could lead the ministry, but he wanted one of us to be present at every meeting. A month later, Ray called to say the first meeting would be at his church.

At our first meeting, both men and women attended, nine in all. It went very well and one member offered his home for the next meeting. We decided to meet every other week, and everything went smoothly for the first few months. Then, one of Ray's board members learned of this outreach. "We don't want any ministry to homosexuals in this church!" he asserted.

Pastor Stedman agreed to put the issue on the next board meeting agenda. The man was persuasive and the board agreed with him. They directed the church elder, who was serving as our leader, to stop attending our meetings. We were left with a ministry without a covering, that is, with no church leadership. The man who had offered his house withdrew, and the group decided to go to a different house for every meeting.

For a month or so, we would each receive a call, telling us where to meet. Then one time, the caller informed me, "We're doing fine on our own; no need for you to come down this way any longer." After a few weeks of no communication, I phoned Ray and asked what was happening. He seemed quite depressed. "I hear the gays have taken over the meeting, and it's now promoting homosexuality," he told me.

By this time, we had also started outreaches in Danville, Oakland, and Santa Rosa. In retrospect, I can see we were spreading ourselves much too thinly, and that we really did not have enough maturity or experience to run satellite ministries.

Nevertheless, other things continued to move forward. Barbara Johnson and I were talking on the phone almost daily. Barbara told me the meeting I had requested with EXIT's leaders was turning into a full-fledged conference. The ministry had a Watts telephone line, which charged a flat fee and allowed them unlimited calls. The staff was calling churches and organizations all across the U.S. to see if there were any other ex-gay ministries operating. Indeed there were. We were as excited to know about them, as they were to know about us. This was the beginning of something bigger than any of us could have imagined at the time.

Chapter Nine

A Movement
is Birthed

The meeting did, in fact, become a conference—in September of 1976. From that first day, my staff and I were amazed at the organizational skills of the EXIT leaders. We had been assigned rooms in a nearby hotel, which was an easy walk to Melodyland Christian Center. It was a hot day in Anaheim, and we were glad to get into the air-conditioned building. Everything went very smoothly, with 62 people in attendance. Dr. Walter Martin, who had a daily radio broadcast as the "Bible Answer Man" was our keynote speaker, and he reviewed for us the Scriptures on homosexuality. Most of us had already studied long and hard for ourselves, but it was good to begin with a Biblical overview. Then, when the EXIT staff members gave their presentations, we learned a great deal about the root causes of homosexuality—a subject which we were eager to understand.

One of the more notable attendees was Perry Desmond. Perry was born a male, had a sex change operation, lived as a woman until he became a follower of Jesus, then realized he needed to return to his God-given identity—that of a man. He had wholeheartedly given himself to the Lord's service, and now spent all his time traveling and preaching the Gospel. Though now a man, Perry still had very large breasts, and some of the ministry leaders decided to collect enough money for him to have them removed. He later died, before the operation could take place. But before his death, Perry's story was published in a book titled, *A Transformed Transsexual*. Through his book, Perry's ministry continued to bless and benefit many lives, even after he was no longer with us.

Everyone's level of energy was high during that weekend conference, each of us filled with excitement. We sensed that something very important was happening. We all realized one weekend together was not enough. We needed some kind of support organization that would help each of our individual groups grow into an effective ministry. We needed an umbrella ministry.

We also needed a name, and there were several suggestions. The first was, "Free All Gays," but we quickly discarded it when we realized what the acronym would be! Someone suggested, perhaps as a joke, "AC/DC Transformers." Finally, Robbi Kenny came up with the biblical name, "Exodus." Exodus, which describes the Israelite's escape from slavery in Egypt, also serves to describe the long road out of homosexuality—which is also a road with many trials and challenges along the way. Just as for the Israelites, our journey ultimately leads to the Promised Land.

So in September, 1976, Exodus came into being. A board was voted in, with Jim Kasper as Chair; Greg Reid as Vice-Chair; Mike Bussee as Corresponding Secretary; and Robbi Kenney as Recording Secretary. I was chosen as Treasurer.

After returning home from the conference, we moved our Love in Action group meetings to my store. The store closed at 6:00 P.M., and our meetings started at 7:30, so we had just enough time to set up a gathering place. Our group members loved this arrangement. They started showing up at 5:00, to arrange furniture and decorate the meeting area. Thanks to the import store, our "interior designers" had a huge selection of decorations to choose from. They would clear an area, find an oriental rug, set a coffee table on it, bring chairs and couches, lamps and vases, arrange artificial flowers, and then prepare a light dinner. Sometimes even today, old friends ask me about our legendary "Brother Frank Salad." The recipe has far too many ingredients to list here; it included just about everything one could ever imagine tossing into a salad. Also, the "Love in Action Dip," Philadelphia cream cheese with a medium salsa over it, was introduced during this time.

It was great fun having the meetings at the store. However, I was continuously close to having panic attacks. I had hundreds of Love in Action letters to answer, a store to run, and merchandise to buy. Managing Love in Action was itself a full-time job and the truth was, I couldn't do it all. Once, alone in the store after the meeting, I remember saying aloud to God, "Lord, I can't handle all this. Do something!"

God responded, but at first, it seemed like bad news. Our store's landlady contacted me. "Your lease is up January first, Frank, and I'm not going to renew it. I've already leased the building to a man who owns a Scandinavian furniture store. He promised me he would invest a hundred-thousand dollars in property improvements. How could I say no?" she added.

I hung up the phone with very mixed feelings. On one hand, I felt relieved and released from the hectic cycle I'd been on. On the other, I was gripped with fear and anxiety. How could we possibly sell a million dollars worth of merchandise before the moving date?

The San Anselmo city government—which had never wanted us there in the first place—was completely uncooperative. They forbade a "going out of business" sale. We could neither post signs nor do any advertising announcing our closing. My business partner, Hal, was not ready to close the business. He diligently searched the Bay Area for a new location. Truthfully, I was praying he wouldn't find anything, and as it turned out, he didn't. Our store was around 27,000 square feet. The largest building we found was only 5,000 square feet.

We marked down all the merchandise and told customers we were going out of business, but they didn't believe us. We had been in that location for 15 years and they seemed to believe that we would always be there. Our last day came, and the store looked as full of merchandise as ever.

We enlisted all our employees to help move the stock to our home that night. I assumed that we would be working around the clock, stacking everything on the front and back lawns, and covering it with tarps. Then along came a miracle. At 5 P.M., with just one hour to go before closing, a man walked in and asked if I would sell him the entire contents of the store. He didn't offer a huge amount of money, but I couldn't have been happier to take him up on his offer. He, Hal, and I made an agreement and at 6 P.M., I handed over the keys and walked away from more than 18 years of business. I was free as a bird, but had no idea how I was going to make a living.

With the store gone, our Love In Action group had no place to meet. Since I was now unemployed, I had time to search for an office for the ministry. Although I found an affordable office, it was not big enough for the group meetings, so for a while, we once again met in Kent's office.

About this time, we learned that Jake—who had rather flamboyantly hosted some of our early meetings—had admitted himself to a local mental hospital. A few days later, I got a call informing me that Jake had committed suicide. We were all horrified by the tragedy of this vibrant young man ending his life. Jake left a note, which revealed the intense struggle he'd been going through. In part, it read, "It is the constant failure that has made me make the decision to terminate my life here on earth...if I remain it could possibly allow the devil the opportunity to lead me away from the Lord. I love life, but my love for the Lord is so much greater, so the choice is simple."

Clearly, Jake was torn between his sin nature and his love for the Lord, but I think the split in our group played a part in his pain, too. Jake was torn between those who had renounced their homosexuality and those who were celebrating it. I believe Jake knew the truth; I think he was convinced that acting out homosexually was wrong. But the gay lifestyle was firmly entrenched in his life. It had met his social needs and he couldn't find the strength to separate himself from the superficial affirmation it provided.

Dr. Ralph Blair opportunistically used Jake's suicide as a way to condemn ex-gay ministries in general, and Love in Action in particular. In his booklet, *Hocus-Pocus & Homosexuality* he wrote, "Are we to believe the people who experience the 'ex-gay' miracles then kill themselves? Or rather, do they kill themselves, believing that they need that 'miracle' and they do not experience it, no matter how hard they try?"

For more than thirty years, Love in Action has been blamed for Jake's death. However, Jake had spent more than a year with his new pro-gay group after leaving Love in Action. What responsibility do they bear for Jake's death? In reality, Jake chose to take his own life—it was his decision, and we all felt great sorrow.

One day when I went to the Post Office, I found a disheveled young man waiting for me next to our Post Office box. His name was Fred, and he had arrived from a town about 100 miles away. "What are you doing here?" I asked him.

"No one understands me," he explained. "My church has thrown me out, my parents don't want me, and you are my only hope."

I took Fred with me back to the office, where I learned he had no money for food or lodging. Hal and I were in the process of moving out of our house; we could no longer afford the rather lavish home we'd been living in, and we were overwhelmed with packing up our belongings while looking for a condo. We couldn't take him in.

When it came time to go home, I didn't know what to do with Fred. Our office building had a guard who came in the evening and stayed until morning. No one was allowed to live there. However, since we sometimes worked until late at night, I told Fred he could stay there. "But after about 10 P.M. you must turn the lights off, be utterly quiet, and please—don't go down the hall to the bathroom," I cautioned him.

The only place Fred could stretch out in our cramped office was under my rather large desk. The next morning, I found him asleep under my desk, with a bottle of urine beside him. I still don't know where he got the bottle.

This went on for two weeks until Brother Arnold from Colusa came to our group meeting and said he would take Fred home with him. Brother Arnold had often made his house available to any man who needed a place to stay. Several had taken advantage of his hospitality, and now it was Fred's turn.

For several years, now, I had been paying Agape Fellowship's rent for their church services at Stewart Chapel. Now that I had no job, I could not afford it any more. Kent Philpott had been urging me to transfer my membership to Church of the Open Door, so I decided the time had come for me to make the move. Sadly, soon after, Agape Fellowship disintegrated, but I was glad to see many of my former church mates join me at Open Door.

Two years prior, Pastor Robert Hymers, one of the Open Door pastors, had moved to Los Angeles to plant some Open Door churches there. He had been quite successful, and in the past year he'd also started a Love in Action group, which had now grown to twice the size of our home group. When Kent mentioned that our San Rafael ministry now had an office but no office workers, Pastor Hymers sent two ex-gays from his group to help us out. One day, while I was trying to focus on some paperwork, I heard a rather loud motorcycle outside the window. I looked out and saw two women climb off the bike. Moments later, Dolores and Shirley charged into my office and informed me they were from Love in Action, Los Angeles, which would be paying their salaries. This was good news since we didn't have a dime, much less a donor base.

Dolores was a take-charge kind of gal. She asked me to take the next day off so she could organize the office. These two industrious young women moved everything out, cleaned every square inch, and then rearranged all the furniture. From that point on, we had a workable office. Kent had agreed to find places for Dolores and Shirley in his Community Houses. Within a month or so, Dolores was house leader of one home. The church elders warned me they did not want two same-sex, ex-gays in the same house.

Soon after Dolores and Shirley's appearance, a young man named Paul arrived at my office. His face was bloody, his skin discolored, and he was weeping. I had known Paul as an ex-gay leader in Arizona, where he'd been a married man with two children. Now here he was, a very confused and battered soul. Despite his sorrowful condition, it was evident that Paul was a very attractive man. At six foot two, with a well-built body, no doubt he attracted both men and women.

He told me his story. He had fallen sexually and when his wife found out, she threw him out of the house. His church sided with his wife and told him to leave the area. He had moved to the Castro District of San Francisco and had entered into a "committed relationship" with another man. This morning, however, Paul's new life had fallen apart. There had been an ugly argument over Paul's unfaithfulness, and Paul's partner had bashed him over the head with a brass candle-stick. We tended his wounds, and Dolores took him home to the community house she was leading. We now had two ex-gays in the same house, but they were not of the same sex. As a ministry, we would have a long relationship with Paul.

From time to time, other people arrived at our Post Office box. Some phoned the office and asked for our street address, intending to come live with us. We were soon swamped with people who had been discarded by their families and churches. Following our elders' rule, we placed one man (and occasion-ally a woman) in each of the church's Community Houses. It probably was the right idea, but things did not go well.

The Community Houses were filled with men and women who had been homeless, and often on drugs and/or addicted to alcohol. Some had invited Christ into their lives, but most had not yet made that decision. When residents discovered their new housemate was homosexual, they began to ridicule him, mimick-ing his walk and mannerisms. Our people felt as if they had never left home—they were living in Christian houses, yet suffer-ing the same rejection and humiliation they'd had at home.

We couldn't help them all, and some returned to the gay lifestyle, angry and embittered. I intervened on behalf of one young man, moving him to Dolores' house where there was already an ex-gay man. It worked out well, and no one seemed to notice that we had broken the rules. Then I grabbed another, and another, and still no one noticed. Soon, Dolores' house had seven ex-gays and no straight people.

The church elders told me that most of their houses were not doing well. There were drunken fights, complaints from neighbors, and yards littered with beer cans and trash. It seemed the houses with women were somewhat better; most of the disturbances seemed to be in the men's houses. After sufficient time had passed, I casually mentioned at an elder's board meeting, that Dolores' house was doing well. One of the elders confirmed, "Yes, I see they put up new curtains, and everything is neat and clean."

"Have you realized," I pointed out, "that this house has been entirely ex-gay for almost a year now—and there has not been a single problem?"

They agreed. Then and there, the one-gay-man-to-one-house rule was discarded.

Meanwhile, the new XX-Gay group was growing in influence. In an "Evangelicals Concerned" newsletter, Ted reported, "All of the six testimonies in Philpott's book, *The Third Sex,* have quit Love in Action and are living quiet lives as gays." Ted was badgering the publisher, Logos, not to reprint the book. However, Kent Philpott was just completing a second book along similar lines, which would be published soon. It was titled, *The Gay Theology.*

It was true that four of our original six members had joined Ted when he formed his new group. Another man, named Jim, seemed to belong to both groups. Our sixth original member, Bob, remained with Love In Action and continued to write our newsletters. To find out whether Ted's assertion was true, I phoned one of the women who had been in our original group. She confirmed that she and another woman from our initial group were living together, but said they did not have a sexual relationship. She believed that God had made her gay, but that it was wrong to engage in homosexual behavior. I don't know if she persevered in that commitment, but at the time, she was not homosexually active.

Meanwhile, Ted was very adept at marketing his views. Soon, one of his pro-gay organizations challenged us to a debate. On April 22, 1977, we met at a church in Sausalito. Several reporters from gay newspapers were there. The *Gay Liberation Alliance* presented the following charges against both Love in Action and Exodus:

1. You are a deprogramming organization allied with Anita Bryant.
2. You kidnap gays and put them into concentration camps.
3. You are promoting oppressive legislation.
4. You have forced gay bars to close and have caused street disturbances.
5. You are influencing the American public's attitude through the President of the United States.

These charges contained some half-truths. We did house gay people in our Community Houses, and supported them in their desire to change. We certainly were not allied with Anita Bryant. In fact, were very distressed about her campaign. She raised millions of dollars to fight gay rights, but paid no attention to helping gay people who wanted to leave homosexuality.

Although political leaders did call us, and some used the name of Exodus in their presentations, we were completely non-political. We refused to testify for them or to be involved in any way in their political agendas. We did have a street-witnessing team which, although rather quiet and unassuming, possibly could be accused of causing a disturbance. We had never once caused a gay bar to close—we only wished for that much power! And yes, President Carter's sister, Ruth Carter Stapleton, had endorsed Exodus.

I responded to these charges by giving my testimony. Kent tried to set the record straight by presenting a press release entitled, "To show gays the love of Jesus and freedom from homosexuality," which he had written prior to the meeting. At the end of the evening, the Gay Liberation Alliance issued this statement, "We will do everything in our power to wipe out Exodus, and will not rule out the use of violence."

Every weekend, our witnessing team went to the Castro and Polk districts of San Francisco, talking to gay people and telling them about our ministry. One San Francisco gay paper wrote an article accusing Love in Action of "...kidnapping gay people and sending them to a lockdown in New York." There actually was an ex-gay residential program in New York at the time—not connected with Love in Action—but it certainly was not a lockdown. Nevertheless, this rumor led to an interesting conversation. I was working in the office one day when a gay man called and pleaded, "What corner do I stand on to be kidnapped, so I can get out of homosexuality?" In that instant, I realized that any publicity, no matter how derogatory or ridiculous, was helpful to our ministry.

The Love in Action witnessing team was a mix of ex-gay and straight Christians from various churches, led by Larry Rosenbaum. Here is how Tim, a team member, described going out to witness:

After we all had gathered together, we prayed, asking God to bind the enemy. We divided up our tracts and were on our way. I always sense tightness in my stomach as the car I am riding in nears the corner of Polk and Bush streets. This is a street where almost everything glitters, from the bright lights in the discos to the jewelry that the weekend revelers wear. They are a strange mixture of men and women, straight and gay. They range in age from 14 to 60, and all of them have one thing in common—they desperately need to meet Jesus Christ. Some are bored with hearing about Jesus; many are curious. There's a fairly large element that is openly hostile to the truth of the Gospel. "Here's what I think of Jesus!" a man snarls, ripping up the tract into tiny pieces. I pray for him and so the night wears on...

The gay community had their own take on our witnessing team, accusing us of being arrogant, hateful, insulting, and terrorizing. Many of them would picket all of our future events.

I had agreed that Love in Action would host the second Exodus conference. Shiloh Temple in Oakland had decided to join us as co-hosts, holding all the events at their church. The fee was $15 for the week, or $3 per day. Shiloh church members would provide free housing for most attendees. Now, the conference date—June 27 to July 1, 1977—was just around the corner.

Exodus Vice-Chair, Greg Reid, came up several weeks beforehand to help with preparations. Many attendees arrived a week early, eager for fellowship with Love in Action staff and members. The first day of the conference, we were confronted by sign-carrying picketers and the news media. We hurriedly put out a table with coffee, donuts, and cookies, hoping to calm and welcome them.

Just as I was about to give the opening address, the doors burst open and a flood of protestors and media filled the sanctuary. One man in drag ran screaming up and down the aisles and through the pews, with a police officer in pursuit. Press videographers focused their cameras on me and shined such bright lights in my face that I could not see my notes. This was my first major speech, and I was completely unnerved. Nevertheless, we proceeded with our conference. Jim Kaspar and Mike Bussee presented an excellent seminar called "The Ex-Gay Reality, Position, and Process." Barbara Johnson gave her testimony, which, as a mix of riotously-funny anecdotes and heart-wrenching tragedies, brought down the house. We were all on the 6 P.M. news.

The biblical theme for the conference was taken from Esther 4:14, "And who knows but that we have come into the kingdom for such a time as this?" The welcome letter in the conference packets contained this statement:

In a year when homosexuality has become the most explosive issue in the public eye, Exodus International has the chance, and more than that, the calling, to be vessels of the love of our Savior to the gay community. On all sides there is animosity and bitterness, but God has called us to stand in the gap, to bridge the troubled waters, and to heal.

Before the conference closed, a statement of faith was agreed upon, which read, "We uphold God's standard of righteousness and holiness, which declares that homosexuality is sin, and we affirm His love and redemptive power to recreate the individual." Through the years, this statement would be modified to some degree, but today remains much the same.

The *San Francisco Examiner* ran an article on the conference. They pictured Greg Reid with the caption, "I released my sexuality to God," while my picture was captioned, "Homosexuality is sinful." The *Gay Crusader* reported the following:

...the whole conference was a big shuck and jive trip...many of the people present were pathetic messes. A person who had the sex change now was trying to be the man he was before, a most sad situation...The person who did not show up for the morning meeting—known to our editor here as 'Satan himself,' was the Rev. Kent Philpott of the Church of the Open Door in Marin County. He was the one who led the first anti-gay demonstration in the history of San Francisco, just a week before the gay parade. Philpott has been accused of causing one or more young men of either committing suicide with his 'ministry to gays' or having them collapse from nervous breakdowns.

This article pictured Jim Jones, Adolf Hitler, Anita Bryant, Kent Philpott, and me. It did result, however, in many inquiries about the ministry.

When Dolores and Shirley first came to work in our office, they had encountered boxes of unanswered mail. Their great work had helped us catch up a bit, but Shirley had now moved on to a different job, and Dolores was left with far more than she could handle. When Kent Philpott's second book, *The Gay Theology*, came out, our office was soon flooded with more letters asking for books, advice, and literature. The phone rang all day long, with churches requesting seminars, and people wanting one-on-one counseling. It was impossible for Dolores and me to keep up.

Many letters we opened said things like, "I have written two times, but still no answer!" or, "I sent money for books. Where are they?" or, "We asked your team to come to our church, but they didn't respond." In reality, there was no "team," there was just Dolores and me—completely overwhelmed.

Then help arrived.

First, a man named Bill walked through the door, asking for me. He had heard good things from a friend who had attended one of our Love in Action seminars. He decided to find out more. I invited Bill to attend our next group meetings and he became very excited about what we were doing. After about four weeks, Bill quit his job, moved into Dolores' Christian house and went to work in our office, donating his time.

Bill was very gifted, and soon the stacks of letters began to diminish as he plowed through them. He loved counseling, too, and wrote long letters of advice to strugglers. Those who received his letters wanted to meet him in person. Soon, many were in private counseling sessions with Bill, and attending our group meetings as well.

Then Dan, a gifted Bible teacher, arrived. At this point,

Dolores' house was full. The church's other Community Houses were full, so we leased a house and appointed Dan house leader. This new residence had a large living room and was ideal for our group meetings, so we did not need to use Kent's office any more.

Dan was self-employed and made his own hours, so he was available to help in the ministry. Before long, he suggested we launch a San Francisco group meeting. The Nineteenth Avenue Baptist Church offered their social hall for our meetings and, almost at once, the group was a success; it was not unusual to have 50 people attending. We met there for several years, until a pro-gay pastor asked us to leave.

Naturally, the gay activists were not happy that we were holding ex-gay support meetings in "their" city. They began demonstrations, and assigned two activists to stand at the entrance, to dissuade people from coming in. Some seekers did turn away, but most pushed past the picketers and joined our group.

Since this meeting hall had a large kitchen, we were able to serve full dinners, rather than just light refreshments. A group of five or six people from Fresno made the long drive to San Francisco every Friday night. With them was Wilma, a mother whose son was in the lifestyle. She was an excellent cook and brought mountains of food in large casserole dishes. Many came, I think, just for her great cooking. Wilma was very devoted; she went on every outreach we hosted, even when it was in another state.

We always invited the picketers to come in and eat with us. Usually they did. One activist brought his full-sized harp and would play outside the door. Often, we would invite him inside to play for us, and it blessed everyone because he played so beautifully.

Another of our long-time picketers had AIDS, and we could see him failing. Soon he was in a wheel chair, with an intravenous-drip bottle on a pole attached to his chair. Whenever I was asked to speak on radio or TV, this same man had often been selected as my opponent. Afterward, he and I would always have lunch or coffee together. He died shortly after wheeling himself up Market Street in the Gay Pride Parade. I missed him after his death; he had become a friend.

Frank, Perry Desmond and Barbara Johnson 1976

Frank teaches at an Exodus conference. (c. 1977)

Chapter Ten

"Lord, Don't Do This to Me!"

Despite some encouraging and inspiring successes, those were hard times for ex-gay ministries. Between Exodus Two and Exodus Three, a number of our leaders fell back into the gay lifestyle. As I see it now, we were disorganized, had no guidelines, and—in all honesty—unqualified to run a national organization. Many of the various ministries had become gay social clubs and pick-up points. Meanwhile, a new model for group meetings had evolved, called "leaderless meetings." I vigorously opposed it. This kind of program had no accountability; there was no responsible, godly leader to point the way to Christ or to encourage strugglers.

A leader is a role model. In ministering to people struggling with same-sex attraction, he or she should be well advanced in the change process and able to answer questions from experience. Without a leader, there can be no informed instruction, and meetings can easily become nothing more than gay parties. In fact, some of these groups even went together to gay bars after their meetings! As I look back, these leaderless meetings upset me more than all the distortions of truth from the gay community.

Even before returning to Christ, I had felt uncomfortable with the childish behavior of many homosexuals. I saw my first gay parade in 1972 ("Christopher Street West"), where grown men in feather costumes rode on tricycles decorated as swan boats. It made me sick to my stomach. *Am I part of this?* I asked myself repeatedly. *What's wrong with these people?* I had not yet reached the point that I wanted out of the lifestyle, but I already wanted to separate myself from gays who acted in such infantile ways. Now, I was even more disturbed, as true seekers were joining our ex-gay groups, only to be led in the wrong direction. My desire and intention was to help them discover a more mature, meaningful life, but instead, they were being exposed to the same superficiality and frivolity that characterizes the gay lifestyle.

In the years after I left homosexuality, I grew in maturity, not by my own methods, but by taking God at His Word. I still remember the first time I read 1st Peter 5:10, which says, "And the God of all grace, who called you to His eternal glory in Christ, after you have suffered a little while, will Himself restore you and make you strong, firm and steadfast."

Early on, this verse had warned me that I would suffer a little while. I most certainly had, and the suffering had come from many directions. The gay community I had so badly wanted to reach had mostly rejected and ridiculed what I was doing. In the Christian community, many churches declared gays could not change, and refused to listen to anything I was saying. The media represented us more or less as a crazed, fringe cult. To make matters even more complex, I was still working through my own struggles.

This scripture, however, offers a great promise to us all. The God of all grace will make us what we ought to be, and will settle us and ground us securely. The first day I heard that promise, I believed God could and would keep it. With careful study, I also saw that no scriptures condone homosexuality. As time went by, I became firmly convinced that God's norm for people is opposite-sex marriage. Yes, I know St. Paul said it was better to remain single, but I believe he said that because of the severe persecution the early Church was facing at that time.

Now, after about five years of celibacy and radical changes in my life, I had the feeling that I could be married, that I had matured enough to handle marriage. Whether that was true or not—and I wasn't looking for marriage quite yet—I realized that my maturity now exceeded that of some heterosexuals in my acquaintance.

Above all else, my desire was to bring pleasure to God. I knew beyond the shadow of a doubt that being "gay but celibate" was in conflict with God's original intention for His people. I am entirely convinced that trying to remain celibate while accepting a "gay identity" leads to unnecessary mental stress, guilt, and frequent relapses.

Holding on to the gay identity encourages self-defeating illusions. Many who try to maintain the balance between gay identity and celibacy are addicted to gay porn. They often frequent gay bars and parties, telling themselves, *These are my people, and I can't cut myself off from my gay brothers and sisters.* If they call themselves gay Christians, their focus is primarily on the gay part of the equation and very little on the Christian part. I am often asked, "Can you be gay and Christian?" My answer is, "Not forever."

As Christians, we all have any number of faults and deficits, and God does not reject us. Instead, He provides a way out for all our besetting sins, and fully expects us to walk through the doors of deliverance, as He opens them. He calls us to repent, right up to our last breath. God is a God of truth, and He has told us the truth. Some of His truths are gentle, loving, and kind, but some are severe. 1st Corinthians 6:9 says, "Do you not know that the wicked will not inherit the kingdom of God? Do not be deceived: Neither the sexually immoral nor idolaters nor adulterers nor male prostitutes nor homosexual offenders...will inherit the Kingdom of God." This is a hard word, but it is true.

As time passed and I reflected on the possibility of marriage, I had no idea what it would be like, but I trusted that God would make me equal to the task, just as He had made me equal to the demands of our cutting-edge ministry. I often found myself saying, "God doesn't lead us half way on a journey, and then abandon us. God completes what He starts, as long as we do not oppose Him."

Sadly, however, it seemed as if some "leaders" in our fledgling ex-gay movement were opposing God. Often, I felt as if more were going wrong than going right, and I had very mixed feelings about our fallen friends and colleagues.

On one hand, I knew the temptations. I too, had struggled greatly, and only by God's grace was I not in their situation. On the other hand, I loved God, wanted to please Him, and loved the calling He had given me. From that perspective, a fallen leader had betrayed both God and man. A fallen leader brings sorrow to God, and disheartens all those who had trusted and looked up to him. Hope is a primary ingredient for change. When a leader falls, it only verifies the dismal, hopeless message the gay community is constantly restating, "There are very few ex-gays." To this day, I feel protective of those who were entrusted into my care, and I am angry when their leaders betray them.

During this time, I was very disheartened by all the chaos and controversy we were confronting in our work. After much prayer, I felt the Lord wanted me to address these issues in a book. I had helped Kent with his first two books, but this would be my first solo venture. I wrote my first book,

Establishing Group Meetings, out of pure frustration. Since then, new ministries have used this book to help them avoid the pitfalls of an out-of-control group. Soon, however, I began to realize that groups were out of control because the leaders were themselves unhealed. Moreover, many were uncommitted to their church or their pastors, and they were not being held accountable. I decided an instruction book on leadership could resolve some of these problems.

As I wrote, more sorry tales crossed my desk. Leaders were making very unwise decisions and jeopardizing not only their own ministries, but also Exodus and the entire ex-gay movement. Some of these reckless leaders were traveling with their group members and sleeping in the same bed with them. Others were into something they called "re-parenting," which included "hug therapy." They believed that the process of desensitization would work with homosexuality. In other words, if you did something enough times, it would become commonplace and no longer elicit a sensual/sexual response. They even instructed group members to hug each other bare-chested, in the hope that the arousal factor would eventually disappear, and they would then be normal men. Sadly, this did not happen. Instead, it led some back into homosexual activity.

Nonetheless, hug therapy was vigorously defended and, in some circles, still is. It is true that we are all created for skin-to-skin contact, but that is supposed to be enjoyed within the bonds of marriage. Outside of marriage, it heals nothing. And, in our case, it only tempts us to move further into homoerotic behavior. It seems to me that desensitization works much better in overcoming fear than desire. Along similar lines, a man once said to me, "If parents would just trust me with their children, I might be able to overcome my pedophilia." I just stared at him in disbelief. I thought to myself, *Oh, okay, here are my kids! Glad to help! ...No, I don't think so!* Exodus finally had to issue a clear statement that no Exodus agency is allowed to engage in hug therapy. Exodus also carefully monitors other fringe therapies and unsavory practices.

Although my book on group meetings had become a kind of textbook for new ministries, my *Leadership* book was not well received. It demanded reform, while our current leaders wanted to keep the status quo. Truly, many leaders were "serving" only to meet their own needs. They knew very well that with new standards and accountability, they would not qualify for the positions they now held. Over the years, however, Exodus ministries have now regained credibility.

Opposition within our own ex-gay movement was not our only source of frustration. Both Exodus and Love in Action were constantly under attack from pro-gay activists. In 1977, Love in Action established a telephone help line. We first called it "Gayline," but changed it to "Homosexual Helpline" because the activists were so offended by our first name. Even then, for days, we could not place calls from our office because they had blocked our phone lines with continuous rock music. We didn't give up, though. We advertised the Helpline in local papers and received around 30 calls a day.

The Helpline had a recorded message of hope for change, and a partial testimony. To hear the whole testimony, the caller would have to call in each day for about a week. At the end of the tape, the caller could leave a message. Activists often used this as an opportunity to berate our ministry, and sometimes to threaten us. Once we had a bomb threat and to our great embarrassment, the bomb squad emptied our entire office building. Since the other tenants did not know the nature of our ministry, they were quite puzzled why anyone would threaten a Christian organization.

Sometimes the messages left on our tapes were hilarious. I especially remember this one, "There are three terrible things in this world: one of them is a faggot, the other is a Bible-beater, but the worst thing is a combination of the two, a Bible-beating faggot!" Although we were much maligned, we often enjoyed their inventiveness. One headline in a gay paper read, "Nazis and ex-gays join forces." A flyer distributed in the gay areas of San Francisco urged, "Build a New Order. Join us! Love in Action/Gay Nazis."

The year 1978 was one of great turmoil and drama, and brought some divisions that remain to this day. Several cities were suggested for our Exodus Three conference, but didn't work out. Then Robbi Kenny, founder of Outpost Ministries, offered to host the conference in Saint Paul, Minnesota. She and Ed Hurst did the organizing. I wanted our office staff to attend, but no one had the money to fly to Minnesota, so we packed everything into my American Motor's Pacer and the four of us headed for St. Paul, camping along the way. As we neared St. Paul, we were only a few miles ahead of a tornado, also traveling north. We wondered if we could outrun it, as we drove by people boarding up their windows and shouting at us to take shelter. Somehow, we felt safer trying to keep ahead of the storm, which we managed to do.

That was not the only storm brewing. Nearly a hundred people attended opening night of Exodus. Sadly, our bright, young EXIT director, Jim Kasper, was not there. Prior to the conference, Troy Perry, the founder of the gay Metropolitan Community Church had challenged Jim to a debate. Troy was very articulate and clever. He out-maneuvered Jim and won the debate, hands down. Afterward, when Jim had returned to Melodyland Christian Center, the church leaders—upset and embarrassed by his performance—had promptly asked for his resignation. This was a tragic decision, and a major setback for the ex-gay movement.

At our Exodus conference, the opening speaker was an affable young man named Marty. Marty stated he did not believe gay people could change, but could successfully be celibate. I was horrified that he would promote celibate homosexuality rather than change. That was not our message at all! *What should I do? Should I try to stop him?*

I grabbed Robbi and Greg, took them out to lobby and asked, "What are we going to do?" We could hear some general agreement, as there was scattered applause and shouts of, "Right on!" This was the very core of our biggest challenge. Because the way out of homosexuality is so difficult, and because the movement was so new, we really did not have proof that gays could change. At this point, our message was one of faith, based on scripture; it was not yet the proven fact that it is now.

We decided I should speak after Marty finished. I would read the Exodus statement—that God's love and redemptive power can recreate the individual. That's what I did, but it didn't go over very well with the crowd. They moaned and groaned as I read the statement, growing increasingly noisy and unmanageable. They liked the idea that they could not change, because it lifted a burden of responsibility off their shoulders. It takes enormous work to go through the change process. Most want an easier path—to simply remain gay and celibate.

Meanwhile, I was trying to find my own way into a new life. The year before, at Exodus Two, I had met a woman I liked and we had corresponded during the year. We had even talked about the possibility of marriage, sometime in the distant future. I was very happy to see Jackie again at this year's conference, and we spent some wonderful time together. I was thinking to myself, *When I am ready for marriage, this is the one!* What happened next, I can only speculate about.

Jackie was housing a group of women at her home during the conference. I knew Jackie had been out of the gay lifestyle for ten years, and I felt confident in her maturity, and secure in our relationship.

On the last day of the conference, one of her friends told me that during the week Jackie had gotten sexually involved with one of the women staying at her house. Suddenly, I was flooded with memories of cheating and being cheated on. I was crushed and devastated. Everything I stood for—new life, integrity, and hope for a heterosexual life—suddenly seemed in ruins.

The "other woman" had just fled an abusive marriage. Years later, when I read her testimony, it was obvious she'd had deep, long-standing resentment toward men: "My father molested me when I was 14, and for six years I hated everybody, and everything. I especially feared and distrusted men…" Looking back, I now think she had a strong desire to save Jackie from falling under a man's control.

Jackie's girlfriends and my staff urged me to forgive and forget, and to go on with the relationship. I did forgive her. I understood so well that we are all vulnerable to the enemy's snares. Beyond that, however, I felt a great sense of violation, which I couldn't quite articulate—a deep sense of loss and abandonment. From that point on, I could think of Jackie only as a friend, not as a future wife. I honestly wanted to feel differently, but I just could not.

After this incident, I abandoned all thoughts of marriage and gave the ministry my full attention. However, inside I felt a deep sadness over the death of a dream. A few months later, Jackie called. I expressed my forgiveness, but told her I was now convinced I would never marry. She was her usual sweet self, and encouraged me not to close that door. That was our last conversation. Surprisingly, rather than causing me to reconsider the gay lifestyle, that experience made me even more determined to separate myself and others from such a deceitful, life-destroying pattern of behavior.

Soon we were planning Exodus Four, in Johnstown, Pennsylvania. Because of the division we had experienced at Exodus Three, Greg decided Exodus Four should be for ministry leaders only, so we could iron out our position. Sadly, Exodus Four would prove to have even more problems than the previous conference.

Once again, sexual temptation had proved too much for some of our leaders. Mike Bussee, the remaining EXIT ministry leader, had been traveling to a conference in the Midwest with one of his office mates, when the two had concluded they were in love. Arriving at that conference, they had announced their mutual love, and upon returning home, they had left their respective families, in order to start a new life together. EXIT, the shining star of ex-gay ministries, limped along for a few more years, and then folded.

Meanwhile, in San Rafael, Love in Action was growing at a phenomenal rate. The witnessing team was finding many who wanted out of the gay lifestyle. Kent, Dolores, and Bill were featured in a Christian film called "Family Gone Wild," in which Kent spoke about ministering to gays from a pastor's perspective and Dolores and Bill gave their testimonies. With both residential houses filled, we were now searching for a third ministry house. It was not easy convincing landlords to rent to six or eight singles. Most landlords wanted families, so it took months to find a willing owner.

Dolores located a rather new house that had been on the market for several months. Since houses were so hard to find, we wondered why no one had rented this one. On the day we got the key, Dolores learned why. When she opened the kitchen cupboards, literally thousands of cockroaches poured out on the floor. We decided the roaches were a blessing, since we got a very good deal on the lease. We had no money for an exterminator, but Dolores somehow got rid of the roaches, and soon had everything clean and tidy. Before long, we filled the house with both men and women.

Dolores was counseling one of the women, who had just left her female lover, and was very depressed. The spurned lover kept calling the office, trying to lure her girlfriend back. As was the practice with abused wives, we kept her location secret, but in a moment of weakness, our grieving resident called her ex-lover and revealed her address. The angry woman marched in, demanding that her "ex" return to their apartment; our new resident refused, trying to communicate that she wanted to be friends now, but not lovers.

The angry girlfriend wasn't buying it; she went away in a rage. In a few days she returned, and to show she meant business, she put her foot through the front door. There was an angry confrontation, but finally she left, never to return. Unfortunately, we didn't have the money for a new front door, so for a year or two, everyone who visited asked, "What's up with the foot-shaped hole in the front door?" Later, we learned this irate woman had found a new love, but the relationship had gone from bad to worse. When her new lover objected to her controlling behavior, she ran her motorcycle over the poor woman, killing her.

One challenge followed another. One day at the office, we received what we thought was very bad news. The City of San Rafael had bought our office building and was going to demolish it to build low-income housing. In short, we had to vacate within 90 days. By this time, we had been renting three separate one-room offices. I now hoped to find affordable space where we could all be together.

Seemingly out of nowhere, we received a check from the city for $2,000. We were dumbfounded. What was this? There was a note on the check stub that read "Moving Expenses." The largest donation we had ever received had been $50, and now we suddenly had $2,000 in the bank! Kent found us a seven-room office for $600 a month. We wondered and prayed about whether we could afford it. We were now paying only $100 each for our three offices, so this would double our rent. After much prayer, we decided to go for it. We felt convinced that God had great things ahead for us and that we would eventually need the space. Someone in our church gave us furniture and decorations for the new office and before long, it looked fantastic. We could hardly believe how blessed we were.

Another new blessing was Lori Torkelson, who joined our staff in 1979 and stayed with us for many years. Lori was trained in journalism so we were soon overflowing with literature, both for strugglers, and also for their loved ones. Lori developed a seminar called "Help! My Loved One is Gay." Later she wrote a booklet that is still a classic, *Emotional Dependency*, published by Intervarsity Press. Now that we had additional help, I found the time to return to college. For the next two years, I studied psychology and human sexuality. Because I was learning new information almost every day, I asked Lori to set up an information bank on homosexuality, so those of us who were writing articles and books would have first-rate information at our fingertips. Several authors eventually spent time with us, putting to good use the information we had collected. Lori also helped by assembling all our teachings and organizing them into what would eventually become our "Steps Out of Homosexuality" program.

We were thriving, but life was not easy. Our residential houses were becoming unmanageable. In a six month time period, all three guitars we used for worship had been stolen. We also found drugs under one man's mattress. Our people were restless, and wanted more help than we were offering. One night, our women had a hair-pulling fight. We decided we should limit our program to six months, as the open-ended method was not working. Having a departure date for each resident did seem to solve some of our problems, and before long, calm returned to the program. Later, we extended the program to a full year.

At about this same time, a Methodist minister we called Pastor Bob, whose church was near the gay area of San Francisco, volunteered to teach at our San Francisco drop-in meetings; we all thoroughly enjoyed his teachings. Then, however, the local gay activists decided to play hardball. A committee of gay men visited Pastor Bob, telling him to stop teaching our ex-gay group, or they would make sure he lost his church. Pastor Bob didn't take their threat very seriously. However, a month later, he was called before a church review board and was relieved not only of his church, but also of his license to be a Methodist minister. We felt terribly sorry that he had lost both his job and his calling on our behalf.

Yet, despite the opposition, we continued our outreach, which included a ministry team we sent into the community. Here Lori describes one of her nights with the team:

One thing you learn in street witnessing is to expect the unexpected. People are going to have a wide variety of reactions to the gospel. For instance, one night I was talking about the Lord to two young guys. They must not have liked what they heard, because one of them said, "You Jesus freaks come out here to Polk Street because you like the attention, just like everyone else." After that, he literally picked me up off the ground and proceeded to carry me off to who-knows-where, probably somewhere where I'd be less offensive. I'm about 5'1" and this guy was about 6'1", so rather than argue, I just prayed that God would prompt him to put me down...which he finally did. I didn't get hurt, except for my pride, but I did learn the importance of total dependence on God in doing street evangelism. I also had some explaining to do to other Love in Action members who'd heard that I'd been picked up on Polk Street.

Although we were facing problems at home, needs and opportunities motivated us to reach out overseas. In May of 1979, Church of the Open Door sent a team to London, England, to start a church. Since the team members were familiar with Love in Action, they also founded a Love In Action ministry at the same time. I went over to check out the progress of the ministry, and was very impressed. There were already a number of ex-gay people in the group, and they were reaching out to the homosexual community in a variety of ways.

They had created an intriguing sticker, which they posted in telephone booths near gay bars, in rest rooms, and even on park benches. It read simply, "Want Out?" and included the ministry's telephone number. It became the most effective of all their outreaches. Often, they would get a phone call in the middle of the night from some gay man, depressed about not finding a partner.

Through networking with other ministries, our team found a Christian businessman who happily provided us with a three-story mansion that had a backyard as large as a baseball field. We used this building as a church, a place for group meetings, as well as a residence for our leadership team. Some of the new group members also moved into the house, along with other Christians who were active in the new church.

In California, wonderful things were also happening. In the summer of 1979, a young man attended Church of the Open Door. Locating me after the service, he said, "I'm Bob Davies. You were expecting me." I guess I looked puzzled, so he went on. "I sent you a letter a couple of months ago, telling you I was coming. In the letter I said that if I didn't hear "no" from you, I was coming anyway."

Of course I knew what had happened. In the past few months, we had received hundreds of letters. Sadly, we had boxes full of unopened letters. We simply could not keep up with all the requests for materials, seminars, and counseling.

Fortunately, Bob was undeterred. He continued, "I'll be here about six weeks to help in the office, then I have to get on with my career." The very next day, we put Bob to work answering letters. About four days later, Bob waved a letter around the office exclaiming, "Here it is! Here's the letter I wrote you!" Now he had one less letter to answer. Neither he nor I could ever have imagined what God had in store for him.

Bob Davies would eventually become CEO of Exodus for about 20 years.

Finally, the time had come for Exodus Four, and I went to Johnstown, Pennsylvania. Greg Reid and his friends had decorated the church and it looked very festive, but this would not be a festive event. The purpose of this conference was to settle the issue of celibate homosexuality vs. change to heterosexuality. Most people attending did believe gays could change, although few had any idea how to do so. However, the main issue we came to solve was pushed to the back burner. We had invited only leaders, but because Exodus was still a loose organization, a few non-leaders also showed up. These people had their own various self-serving agendas, based on their own needs.

The entire week was wasted in un-ending petty arguments about every imaginable topic. It was unbelievable and unbearable. We now had more divisions than before we started. The only clear result of the week was that I was voted in as Exodus President. When I returned to Love in Action, Bob asked me how it went. He was startled when I said I didn't want to discuss it—ever.

Since Kent Philpott was Director of Love In Action and I was Assistant Director, when he asked about the conference, I had to tell him everything. After hearing about all the drama and trauma, Kent declared, "We don't need Exodus! Nobody needs Exodus! You may be President, but you are president of nothing. As President, you can kill it off. Don't have any more conferences, and disband Exodus. Kill it now! Love in Action is going international; it can take the place of Exodus. We don't need all the problems that are attached to Exodus!"

I was very tempted to do exactly what he suggested, but I could not. I strongly felt the Lord did not want that to happen. I couldn't have known, but Exodus was going to have a rebirth the following year.

In the meantime, Love in Action, London—which had been a flourishing new ministry—inexplicably vanished. Because we were not in daily contact, we had not realized the ministry had been gone for several months. The huge house we had been provided was now being used by another group. We were puzzled and confused. One day at an Open Door Church board meeting, Kent held up a picture of a fabulous mansion and announced, "This is our new ministry base!" He then filled us in on the details. Our church missionary to London had been invited to speak for a seminar at a Christian school in Wales. While there, she marveled at the beauty of the mansion that housed the Christian school. The school's director responded, "It's yours if you want it. We're closing down."

So, within a few weeks, our entire Open Door outreach had moved to Wales, and Love in Action, London, had been abandoned. Our Open Door director intended to run a retreat facility and establish a new Christian school. Although Open Door Church elders were enthusiastic about this new venture, I was devastated.

I resolved to maintain Love in Action, London. As I sadly related this situation to my office staff, Bill volunteered, "I'll go to London." When we took Bill to the airport, he had with him just about everything he owned. Today, he would never be allowed seven carry-ons, but remarkably, no one said a thing. He stayed with one of our missionaries in London until he found a room to rent in a home. Bill soon reported that the cold, damp weather did not agree with his Latin blood, and that if he stayed too long, it would eventually kill him, so we considered his role in London to be temporary until we could find a local director. Bill successfully kept our ministry alive in the interim.

Meanwhile, Paul, who had arrived beaten and bloodied on our doorstep, and had lived in Dolores' house for eight months before disappearing, returned from his most recent misadventure. After leaving us, he had moved to the gay area of San Francisco. It had been two years since we had heard from him, but now he was back. This is what he wrote for our newsletter:

I was trying to ignore God, but I got hit by a car. It turned out to be one of the best things that ever happened to me. Lying in the hospital with torn ligaments and a broken knee, I couldn't cloud the Lord out anymore. I asked the nurse for a Bible and turned to Galatians 1:6 which read: "I am amazed that you are so quickly deserting Him who called you by the grace of Christ..."

Because of his injuries, he could not work at a regular job, so he joined our office staff for a period of time. There would be more misadventures in Paul's life, still to come.

It was now June of 1980, and twelve of our staff members went to Seattle for the Exodus Five conference. As soon as I arrived, I sought out our primary conference speaker, Arthur Katz, a leader in the Hebrew Christian movement and author of two books, *Ben Israel* and, *Reality*.

As President of Exodus, I wanted to greet our guest speaker and acquaint him with Exodus and with the conference agenda. Art gave me a warm greeting, but then informed me, "Look, Frank, I'm throwing out the agenda. I only do what God tells me to do, not man." I didn't quite know how to respond. I also wanted only what God wanted, but I believed agendas were good, and kept things from getting out of control. However, in the back of my mind I felt God saying, *Just let it happen. I'm in charge.*

The conference opened with a time of worship, and then Katz went to the podium. "First thing I want you to do is look in your conference pack and pull out the agenda. Okay—everybody find it? Now, tear it up. We are not going to go by an agenda; we are going to go by what God tells us to do."

I was worried. Would this conference turn out to be an even greater disaster than the last one? As Art Katz got into his message, I found it very challenging. The point was if we want to serve the Lord, a sacrifice is required. There must be a death to self-rule. He continued, "Are you willing to let God bring you to the end of yourselves? Will you allow Him to put to death all of your personal goals, ambitions, and desires? Will you sacrifice your strengths as well as your weaknesses? Will you let Him put to death any identity you may have apart from Christ, so that He can raise up within you the life and character of Christ—so He can do His works through you?"

At the end of his presentation, Art declared, "Most of you were not called to be doing what you are doing. You are doing it for the wrong reasons, to meet your own needs. If so, you should pack up now, go home and shut down your ministries!" The auditorium was filled with weeping, moaning men and women on their knees, begging God for forgiveness. Those of us on the Exodus board also felt painfully aware of how far we had to go before we would become Christ-like.

During the conference, two men had put pro-gay literature on our book table, while several others had vocally proclaimed they did not believe gays could change. After his speech, Katz said to me, "I want you, as President, to find these people and get them out of here!"

I immediately held a meeting with Robbi Kenney and other leaders, and then we did what he asked. This was a pivotal event, and never would have happened without Katz's urging. Although the controversy about celibacy vs. change continues to this day, as of this writing, it has never been a divisive issue at any Exodus conference since then.

We owe much to Katz's discernment, and I believe the Father sent him to give us a new beginning, and to purify the ministry. Sadly, Katz was also right about most of our ministry leaders serving to meet their own needs. Most of the ministries represented there quickly vanished.

Soon, however, we had new people entering Exodus who would take their places—dynamic and dedicated workers who would form a new Exodus. One key figure was our own Bob Davies, who would lead Exodus for many years. Another was Alan Medinger, who would serve as a long-time board member, and launch both Regeneration Ministries and Regeneration Books. A third was Doug Houck, who would become our gifted conference organizer. These men would soon be among the new pillars of Exodus. Exodus Five turned out to be a time of cleansing, after which the old passed away and the new arrived. The Exodus we know today began here. Art Katz and I became friends, and I will never forget how God used him to revitalize Exodus.

At about this time, my church, Church of the Open Door, was having difficulties with our Senior Pastor, Kent Philpott. In 1979, the church had ordained me as an Associate Pastor, so now I was involved in the board decisions. To my great shock and disbelief, Kent had been accused of adultery. In my loyalty to Kent, I could not believe the charges could be true. I defended him for months. Kent was Director of Love in Action and my encourager. I was his Assistant Director. Together we had planned Love In Action's future; he was vital to our ministry.

Nonetheless, as people came forward and confirmed the charges against Kent, I was compelled to face the truth. On one of the worst days of my life, along with the rest of the board, I voted for his expulsion. I know Kent felt I had betrayed him, and it was hard to face him. On the other hand, if the charges were true—and it seemed obvious they were—then he had betrayed all of us. For a while, Kent fought the expulsion and refused to leave. Then he capitulated, saying, "I will leave the church, but I will not leave Love in Action." Kent still had great plans for Love in Action; he wanted to make the ministry not only national, but international. Now, believing the charges to be true, I realized I could no longer work with Kent. Sick at heart, I turned in my resignation as Assistant Director.

A few weeks later, Kent called me, "Okay, you can have it, I quit." Kent had originally incorporated the ministry under his name. Working for several weeks, Dolores now succeeded in getting us incorporated as Love in Action. I then became Director. When the turmoil finally subsided, Kent and I were able to continue our friendship. After a couple of years of "finding himself," Kent became pastor of a Baptist church in Mill Valley and has now successfully led that church for more than twenty years. Mike Riley, who had been with Church of the Open Door from its beginning, became Senior Pastor after Kent's departure.

Our church's missionary to Mexico, Donna would return to San Rafael once a year. One day, she phoned me and invited me to lunch. When I arrived at her apartment, it was clear she wanted to talk with me about early events in my life. I was somewhat uncomfortable with the direction the conversation was taking. She was convinced I was still seeking affirmation from men, and that this tendency was due to my distant relationship with my father. She was certain I needed spiritual deliverance. She began to pray, asking Jesus to bring up the scene from my early childhood that was the root cause of my insecurity.

As Donna prayed, an unwelcome picture came into my mind. Father had decided to divorce my mother and was walking down the front steps of our San Jose home with his luggage in hand. I was screaming, "Take me with you, Daddy!" My father either did not hear me—or didn't want to—and getting in the car, he drove away. I ran down the street after him, until he disappeared in the distance.

Donna prayed that God would heal the brokenness this tragic scene had inflicted on my heart.

A few days after Donna's prayer and counsel, I had to admit that I did feel much better. Somehow, I had begun to feel more complete within myself, no longer needing other men's approval. I firmly believe that Donna was led by God in order to release me from the past. The next year, she would again have a word for me, which would drastically change my future.

When Donna came home the next year, I ran into her again. She studied my face with a knowing look in her eyes. *Uh-oh,* I thought. *What is it this time?* She told me she wanted to speak to me alone, so we went to my office. "God has told me some things about you," she said, "things He wants me to tell you. To begin with, you have dated an ex-lesbian woman, but He wants you to know you will not be marrying an ex-gay woman. The woman you will marry is 38 years old now, and she has one child, but she cannot have any more children. She is in ex-gay ministry and will work side-by-side with you in this ministry."

I immediately assumed the woman she was describing was an advisor to my staff, since this woman seemed to meet every qualification of the prophecy. I said her name, and Donna nodded. *Could this be?* I asked myself. I knew this woman fairly well; she sat behind me in church every Sunday morning. Even though she was a very pleasant, sweet, and caring woman, I had no romantic feelings for her.

Donna departed, leaving me somewhat terrified. By now, I was very comfortable in my single life. I spent most of my time traveling, and I enjoyed it. What would this mean to my ministry? When I wasn't traveling, I worked from eight in the morning to nearly midnight every day. How could I ever fit marriage into a schedule like that?

Lord, I prayed, *I don't want to do this! I am happy the way I am. Don't do this to me!* Then I qualified my prayer a little more carefully, *I have always done what You've told me to do, so I will do this. But I really don't want this marriage, and You will have to do it all. I am not going to cooperate!*

I told my staff I was going out and I went to the beach, to try to talk God out of this, even though I knew I couldn't. I collected a dozen or more stones, brought them back to my office, and made a pyramid of them in my office window. They would serve as my "Ebenezer" (stones of remembering God's help), to remind me that I had agreed to do whatever God asks of me. Not long afterward, I got a call from this woman wanting to get together. My staff was overjoyed at the prospect of having her on staff full-time as my wife. She and I had several long talks. Then, over dinner one night, I told her I was not very happy about this turn of events. That dampened our relationship greatly.

My staff was very displeased by my attitude and said they could no longer follow my leadership, since I was obviously rebelling against God. This made me re-examine everything. Yes, every point of the prophecy fit. Yet, could there be someone else fitting that description? It seemed impossible, so I assumed she must be the one God intended for me.

Celibacy had not been a problem for me. In fact—perhaps mistakenly—I thought celibacy was my gift back to God for all He had done for me. When I read about eunuchs in Isaiah chapter 56, I always felt God was speaking to me. I liked what it said: "I will give in My house and within My walls a memorial and a name better and more enduring than of sons and daughters. I will give them an everlasting name that shall not be cut off." I wanted that. Did I now have to give that all up?

In the middle of this turmoil, Joe, my former lover and wrecker-of-cars, walked into the office with a woman and a baby. It had been years since I had seen Joe. "I wanted you to meet my wife and see my son," Joe said. I was stunned. Joe, married? He declared to his wife that we had been friends for a long time, and that I had done a lot for him. I asked Joe if I could speak with him alone. His wife went to the reception room and I asked, point-blank, "Joe, I thought you were gay, what happened?"

Joe smiled. "Frank, I was never gay! I just needed the money, that's all. I've always been straight."

I could hardly believe what I was hearing. Joe was straight? After all the sex we'd had together?

Joe departed with his little family and left me thinking, *What next*? Suddenly, I was overcome by feelings of guilt. I had kept Joe from leading a normal life. If I had known he was really straight, and only with me for my financial support, I never would have been involved with him. I couldn't help but wonder, *Is Joe telling me the truth*?

Around this same time, our San Francisco group had grown and we were now conducting two meetings a week. Since our original location was no longer available, we found another church about four blocks away. Just as we settled into that location, a contingent of gay leaders paid the pastor a visit. They gave him an ultimatum, "Either Love in Action goes, or your stained glass windows go." The pastor called a board meeting, and the windows won. We were once again homeless. Later, a church a little farther away took us in, and we remained there for several years.

The next year, I spent several months in Europe, encouraging several ex-gay ministries there, and giving seminars. Simon, a man we had trained in our San Rafael office, now had a busy ministry in Zurich, Switzerland. He offered me office space in his home, and from this point on, Zurich became my European headquarters. I purchased a van so I could avoid carrying all my luggage on and off trains. During this trip, I spent several weeks in Stockholm, Sweden, where I attempted to plant a ministry.

I also attended the second Exodus Europe conference in

Battle, England, where I met Chris, a man I felt would be qualified to lead our London ministry. Chris came to San Rafael and trained with us; he would become a good friend. When Chris returned to London as our new director, the same Christian businessman—who had previously provided us with the mansion before our team moved to Wales—now provided an abandoned nightclub to use as our Love in Action office.

Back in San Rafael, some things were moving along better than others. My relationship with the woman I supposedly was to marry had cooled to the point where we avoided each other. I felt guilty for rejecting her, as I had also felt the sting of rejection in my life. Should I go ahead with a loveless marriage? Would this be fair to her? I needed someone to talk to, but all my friends were pushing for marriage. My staff was very unhappy with me and I suspect they were hatching a plot to push me into marriage, believing it was God's will.

One day, the church elders summoned me and said they were concerned that I was living with a man. Hal and I were living on a ranch that I was developing for future use as a Love in Action retreat center. Hal had separated himself from the gay lifestyle several years before I had, and he was quite interested in the ministry that had developed since my rededication to Christ. He frequently donated money and equipment to our ministry, and he visited the office regularly.

I had a fairly large financial investment in the ranch. I had built several buildings, and purchased restaurant equipment so we could feed a large group of people. The church used the ranch for baptisms, Easter, and other holidays. At one event, we fed over two hundred people. Now the elders were instructing me to leave the ranch? I never knew precisely who had brought up this, but I strongly suspected my staff. They knew how contented I was living in a rural area and how happily I was involved in the ranch project. Whoever it was, they probably believed my contentment at the ranch prevented me from considering marriage. I was very depressed by this directive. I said I would pray about it, and I really meant it.

Back at the office, Bill asked to talk with me. Bill said, "Frank, I have a word from God for you. The Lord says you don't have to leave the ranch." Well, that was good news. Then he went on, "But He also says that if you leave the ranch He will make a world leader of you, and if you don't leave the ranch, Love in Action will be a back-water ministry and never achieve greatness." Well, that didn't sound so great after all.

At about this point, a spirit of deep loneliness and alienation came over me. Until then, I had been happy being single, but suddenly, I began to long for a partner in life. Sometimes I found myself crying on the way home, knowing that no one was waiting for me. Hal and I lived in separate quarters on the ranch, so he was not readily available for me to discuss things with. One night, I carefully questioned myself. *Do I want a man or a woman waiting for me?* I knew for certain that I did not want a man in my life. So was it a wife I was longing for? I tried to envision what it would be like if I were married to the one everyone seemed to think was God's choice. It was a nonstarter. I simply could not put that picture together.

After a few days, I told Hal I would be leaving the ranch. He believed I was abandoning him and asked why. When I told him about the elders' directive, he was quite indignant. "What are they accusing me of?" he snapped. He came down to the office and asked my staff what they thought about all this. "I have been surrounded by hundreds of your church people and no one ever said they suspected me of anything, so what is this all about?" he demanded.

Dan, one of our staff members, spent time with Hal and comforted him. After a while, he seemed to accept the fact that he would be alone at the ranch. His response revealed that he was more dependent on me than I had realized. I could see this was not healthy for him or me. I knew this would be a hard adjustment for both of us.

If Hal and I divided the income from our investments, we would have to sell the ranch. Otherwise, there would not be enough money for us to live separately. About that time, a condo we owned became vacant. I knew I should take it. I told Hal I would take the income from one mortgage we held, plus the condo, and he could take the rest, under the condition that if he died first, it all would come back to me. Hal agreed. However, he did not keep his promise. Instead, he left everything—both his and mine—to his gardener!

About this time, I got a call from Chris, the director of Love in Action, London. He was coming for a visit and asked if I would take him to Disneyland. I was not adjusting well to my new living situation; I was in a deep depression. I told Chris I would love to take him to Disneyland, thinking to myself, *Maybe this is what I need, a time away from all this drama.*

Talking to Barbara Johnson, as I still did daily, I said I would be coming down to the Los Angeles area and would stop by to see her. When I mentioned Disneyland, she said, "I have season passes. Stop by before you go, and I'll give you and Chris the passes; it will save you a lot of money." Since I now had a mortgage payment to worry about, I was very grateful for the free passes.

Chris arrived and we headed for Los Angeles.

Chapter Eleven

Matters of Life and Death

The drive along the Pacific coastline is spectacular and as Chris and I traveled south, we both soaked up the tranquil scenery. I pointed out some of the old California missions, the Malibu mansions where film stars reside, and other points of interest along the way. Once we arrived in greater Los Angeles, we headed for Barbara Johnson's house.

Our plan was, after I conducted a seminar for Barbara, the next day I would introduce Chris to "the happiest place on earth"—Disneyland. When we arrived at Barbara's house to collect the tickets, she and another woman came out to meet us. After hugs and greetings, Barbara put—not two, but three—tickets in my hand.

"You know, Frank," she explained quietly, "I have been promising Anita for weeks that I would take her to Disneyland, but I've been too busy. Will you do me a favor and take her with you?"

Chris and I had been looking forward to a fun day at the park and now we had to bring some unknown woman along with us—but what could I say? Barbara had told Anita a slightly different story, confiding that by going with us, Anita would be helping her out, relieving Barbara of a social obligation so she could attend to more pressing things.

As for Anita, she was more than happy to join us. Although she was a single woman, she figured that neither Chris nor I was a possible romantic interest, so she could just relax and be herself. Her presence created an awkward situation. If I went with her on the rides and attractions, which were designed to seat two passengers, I would be leaving Chris on his own, like the proverbial third wheel. Worse, I did not want to be that close to a stranger.

Finally, we decided we would all crowd in together. Chris seemed to enjoy it, so I guessed it would have to do. After the first ride, a roller coaster in the dark, Anita was chattering away, and mentioned she had first met me at a seminar in Eugene, Oregon. *Good Grief!* I thought. *Could she be that hyper woman from Oregon I tried to avoid?*

Through the course of the day, we learned Anita had a son in the gay lifestyle and that our ministry had been sending her materials for a parents' group she had started in Eugene. Anita said her mother lived near Barbara, and that she had felt led to leave Eugene and her ministry, in order to move to Los Angeles to care for her ailing mother. While there, she had contacted Barbara's ministry, and was now active with that group. As the hours passed, I was relieved that Anita was enjoyable company after all. In fact, my depression even lifted.

Chris went back to London and I returned to San Rafael. In the days that followed, during one of our daily phone calls, Barbara mentioned that Anita had liked me. I felt flattered and affirmed, and a warm feeling rushed over me. "Well, I liked her too," I responded.

The next day, Barbara said, "Anita's here and she'd like to talk with you." She handed the receiver to Anita. We agreed we'd had a great time together at Disneyland, and maybe someday we would see each other again. That conversation began a series of weekly calls between Anita and me. A month or so later, Barbara announced, "Some women friends and I are coming up to visit you. There will be five of us."

Five women? I had just moved from Hal's ranch a short time before. It had been a wrenching move and in all the upheaval, I had not yet furnished the place. I didn't even have a bed—I had been sleeping on the floor, without so much as a mattress. I had been too depressed and broke to think about furniture, and spent most of my time at work anyway. Fortunately, I did have a credit card. So in the next few days, I spent at least $2,000 on beds, bedding, living room furniture, and a host of other things.

Shortly thereafter, Barbara's plans changed. "There will be only four of us, one dropped out."

That was good news as far as I was concerned. Then a few days later she announced, "There will be only three of us; another lady dropped out."

The day before they were to arrive, Barbara called, "Sorry, Frank, I'm not coming. I have a last-minute speaking engagement, but Anita will be arriving tomorrow morning in Oakland, on Amtrak.

Anita, alone? Staying with me? I was shocked and all but scandalized. I quickly called Lori. "You are coming to live at my house for the next few days," I told her, "and I won't take 'no' for an answer!" After I explained my situation, Lori agreed, and arrived at the house the next day while I was picking up Anita at the train station. Anita was bubbly with excitement, talking a mile a minute. I dropped her at the condo, and told her to walk down to the office after she got settled. Later that day, I took her for a drive along the coast and when we got back to the condo, she and Lori cooked a great dinner for me. Sitting in my living room after dinner that night, I felt like a married man with two wives! I liked the feeling of having someone prepare dinner and wash the dishes while I did nothing but relax. *How great is this?* I congratulated myself.

The next day was a deadline for my book, *Steps Out of Homosexuality*. The manuscript had to be assembled and sent to the printer within the next 24 hours. Anita joined the staff and we put the book together. This effort went on until the wee hours of the morning, and I found out later that Anita was nearly dying in her high heels. Later she confessed, "Barbara told me how to dress and the high heels were her idea. She wanted me to make the right impression, so you'd think I was a classy lady!"

Unfortunately, that first printing of *Steps Out of Homosexuality* had not been proofread—my staff hadn't had time to do any editing. After the printing, I heard from a man who had bought my book. To my dismay, he informed me that it contained over a hundred typos, and he sent me his red-marked copy as evidence. I used his corrections for the next printing.

The next few days, I couldn't spend much time with Anita because of my responsibilities at the office. While I was away, Anita scrubbed and cleaned my condo, washing all the windows and rearranging the kitchen.

What I asked her why she had done so much work, she said, "I wanted to do something nice for you and the place really needed cleaning. But you didn't have any cleaning supplies, so I had to borrow them from Bob Davies!"

Soon, it was time to take Anita back to the train. She later denied it, but she cried most of the way back to the Amtrak station. Overall, I had to admit it had been a good experience for both of us. Anita's perspective was similar but more expressive. "I fell in love with the whole idea of living in this area," she would later write, "actually the whole package: the town, the condo, Open Door Church, and the office staff. I was very aware that Frank held the key to my being a part of all this. I didn't want to blow it and scare him off by being too emotional. I was already feeling a deeper affection for Frank, but I thought I might not get another chance to connect with him."

In the days that followed, both of us went back to communicating our real feelings through Barbara. Anita told Barbara she wanted to see me again soon, and I told Barbara that I liked Anita a lot. As for Barbara, she was rather proud of herself. "I told you this was a good one," she declared. "I want a star by my name!" I agreed she had earned it.

My annual European trip was coming up at the end of April and I wanted to see Anita again before I left. I drove down to Los Angeles, met Anita's ailing mother, and spent three days getting to know Anita better. The first day, we went to Knott's Berry Farm—and we were already talking about marriage! For obvious reasons, I had many doubts and fears. To begin with, I didn't know if I could respond to Anita sexually, and I thought I should warn her of that possibility. We agreed that if we married, at least we would no longer be alone. After all, we decided, even if there was no sexual element to our relationship, it was still far better than what we had now.

The next day, we visited the arboretum in Pasadena and it was there I first kissed Anita. It was such a beautiful place that we said if we ever had difficulties in our marriage, we would return there and start over again. Then we went on a picnic. We lay on the grass together, and I noticed that, yes, I had a sexual response to Anita after all.

Anita's next visit came at Easter. She arrived in time to join in our church's Good Friday March, up the main street of San Rafael. The church secretary dressed Anita in black and she joined the group of mourners following Jesus, who was carrying a large wooden cross. Anita thought this event was a bit strange, but she went along with it. That evening I took her out to dinner at a German restaurant and presented her with a gold cross necklace.

On Sunday, Pastor Riley invited us to the annual Easter dinner at his house. Most of the elders were there, and wanted to interact with Anita before giving their "approval." Anita charmed them all. Then, just as dinner was ending, the pastor's wife, Mona, brought out a stack of pictures to show Anita. Peering over her shoulder, I could see that they were pictures of wedding cakes. "One of my hobbies is baking wedding cakes," Mona was saying. "So which one can I make for your wedding?"

Anita glanced my way, expecting me to say, "Mona, we are not even engaged yet!" But I didn't. So, Anita went ahead and picked out the cake she liked best.

I had every intention of formally asking Anita to marry me, but I planned to wait until after I had returned from Europe in three months. In my mind, I had set a wedding date for the following year, in June. After the Easter dinner was over and I was opening the car door for Anita, she asked, "What was that all about, with the wedding cakes?"

I noticed, just in time, that a dog had relieved itself right by the car door. I was trying to maneuver Anita away from it. In an awkward moment, I blurted out, "Watch where you step! Will you marry me?"

As Anita straddled the dog poop, she replied, "Yes!"

And I kissed her.

I told her I hoped we could be married the following June, but she said, "Can we have the wedding on Thanksgiving? That way, all my relatives will be on vacation and they will be able to come." So I agreed to November.

The engagement ring would have to wait until my return from Europe. But just before she left for Los Angeles, I bought her a white wooly lamb to cuddle while I was away. I also took Lori aside and pleaded, "You know how inept I've been with women. I don't want to lose this one! Will you help me do the right things?"

Lori nodded gravely and said she would help. "For starters, you need to keep in close communication," Lori advised. "That's very important!"

Knowing how difficult it was to find stamps in Europe, and how hard it was to know how many foreign stamps to put on an envelope, I decided to write all my notes to her before I left. I bought enough greeting cards to cover the three months, and wrote a little note in each one. I got out my atlas, found romantic city names, and wrote such things as, "It's beautiful here in Marrakesh." I asked Lori to mail about three cards a week to Anita. Although she was a bit dubious about this whole idea, Lori did as I asked and faithfully sent the cards.

Of course, Anita figured out my scheme. Shortly before I returned home, one of her nieces, who collected stamps, asked if Anita had any stamps from abroad. Anita told her she could take the stamps off the cards I was sending.

"But they're all U.S. stamps!" the niece complained.

Anita was a bit confused, but thankfully, was not angry at my little deception. In retrospect, I can only thank God for that. In Wales, I found her a very expensive stuffed bear, which I sent with a note, "When I return, Bear must decrease and I must increase."

While in Europe, I revisited a number of ministries and again attended the European Exodus conference. Ministry representatives from ten nations were gathered there—Exodus Europe was thriving. After the conference, Chris and I visited friends in Oslo, Norway, who told us that the pastor of the Oslo Full Gospel Church had been arrested for speaking negatively about homosexuality.

Later we found out he had been convicted and sentenced to two months in jail. Chris and I were scheduled to conduct a seminar in his church, but soon learned that gay activists had burned the church. Upon inspection, we saw that it was a stone building, with only the interior destroyed, so we decided to go ahead with our event. A business next door allowed us to plug in an extension cord for lights and microphones. And so, amid the charred interior, we held a very well-attended meeting.

I was exhausted from traveling thousands of miles in Europe, but still had one more stop to make before returning home. In Baltimore, Maryland, I attended the annual North American Exodus conference. This was the ninth Exodus conference, and by now, it was like a family reunion. Word had spread and everyone seemed to know I was engaged. Of course, they wanted to know all about Anita. The sessions I was supposed to teach turned out to be mostly question-and-answer forums about my upcoming marriage!

I was about to teach a class on counseling the homosexual—and by request, I had a picture of Anita up on the screen—when someone rushed through the door exclaiming, "Jerry Falwell is on the phone and wants to talk to you!" It took a minute or two for me to realize this was not a prank.

When I took the phone, it wasn't Jerry, but his secretary. "Jerry is doing two conferences, one in San Francisco and the other in Dallas. He would like you to join him and do a class on understanding homosexuality." I told her I was in the middle of a conference session. Could she call me back tomorrow? When I came back to the class, everyone was shocked. "You aren't going to do that, are you?"

"I don't think so," I told them.

Later, however, at about three in the morning, God spoke to me. *You are going to do that!* Remembering the last time I'd said "no" to God, I immediately understood that I had to accept. When Falwell's office called the next day, I agreed to do as he had asked.

When I finally arrived home, I was very surprised to find Anita waiting for me at the airport. I had no idea that she had just driven the entire 400 miles from her home to the airport, just to meet me. She had fantasized about this romantic moment for weeks. She was dressed up and looked wonderful. I, on the other hand, was so exhausted I could hardly respond to her warm greeting. I was smelly, badly needed a shave, and could barely mumble, "Hello." Then, as we waited at the carousel for my luggage, I watched my brand-new American Tourister suitcase come toward me on the conveyer belt—completely smashed. Any trace of romantic mood was also smashed.

Anita was overwhelmingly disappointed; she felt terribly hurt and rejected. Later, however, after I'd had a bath and felt more relaxed, we spent a wonderful evening together, talking and cuddling. The next day, Anita returned to Los Angeles and I tried to get back to business as usual. It wasn't as easy as I'd expected.

One evening I was particularly lonely. When Anita called I said, "Why don't you drive to San Luis Obispo? I'll meet you there..."

Anita declined. "You're crazy," she told me, "but I'm impressed by your impulsiveness!"

In the following days when we talked, I pressed the issue and Anita finally changed her mind. Several times, we both drove about 300 miles to see one another. In San Luis Obispo, we met at the Mission, walked on the beach, and ate out. Most of all, we talked and talked.

The date arrived for Jerry Falwell's conference, to be held in a hotel near Union Square in San Francisco. Protestors numbered in the thousands and the police cordoned off several blocks. We had to show our ID to enter the building. I had just met Jerry and his entourage, when a bomb squad ordered everyone to evacuate the building immediately. It took them nearly an hour to decide it was a false alarm.

The "Sisters of Perpetual Indulgence" (gay men dressed as nuns), were parading outside the building, shouting insults at the participants. After I spoke, a number of people told me they'd had no idea there were homosexuals who did not want to be that way. The concept of ex-gay ministry was entirely new to most of the attendees. Now I knew why God had insisted I speak at this conference. The next day, we flew to Dallas, and so did the Sisters. But in Texas, there were only a handful of protestors, no bomb threats, and the conference went smoothly.

About five days before our wedding day, I had a panic attack. I couldn't breathe and felt as if I were dying. Anita rushed me to the emergency room, where I had to strip off my clothes and put on a hospital gown. Anita was standing by my bed, when the doctor came in and unceremoniously yanked up my gown. I flipped out, angrily exclaiming, "We aren't married yet!" Anita was mortified. She was so embarrassed that she fled the room, which did not help my condition in the least.

The hospital wanted to observe me for four days, which would have included our wedding day. The next evening, Anita's nineteen-year-old son, Tony, arrived and I met him for the first time. He had come from Oregon for the wedding, never expecting to find us at the hospital. After he and Anita left, the night nurse came by and gave me a white substance to swallow. Almost immediately, I felt better. I pressed the red button, and when the nurse returned, I asked her what the miracle drug was.

"Mylanta," she informed me, giving me a strange look.[2]

The next morning the hospital released me and before we knew it, the big day had arrived. On November 24, 1984, at the age of 55, I married Anita Thomas. About 200 guests showed up for what could only be called a "poor man's wedding." By now, I had very little income so we had asked the guests to provide a potluck feast, which they did. Mona's beautiful cake

---

[2] Mylanta is an over-the-counter remedy for heartburn, gas, upset stomach, and acid indigestion.

towered over the food table, everything was delicious, and everyone had a wonderful time.

After the wedding, Anita and I rushed home to change clothes and begin our honeymoon—only to find ourselves locked out of the condo. We had given the keys to a friend, who was going to hide our car so it would not be decorated, and he hadn't returned them. As we waited for our keys, a crowd arrived from the reception, and it was party time all over again. When we finally got away, we drove to Castroville, "The Artichoke Center of the World," where we each had a steamed artichoke. Then we drove on to Monterey where our wedding dinner was elegantly served—at Jack in the Box.

I had reserved a cabin in Carmel with a fireplace. I was going to start the fire, but since Anita was from Oregon, and seemed to have a better idea about building fires than I, she did the honors. In a way, it was a relief to have the wedding behind us. It had been a wonderful day, but we were both weary. We had decided not to make love on our wedding night—we figured we would be tired and stressed.

Sometime after midnight, we broke our agreement.

Just a few weeks later, we celebrated our first Christmas as a married couple and then prepared for an extensive travel adventure. I was due to speak in several southern states, and then go to Europe.

Meanwhile, our Love In Action office staff was very excited again. Not only was Lori planning to get married, but Bob Davies also was now engaged. Many more marriages would soon follow in the Exodus organization.

As for our own marriage, people were very curious—they never stopped asking how things were going. They could hardly believe we were having no problems and were so happy. Lori interviewed Anita for our February 1985 newsletter, and her words bring back fond memories:

I feel like a lost homing pigeon that has finally come home. There haven't been any trials between Frank and me. The strains have come from the outside...people calling in the middle of the night, you know how ministry is.

I was prepared for this because the Lord had given me a vision of the type of man I would marry. In that vision, I could see myself with someone in ministry. I could be an understanding wife to someone who might work long hours into the night doing counseling. I saw travel being a part of it, too—life with a "missionary-minister." I didn't see how it could all fit together, but I didn't question it.

Then, Barbara asked me to take Frank and Chris to Disneyland and we had a great time. There was no romance involved, but I discovered Frank's sense of humor; it was a little strange, but I liked it. The next day, the Lord showed me that Frank was everything I had envisioned. I got chills down to my toes.

Then the Lord also allowed me to see Frank at his worst. He was not feeling well and was kind of grumpy. But, as we got to know each other better, I thought, *This man believes the way I do*. The more time I spent around Frank and Love in Action, the more I fell in love with everything, especially the guys in the live-in program.

After my first visit, when Frank drove me to the train station in Oakland, I burst into tears, but for a while wouldn't admit it. Frank probably hates nothing more than a crying woman; he just dropped me off, gave me a pat, and said goodbye. I needed the whole 10-hour train ride home just to get my face cleaned up. So much was at stake. Everything was hanging on Frank saying yes or no. I just had to trust that God would show him what to do.

One thing I can share about our wedding night

was lying next to my husband and praying together. We were both overwhelmed with this feeling: there was no guilt! We had no shame in asking questions of each other. Frank and I have such good times, and our love grows each day. I love him so much more now than when we were engaged. I just put all my tomorrows in God's hands, and I'm so glad I did.

The year 1985 was event-filled. Love in Action hosted the tenth annual Exodus conference, which we held at San Francisco State College. Our office staff did most of the groundwork while Anita and I were on our trip to the southern U.S. and Europe. Our first stop in the south was Tulsa, Oklahoma, where we did a seminar for students at Oral Roberts University. From there, we went to Last Days Ministry in Tyler, Texas, where we presented a seminar to their Intensive Training School students.

In New Orleans, we gave a training workshop for a group of pastors. It was the first time either of us had been to New Orleans, and walking down Bourbon Street was quite a revelation. There were several drag shows (female impersonators) and I recalled that Perry Desmond once had owned an occult shop on that very street.

Our last stop was with a group of pastors in Mississippi. They introduced me as "Brother Frank, from Sodom and Gomorrah," meaning San Francisco. The lead pastor smiled rather smugly and said, "It's good to know about these things but, thank God, we don't have that problem here." I could hardly hold my tongue. At that very time, I had a young man from his church in our residential program.

Before taking off for Europe, Anita and I spent two days in New York City, where we participated in a seminar organized by LIFE ministry (Living In Freedom Eternally). It was great to see my good friend, Sy Rogers, again. Sy had joined Exodus at our sixth conference, held in Las Vegas. At the time, we had not been sure if Sy were male or female. Since then, he had married Karen, had a daughter, and had recently become Chairman of Exodus, for a four-year term. The changes in Sy's life were nothing less than astonishing. As he and I talked about being married men, we found we had much in common. After the conference, Sy said he thought the Lord had told him to start a ministry in Singapore. When I heard this, I felt a twinge of guilt. Earlier that same year, the Lord had told me to go to the Philippines. At the time, it had seemed impossible—I had never been there and I had no successor with whom I could safely leave the ministry. I had dismissed the idea and had told no one about it—not even Anita.

When I mentioned this to Sy, Anita was in the kitchen and overheard our conversation. "We're going to the Philippines?" she countered, "I don't think so!" After such a whirlwind year, this idea was overload for her. She had made our condo into a cozy little home and was continually thanking the Lord for such a lovely place to live. Was she about to be uprooted once again, not knowing what was next?

Sy and I agreed that someday, we would make an exploratory trip together to both Singapore and Manila, and we left it at that. The next morning, continuing on to Europe, Anita and I flew to Zurich, Switzerland. This was an exciting journey for Anita—her first trip abroad—and she was glued to the window as we flew over the Alps. Below us, like a beautiful toy-train panorama, we saw charming alpine villages, with railroad tracks winding through the mountains.

After giving a seminar in Switzerland, we drove to Neuschwanstein, Mad King Ludwig's fabled castle—for a continuation of our honeymoon. We stayed at a hotel on the banks of the frozen lake just below the castle. It was a fantasy setting, beautiful and romantic. From there, we headed for

England, where we were scheduled to give a seminar in downtown London. Our route took us through Nuremberg, Wurzburg, and Heidelberg, all in Germany. Along the way, we stopped to see the Rhine Falls—a breathtakingly beautiful sight. We drove by many castles, perched high on the cliffs above the historic Neckar Valley. Finally, our road trip ended at Oostende in Belgium, where we waited overnight for a car-ferry to Dover, England.

As if announcing that the honeymoon was over, a blinding storm of hail and rain greeted us as we drove off the ferry at Dover. I could not see the vehicle ahead of me and because I was driving so slowly, the cars behind us were honking angrily. I had to find the road to London, and I could not see the street signs, all while trying to stay on the left side of the road. It was a nightmare.

After a great deal of confusion over maps, directions, and off-ramps, we finally arrived. We stayed in a bed and breakfast that night. The next day, I got together with Chris to prepare for the evening seminar. As people began to arrive, I noticed many attendees looked like actively gay men and women. They were quiet during the presentation, but when it came time for questions and answers, they suddenly seized the microphone and took over the meeting.

Revealing themselves as angry activists, they ripped apart hymnbooks and spray-painted gay symbols on the building. The Christian organization that owned the building held Chris responsible for the damage, and it drained his ministry's bank account.

From London, we traveled to Wales and then to Paris, where we spent Easter in a drenching rainstorm. Then, on the way to Amsterdam, I tried to prepare Anita for what she would see. Perhaps nowhere else in the world are light and darkness displayed in such stark contrast. It was early spring, and the Dutch countryside was breathtaking. Trees were arching over the roads, brilliant in pale-green splendor, the sun shining through newly unfurled leaves. Everything was orderly, with immaculate houses and barns neatly arranged against the landscape. Even the cattle looked recently scrubbed.

The city itself was a completely different story. In other places, perhaps equally sinful, the evidence is at least partially hidden. But in Amsterdam, all kinds of wickedness is right in your face. Anita could not believe her eyes when she saw window after window illuminated in red, displaying prostitutes of all nationalities, openly advertising their bodies. Sometimes they wore scant clothing; sometimes they were entirely nude. This was the deep darkness I had tried to explain.

But, where there is darkness, God brings His light.

Many Christians see Amsterdam as a mission field, and have come from all over the world to minister there. One friend of ours has brought many prostitutes to the Lord, and has then spirited them away from their slave-masters to safe havens. We stayed at a haven, called The Shelter, a hostel located down a dark alley. Many seek refuge there when exhausted and near death, whether physically or spiritually. The enemy is not pleased to have so many escape his clutches: sadly, just before our arrival, a man had rushed in from the street and slashed the night clerk to death.

As Anita and I made our way along the street, sometimes dodging cars that unexpectedly drove onto the sidewalk, a friend pointed out a pentagram[3] above a gay bar. The building spanned the entire block, and on the back street was the entrance to a satanic church. Somewhere, the two enterprises were connected.

For a moment, I was stunned—gripped by fear—as I recalled freely going in and out of gay clubs in my younger

---

[3] A pentagram is a five-pointed star drawn with five straight strokes. Pentagrams are used today as a symbol of faith by many Wiccans, akin to the use of the cross by Christians and the Star of David by Jews. Wicca is a form of modern witchcraft. Its adherents are known as Wiccans or Witches. - Wikipedia

days. Now, I realized as never before how tightly I'd been in the grip of Satan. I wondered if such an obviously displayed pentagram symbol would have kept me out of such places. I wished the spiritual darkness and satanic element of the gay lifestyle had been as clear to me back then. I stopped Anita and wordlessly gave her a big hug. I was so happy about the new life the Lord had given me!

We could not honestly say we enjoyed our stay in Amsterdam, except for the pleasure of visiting our friends there. After a couple more stops, I called Jorgen in Copenhagen, Denmark, to tell him we were on our way to see him. He exclaimed, "Frank, you are going to speak in Parliament!"

What next? I thought to myself. We reached Jorgen's house around sundown and his wife had dinner prepared for us. They had a house full of children, all very well mannered and quite mature. I learned I was to address a press conference in the Parliament building.

The event turned out to be a two-hour debate with the representatives of the gay community, which the Danish press covered. Little was accomplished, but at the end of the debate, Jorgen informed me, "Now, you're scheduled for a 30-minute TV interview. The best part is—it's going to be in the lobby of the gay community's headquarters!"

The gay center was a large building covering about a third of a city block in downtown Copenhagen. An angry crowd of gay men and women encircled us, demanding to know what I thought I was doing in their building. Later, Jorgen said something about "taking the fight into the enemy's territory." I was not convinced this had been a good idea, but the interview aired on national television in prime time, so we hoped it had reached someone who might be open to a different point of view. Before leaving, I gave Jorgen an autographed copy of my latest book, *Steps Out of Homosexuality.* He had urged me to write it, and therefore, I had dedicated it to him.

Our next stop was Stockholm, Sweden, and from there we went on to Oslo, Norway. We were scheduled to speak at an evening meeting, but they had not done any advertising. That night to my surprise, the entire church was filled, with standing room only. As I looked across the crowd of over 300 people, I realized that, as in London, these were not ordinary church members. Most were dressed in leather, some had half their heads shaved, others had multi-colored hair and seemed to be part of the punk movement. Before the service, we prayed, thanking God for the opportunity to speak to unsaved people.

Then, about an hour into the presentation, someone gave a signal, and most everyone there stood up on cue and began chanting, "We will not be trampled on!" It was a frightening experience. The volume increased, and soon the air reverberated with shouted obscenities. They began to throw things at me— books, vegetables, cans, whatever they had brought with them. I feared for our lives. Then, as I prayed for protection, they suddenly all filed out. About twenty people remained, women and men who actually wanted to hear what we had to say. We prayed for the protestors, and then finished our seminar.

One protestor had lingered behind. After the meeting he said to us, "I don't know what they were so upset about. I saw only love here." His few words made our night a lot more rewarding. In any case, our time in Oslo was over, and realizing we had broken Norwegian law by speaking negatively about homosexuality, we were happy to leave town as soon as possible. We drove back to Stockholm, where we boarded a car-ferry to Helsinki, Finland. After speaking with officials of the Lutheran Church there, we returned our van to Zurich, to be stored for another year. It was time for us to head home.

We had little time to reflect on our journey or to recover from jetlag, before a new challenge faced us at Love in Action. While we'd been gone, Paul, the resident who had first come to us in a beaten-up condition, then had returned to us briefly after being injured in a car accident, had ended up in the hospital again. This time, he had been hit by a truck. When the hospital had discharged him, again he'd had no place to go, so again our staff had taken him in and cared for him. He was now ambulatory and, once again, was helping out in the Love in Action office.

The previous time he had been with us, I had warned Paul that when his body was healthy again he would face the same temptations, and needed to make a decision: would it be God, or would it be the gay lifestyle? Sadly, just as he had previously, when Paul mended this time, he again returned to the world he knew best. However, this time, it would be a very short stay.

A few weeks later, Paul walked into the office and asked to see me privately. He wanted prayer, he said. He had just been diagnosed with AIDS and was deeply fearful. I learned he had been modeling in the nude for gay magazines and newspapers. Now, with his life on the line, he was thoroughly repentant. This time, Paul's rededication to the Lord was powerful. Neither he nor I knew he had only a few weeks to live. Here is Anita's description from our newsletter, of Paul's last days:

I met Paul after his last return to the Lord, about five weeks before he died. At first, I was careful not to love him too much, knowing he probably wouldn't live long. Besides, I thought, he had only come back to Christ as a last resort. Later, I realized that is why most of us come to Christ! Anyway, I did okay at the beginning—being nice, but detached. Then one day, I had my guard down. I was working at the reception desk when he telephoned. He was hurting, and asked me to pray with him. As we began to pray, the Lord took over, and Paul and I became close friends, praying and sharing often.

Paul went into the hospital the week we sponsored Exodus Ten, in San Francisco. He sounded chipper and said he would be out in a week or so. A few days later, I visited him. On the ride up to the AIDS ward at San Francisco General Hospital, my knees started getting weak. Traveling down the long corridors, I braced myself. My reaction was, *Oh God, they are so young!* Nothing could have prepared me for how helpless I felt. On the walls were pin-ups of half-clad men. I felt sick.

Sitting by Paul's bed while he slept I had time to reflect. I prayed he would be at peace with his impending death. Oh, how I wished I could go into the bars and drag those guys to the AIDS ward, to show them what chances they were taking. When Paul woke up, we handed out copies of an article he had written called, "The Spiritual Aspects of AIDS." A Christian mom read it to her son, who became angry because Paul had written that acting out homosexually was sin. A week later, the young man came to the Lord, calling his family members to his bedside to ask their forgiveness. He died a few days later.

As Paul's condition worsened, he began to let go of the small hope that God would heal him. He was fearful, not of whether he would be going to heaven, but of the process of dying. God gave all of us who visited Paul words of comfort. The tears rolled down my face as I thought of all my "kids" who were still in the lifestyle. Like Paul, they knew the Lord, but their behavior was out of control. *How can I handle this, Lord?* I pleaded.

The Lord spoke to my heart, *You see only a tiny bit of what I see. I see all My children who are turning their backs on Me, choosing the ways of sin and death, and it breaks My heart.*

Knowing the time was short, I had planned to spend that night by Paul's bedside. I put headphones on him so he could worship the Lord. By morning, Paul was with Jesus, no longer struggling to overcome his addictive behavior. At last, he was truly free from sin. Paul's was the first of many AIDS deaths we were to encounter in the near future.

One morning, the office door opened and our friend, Jeff, walked in carrying a computer. "I want you to have this. I won't be needing it any longer," he explained. How we had wanted and prayed for a computer—but not like this! Anita had become a mother figure to Jeff, and he was dear to all our hearts. In a few weeks Jeff, too, was with Jesus. As we grieved, we were all thinking the same thing, *Oh Lord, how many?* Sadly, there would be many more.

All this happened within a few short weeks of our return from Europe. Anita and I we were exhausted from the trip and now, by all the emotional stress. "I wish we were back in Europe," I said. "Even though we worked hard there, at least we weren't involved in all the death and heartache we're facing here at home. Honestly, the one joy in my life is our marriage!"

"And to think that at one time I wasn't open to marriage," Anita said with a sly glance.

"I didn't know that," I responded. Anita then described the event years before that had made marriage a possibility for her. She had been at a meeting, when the group leader asked her if she ever grieved over not being married. She had then realized that she was fully independent, not needing a man to lean on, and that she rather liked it that way. After she had prayed about it, however, God had opened her heart to consider marriage.

On hearing this, I realized I had never told Anita about the prophecy I had received. I chuckled, "You know, a couple of years ago, Donna gave me a prophecy about marriage, but it didn't turn out so well."

"Tell me," Anita said.

"Well, Donna came into my office and informed me I was going to be married. I didn't want to be so, at the time, it wasn't good news."

"She was right though. You're married!" Anita smiled. "Was there anything more?"

"She told me that the woman was 38 years old."

"When was this?"

"I guess about two years ago."

"Well, don't you know I was 38 then?"

I continued, "She also said that I would marry a straight woman."

Anita nodded, "I hope you know I'm a straight woman and always have been."

"Well, you got a couple of points there," I said.

"What more? Tell me what else she said."

"I don't think I can remember all of it. She did say the woman I married would have one child."

"Tony is my only child."

"Well, you just got three points. And, she said my wife-to-be would be in ex-gay ministry."

"I was working with Barbara's ministry when you found me, and I'd had my own parents' support group in Eugene."

"Four points! But she wouldn't be able to have any more children."

Anita paused briefly. "Well, I guess we never discussed this, but because of some earlier health issues, the doctor told me I would never be able to bear children again."

"I didn't know that! I thought we might have a child! Anyway, I guess you now have five points! But that's all the points you are going to get, because the name given wasn't your name."

"Did she actually give you that name, or did you both think it was that woman because all the points fit her?"

I reflected for a minute. "Yes, I guess that's what happened." We were sitting in our cozy living room overlooking the San Rafael canal, with boats passing by every so often. After a moment or two, I turned to Anita and said, "I'm so glad you turned out to be "point number six!" I gave her a kiss and a hug. It was one of the rare quiet, peaceful times in our lives.

A few months after Anita and I married, Anita's nine-teen-year-old son, Tony, had come to live with us. Knowing what I did about the roots of homosexuality, I was hoping to become a surrogate father to Tony, but I never got the chance. One day Tony was very restless, and that evening he said he was going out. My heart sank. I knew the dangers out there, and I was particularly concerned about AIDS—it was still a mysterious disease and more young gay men were dying of it every day.

I did not sleep much that night, hoping to hear a key in the door, praying that Tony would come home safely. By morning, I was very distressed; Tony had not returned. I tried not to show my concern to Anita, but in my heart, I knew something bad had happened.

Later that morning Tony returned home, very happy. He had found a lover whom he would live with for the next ten years. Soon, the two of them found a house together and we saw very little of Tony. Unknown to either of them, Tony's new partner was HIV-positive. At this point, we had no idea of the trauma to come.

In 1986, six men in our Steps Out Program wanted to be baptized. I believe baptism should be a public affair, so one Saturday, 30 of us took off for Santa Cruz. I had designed and printed a tract that explained what we were doing, and our guys handed them out on the beach. It was a beautiful summer day and the beach was packed. I found a place where the river met the ocean and the water was rather calm. A group of spectators surrounded us as I baptized the men.

Suddenly, I noticed that one of the spectators was totally naked. I thought, *The enemy of our souls is here, trying to distract our guys.* As I was pondering this situation, a "sleeper wave" hit me, and I found myself under about six feet of water. When I came up, I immediately thought, *God just baptized me, too!* In the meantime, the naked man had disappeared.

One of our men wrote a poem about that day:

> I saw the power in the ocean as we stood upon the shore,
> I saw the power there among us that comes from Christ the Lord.
> And as my brothers walked in faith and followed His command,
> I watched them die, to live again by the power of His hand.
> While the waters stirred around them, the Spirit stirred within
> To break the bonds, to set them free, and draw them close to Him.
> They took a stand before the world and lifted up His name.
> There is no doubt within my heart they will never be the same.
> And, like the power of the ocean that beats upon the shore,
> There's a power beating in their souls that comes from Jesus Christ, their Lord.

All of us felt the power of the Lord that day.

Weeks turned into months. Now and then, Anita would ask me about God's call to the Philippines and I always said the same thing, "There's nothing I can do about it. God hasn't brought anyone to take my place at Love in Action."

One day in the fall of 1986, Anita was at the reception desk taking calls. I heard unusual excitement in her voice as she spoke with someone. After hanging up the phone, she said, "Well, you got your man!"

I looked at her blankly, with no idea what she was talking about.

"Frank," she announced, "I really believe I've found the man to take your place so we can go to the Philippines."

How on earth could she know all that after talking to a stranger on the phone for a half hour? She had never even laid eyes on him. Nevertheless, he was already on his way from Nebraska to San Rafael.

John Smid was a youth leader who had come out of homosexuality some years before. When he arrived, I also felt that he was the man. I found him to be extremely capable, and he was dedicated to ex-gay ministry. In the years to come, I gave John more and more of the load I was carrying, and he was always up to the task. It was clear that God had released Anita and me to embark on our next missionary journey.

At that time, 101 men and women who had been in, or were going through, the Steps Out Program were attending Open Door Church. I was very pleased about this, and had never seen it as a problem. But one of our church board members thought otherwise. He told the board of a book he was reading about church demographics. He said the balance in our church was off, and unless we maintained the right percentages of "people groups," we would never grow. He stated what I already knew—that about forty percent of our church body was ex-gay.

I was offended, bur I resolved not to show it. He didn't seem to consider that some of these ex-gays were now married, a few already had children, and they no longer saw themselves as ex-gay, but as normal people with families. Having these people in our church was a rich resource. For example, most of them were very talented; some were in the worship team, others were Sunday school teachers, and those who were single volunteered for the tasks that families did not have time to do. Furthermore, when new men and women with homosexual struggles entered our program, they found a church with people who fully understood what they were going through, who rallied around to help them find the way out.

This issue would continue to gain ground for several years and, eventually, the church board would decide to break up our ex-gay majority. The new men coming into the program would be assigned to other churches, and some who already belonged to our church would be asked to attend services elsewhere.

The problem would fall into the lap of John Smid, the new Director of Love in Action, after I was in Manila. It would become his job to distribute our men among other churches in the area. Thankfully, these churches would welcome our men with open arms, and the men would report back that they were glad to have made the change. Now, some 20 years later, many of these men are still in those churches, some in leadership positions.

No one knew it at the time, but this would be the beginning of the end for Love in Action in San Rafael.

Sy Rogers and I had kept in touch. Three years later, now, it was time for an exploratory trip to the Philippines and Singapore. On May 20, 1989, we took off. There were a few obstacles along the way. First, a typhoon delayed our flight nearly a full day; then, the airline lost our reservations and we had to go on standby. For me, this was just the beginning of spiritual warfare that would continue for several years. It was obvious the enemy did not want an ex-gay ministry in Manila.

Mary Bains, of Youth with a Mission (YWAM) in Manila, acted as our booking agent for speaking engagements. Mary eventually became a team member of New Hope, Manila ("Bagong Pag-asa" in the Tagalog language). Nearly everywhere I spoke, a pastor would confide, "We have a great homosexual problem here in Manila and we need you! Please don't go home! Stay and minister to our people."

Of course, I couldn't stay quite yet but it confirmed my calling. The same welcome greeted Sy in Singapore. There, I had my first experience of ministering to people who were Buddhists. They did not take offense at our Christian message. One mother even said, "If my son will change his ways, I will become a Christian!"

Sy and I both returned home, eager to start the ministries to which God had called us. In July, Anita and I attended the 15th annual Exodus Conference in San Antonio, Texas. Along with Sy and Karen Rogers, Anita and I were commissioned as official Exodus missionaries. Anita and I now planned to leave for Manila at the end of the year.

Understandably, it was difficult for me to turn over Love in Action to John Smid. I wrestled with myself. I knew he would do a great job as director, but I had birthed the ministry and had seen it through many hard times. I knew I couldn't direct Love in Action from seven thousand miles away, and this wasn't going to be a visit—Anita and I were going to be gone for years, although we didn't know how many. Painful as the decision was, I realized John was right to ask for full directorship. Finally, I was able to make the break.

I had walked away from many things in my life. At last, I came to see this parting of ways simply as another sacrifice the Lord was asking me to make.

Pastor Mike Riley presiding at Frank and Anita's wedding. (1984)

Chapter Twelve

Please...Not Another New Beginning!

In November 1990, Anita and I were preparing to travel to Manila for our "new beginning" in Asia. As has so often been the case, we had to keep moving forward without any absolute certainties. In His mercy, and true to His word—"Your Father knows what you need before you ask (Matthew 6:8)"—the Lord provided us with a house just three days before our departure. A pastor from a village in the outskirts of Manila contacted us. He said he was moving into a new home, and we could rent his old house for just $70 a month!

Regarding this as an answer to prayer, we told Pastor Lamitar we would rent the house, sight unseen. Naturally, we couldn't help wondering what it looked like. On my fact-finding trip the previous year, we had seen people living in bamboo houses on stilts, with animals living on the ground level below. Would our new home be something like that? So far, we had learned only one very important detail from Pastor

Lamitar. This house had a telephone, which was very exceptional. Only one family in a hundred had a phone, and there was a seven-year wait for telephone installation. For obvious reasons, a phone was vital to the launching of our ministry.

When the time arrived for us to depart, we were thrilled to learn that our trip was entirely free. I had enough air mileage for both Anita and me to fly to the Philippines—and to our surprise—the itinerary also included three nights in Hong Kong, at no charge. On arriving in Hong Kong, we found ourselves at the swanky Conrad Hotel. Our room was on the 45th floor, with a stunning view of the whole harbor. The bathroom was a marvel of marble, and the hotel was delightfully luxurious.

When we arrived in Manila, it was quite a contrast to the opulence we had enjoyed in Hong Kong.

Pastor Lamitar met our plane. He took us to his home for the night, where we slept on a mattress on the floor. It was both surprising and distressing to spend the night at eye level with the largest cockroaches we had ever seen. Later, we learned they could fly as well as crawl. When we drove to our new home the following day, we experienced a more pleasant surprise. We saw we had rented a very livable three-bedroom cinder block house.

Our team included four people: Anita and me, Mary from YWAM, and a young man named Jerome—so there were just enough bedrooms. We spent the next several days furnishing the house. The local shopping district was about a mile away and had several furniture stores that made furniture on the premises, so they had a good selection. All the stores delivered their merchandise, which arrived by motorcycle with a sidecar, rather than on a truck. We hired a housekeeper from Pastor Latmitar's church, and after a couple of weeks we had created a livable home.

Before leaving the U.S., I had been concerned about how I would start a ministry in a foreign country, from nothing. I believed God had given me a word of encouragement, *I only want you to go there. I will do the rest.* In the days following our arrival, that promise seemed to come true, because once we were well situated in Manila, the telephone began ringing off the hook almost immediately. People were calling, wanting to be part of this new ministry, and within just twelve days, we held our first group meeting. Our telephone was proving to be indispensable, just as I had imagined.

What I hadn't counted on, however, was that the phone was one of a very few in our village, and our neighbors expected to use it any time they wanted. Since Pastor Lamitar had allowed them that privilege, the locals considered it their right, even though he had moved out. Now and then, I'd wake up in the morning and on my way to the bathroom, I would have to say good morning to strangers who were lined up for the telephone! Our housekeeper always let them in, and sometimes they would hang around all morning, waiting for a call. Even worse, callers from overseas would sometimes demand that we run down the street and call someone to the phone. On our main road, there were telephone booths every two blocks. The problem was, the wires were just flapping in the wind; they had never been hooked up to the phone lines. This was typical of the Philippines in those years.

We learned a few things about Philippine history that gave us a better understanding of the culture. The Spanish arrived in 1521 and put the tribal people under harsh authority. The Spaniards were exploitive and were responsible for many atrocities. They lost control of the islands during the Spanish-American war in 1898. For a brief moment in time, the Philippine people enjoyed a democracy—until we declared them a U.S. possession. A war for independence ensued with great loss of life, but the United States prevailed. During American rule, several school systems were established, the most comprehensive being the Catholic one. In 1946, we granted them independence, and the Philippines operated as a democracy until President Ferdinand Marcos declared Martial Law in 1972. Because of flagrant corruption, Imelda and Ferdinand Marcos were deposed in a 1986 uprising.

Investigators have alleged that when Imelda Marcos left the country, she emptied every utility company's bank account, and deposited around $5 billion in a Swiss account that remains hidden to this day. The evidence of this was all too apparent. We arrived just as the country was slowly grinding to a halt. Without funds for repairs, the generating plants now began to shut down, one by one. At first, we had sporadic disruptions in our electric supply, but it got to the point where we had electricity only from about 1 A.M. to 9 A.M. each day. The water situation was worse. We had running water for only about two hours, from around 3 A.M. to 5 A.M.

Anita took it upon herself to get up at three each morning and fill six or eight five-gallon buckets, so we could bathe and wash the dishes. On some days, there was no water at all, and Anita and our housekeeper would walk two blocks to the communal water pump and bring buckets of water back to the house. For some reason, Anita really enjoyed her role as water provider. Thanks to the hour, she began to have an early morning quiet time with the Lord, which she continues to this day. It was not only spiritually nurturing—she also confided that it was the only way she could beat the heat and enjoy a cup of coffee.

Although there were difficult times, Anita and I loved sharing adventures together, and we had many laughs despite the hardships. Our first night in our new house, Anita and I had gone out and sat on the front steps, to watch the sunset. It was beautiful, with the sun setting behind a tall palm tree in the neighbor's yard across the street. Just as we were rejoicing in the beauty of the moment, a man with an axe came out of the house and started hacking at the tree. Before long, it crashed to the ground. I know I was battling depression, but I could not help but wonder if the tree's demise was symbolic of our venture.

We certainly felt as if we were under attack, somewhat like the palm tree, in the weeks and months that followed. True, churches welcomed us with open arms and from day one, it appeared that our ministry was a success. But I'd had no idea how the enemy would try to cut us off at every turn. Much of this came through physical illness and injury. Although our struggles brought forth unexpected blessings, the time we spent in the Philippines proved to be one of the most difficult chapters in my ministry.

The first major challenge came within a month of our arrival, when I contracted a type of typhoid fever. It lasted close to three months and relentlessly sapped my strength. Since the ministry was just in its beginning stages, I had to drag myself to seminars, meetings, and visits with pastors. Shortly after my recovery from that, another frightening episode occurred. As Anita remembers it,

After a meeting, Frank and I were lying in bed, feeling very content. Then he matter-of-factly said, "I have something to tell you but I don't want you overreacting, I had a small stroke, but it's all over now."

"You what!?" I nearly screamed.

Frank went on to say, "The whole side of my face became paralyzed about an hour ago but it seems to be all over now, so just go to sleep."

Well, there would be no sleep for me that night because I knew that often a small stroke is a prelude to a major stroke. What would I do, two hours from Manila, if Frank took a turn for the worse? In Pacita, there were neither ambulances nor anything resembling them. I had to strong-arm Frank into taking the next day off and going to the hospital for a checkup in Manila.

At the hospital, they confirmed the left side of my face had gone dead. My vision was impaired and it was difficult for me to read. The doctor explained, however, that I had Bell's palsy, not a stroke, and that it would be a permanent affliction. "People do not recover from Bell's palsy," he told me.

Nevertheless, after a month or so, the symptoms left.

Not long thereafter, I scheduled a leadership retreat in a rural area. Developing leadership for this new ministry was of primary importance. Someone warned me that dengue fever was rampant in that area, and that we should be careful. To my alarm, the bus we'd hired for transporting our group to the retreat had no glass in its windows. I saw a mosquito come through the window opening and light on my arm. I swished him away, but it was too late—he had already bitten me. I remember thinking, *I wonder if I'll get dengue fever?* Then another thought came into my mind, *I don't think Anita can live through another of my illnesses. She'll be upset with me for taking too many risks.*

As it turned out, I did have dengue fever and Anita was upset with me, but she faithfully saw me through another difficult time anyway.

It took months to overcome this disease. Sometime around August, I started feeling better, so I agreed to present the largest seminar we'd organized so far. Several hundred people were registered. As our staff was getting prepared to go, I slipped on a throw rug that was on our highly waxed concrete floor. I could see my leg bone hanging just under the skin, down alongside my ankle. Our housekeeper helped us locate a hospital. In pain and shock, I remember being stretched out on an operating table that was literally crawling with ants and cockroaches.

When I woke up, the doctor told me that he had examined my leg. "I can't set the bone until the swelling goes down," he said, and simply taped it up. They put me in a room, but like the operating table, it was full of cockroaches. Also, there were cats in the hallways, eating food leftovers that had been placed on the floor. They said they were going to transfer me to another hospital for the surgery. Anita recalls:

Frank was returned, unconscious, to a hospital room, where I picked the ants off of him. When he woke up, he was determined that the seminar must go on, and I was too traumatized to argue with him. I realized this big event was now in my hands.

I looked for a bell to call the nurse, but there was no nursing staff. We were supposed to make sure a relative or a friend would be there to take care of him. Now I understood why the housekeeper had protested when I'd sent her home! But it was too late! I couldn't call anyone to care for Frank because the hospital had no phone. I went around like a mad woman, waving money until I found a young student-nurse to watch over Frank while I was gone.

Frank was given a plate of food that consisted of rice and fish heads (no eating utensils), this only traumatized him further. When I returned from the seminar, I had to go out and find him a hamburger. I liked the idea of cats in the hallway. I was sure they were there to keep the rat population down.

Soon they took me to Makati General Hospital in central Manila, the newest and best hospital available. I was given a private room, with an extra bed for Anita, for $38 a day. In this recently constructed facility, cats and ants were missing, but the cockroaches still looked me in the eye from my night stand. The room seemed much more American than the one in the village hospital. The hospital bed cranked up so I could eat, and there was an adjustable tray that swung over the bed—

although this seemed only to make it easier for the cockroaches to get eye-level with me. It took six days for the swelling to decrease sufficiently for my broken leg to be set.

During my hospital stay, some church members came to visit. Only now were we beginning to discover what generous and loving people they were. More than twenty of them crowded into a Jeepney (a Jeep with an extended body) and made the daunting journey to downtown Manila. My room was on the fourth floor and all these people were huffing and puffing as they came through the door. One of them sheepishly said, "We walked up because we didn't know how to use the elevator."

This was a big adventure for them. Almost none had full employment; most did part-time work. Some worked for pennies a day at a factory that produced Christmas ornaments. Their faith put us all to shame. Every day, they went out witnessing to others about Christ. They financially supported their church, despite incomes so low that they often went without food. It was common to learn of family members dying because medical attention was out of the question. Yet, although some lived in houses made of cardboard or under plastic tarps, they were a happy people.

In the meantime, I was not a happy man. My leg was set and in a cast, but when I tried to get out of bed to walk, the pain was unbearable. I would be released from the hospital only when it was safe for me to put some weight on my leg. Needless to say, I wanted to go home. However, when I tried to walk on crutches, the pain was so intense that I simply could not move. The nurse smiled, "Okay. We'll try again tomorrow." She was far less troubled than I.

Long before Anita and I met, she had worked for several years in a rehabilitation facility, and she knew how to teach people to use crutches. She was, however, unsuccessful in getting me to walk. My attitude was, "I just want to die! Leave me alone and let me die."

Anita was not going to put up with that. "You are going to walk!" she proclaimed. "We have a trip to Australia coming up, and I'm not going alone. If you choose not to walk, I will take care of you as a cripple, but it won't be here in the Philippines!"

I knew from the look in Anita's eyes that she meant what she said, so I tried my best. Gradually, I was able to make it across the room, and eventually I checked out of the hospital, still trying to perfect my use of the crutches. I had a seminar scheduled in a few days and I was determined to keep this engagement.

On Saturday, we arrived at a mega-church, where we hoped to find some financial support. We also hoped to interest the church in starting its own ministry to ex-gays. There were a few steps up to the foyer and my team practically carried me. The pastor greeted me, then said, "All right, follow me, and we will get you set up for the seminar." He rushed up a flight of steps ahead of me. I had not yet mastered steps on crutches. Again, the whole team had to help me and we finally managed to get to the second floor, where the pastor announced, "Just one more floor." When we got to the top floor, I then had to go down several steps to the pulpit.

After that day, I knew how to use crutches.

Shortly thereafter, it was Anita's turn to be hospitalized. She was suffering from serious health problems due to early onset of menopause. As I was returning home from a visit with her, another disaster struck, and this one almost cost me my life. My driver and I were stuck in traffic. All at once, I heard the whistle of a train and realized we were trapped on a railroad track. We couldn't go forward as we were already just touching the bumper of the car ahead, so we tried to back up. I heard a crash as we backed into a tricycle behind us. (A tricycle is a motorcycle that has been modified to carry several passengers.) The enraged tricycle driver started yelling at my driver and they went back to access the damage, leaving me alone in the car. I could see the train slowly rolling toward me and picking up speed. Getting my leg—cast and all—out of the car was not easy, but somehow I scrambled out the door and out of the way, just before the train demolished the front of the car.

Life was difficult for everyone in the Philippines. The poverty surrounding us was draining the life out of good, decent people. While I traveled around speaking, Anita was never idle in her efforts to help the poor. Surrounded by hungry, begging children, she took it upon herself to organize meals for them.

It wasn't long before we were facing more than hunger. One day, our housekeeper pointed out that a nine-year-old girl from the feeding program was wasting away with sickness. Anita and I looked at each other, silently asking the same question, *What should we do?* Anita remembers:

We had just enough money for our ministry and we felt strongly that we were not to get involved in the endless medical problems in the Philippines. Yet we knew this little girl, and we couldn't just let her die. We feared that if we paid for medical attention, before long, dozens of people would want us to pay for all kinds of medical support. We were both praying for Shelly and asking the Lord what He wanted us to do.

At the same time, I was trying to get Frank to take me to see "Phantom of the Opera" in Manila for my upcoming birthday. It felt so wrong to be praying for this luxury and for Shelly at the same time. I would start my prayers asking to see Phantom and then later at the end, I would pray for Shelly's healing.

After a few days, I knew I would have to choose between the two things. Of course, I chose to help

Shelly, so I told Frank to forget the play. "Let's go see Shelly instead," I said, only a little regretfully.

Anita and I went to see the child. She recognized Anita, but by then she was in a partial coma, too weak to raise her head. We looked at each other and silently agreed to provide whatever was necessary to save her life. Anita took her to a hospital, where they flatly stated they could not help. However, when they understood that Anita would pay, they suddenly changed their minds. The doctor later said Shelly had been very near death, and that she definitely would have died if Anita had not intervened. Afterward, in reviewing how much we had spent for Shelly, we were awestruck to find that the total bill was almost the same amount the show tickets would have cost us.

A week or so after Shelly got out of the hospital, her mother brought her to our house and, through our housekeeper's translation, told us, "You saved her life, now she is yours." We declined to adopt Shelly. Instead, we enrolled the mother in a class on how to prepare nutritious food. Shy Shelly leaned on her mother and watched us with a smile, all the while clutching an anorexic-but-bosomy Barbie Doll. As the days went by, Shelly continued to get better. And, to our relief and surprise, no sick people lined up at our gate looking for free medical care.

After the first year in the Philippines, my body seemed to adjust to the germs around me and I was relatively healthy for the rest of my stay. But still, our circumstances fluctuated wildly between "good" and "bad." For some time, we had been searching for a house to use for a residential program. Finally, we located one about a mile from our house. Despite some serious complications during the remodeling, we soon had seven or eight men living there. They could easily walk to our house for the group meetings that were part of the Steps Out Program.

When the men moved into the residence, they all promised to pay the small sum of about $30 a month, but few of them did. I wanted them to get jobs, but I had not yet realized that it sometimes took two or three years to obtain employment. I talked this over with some men at the church. One of them said that he was tired of his management job and would help us start a bakery, which could then employ the men in our program. I called a meeting of all our leaders and program members and asked if they would participate in this venture. Everybody thought it was a great way to finance the residential house. It seemed like a good idea at the time...

Little did we know that this bakery would be one of our biggest disasters. To equip the bakery, the start-up costs amounted to about $26,000. And, as weeks turned into months, one mishap followed another. Strangely, although the bakery was successful for a while, it continued to lose money. After some internal auditing, we found that our manager was better at cooking the books than at producing cookies. Finally, when our drunken baker dropped the $2,000 mixer and shattered it, we decided it was time to close the bakery and chalk it up as a very unpleasant learning experience. Our new ministry was growing, and despite the challenges, we were making progress.

In the meantime, while one distracting calamity followed another in the Philippines, Anita's son, Tony, and his partner, Rick, were facing an enormous crisis in California. During one of Anita's monthly calls to Tony, he mentioned that both he and Rick were feeling constantly sick and didn't seem to be able to overcome their flu-like symptoms. They both were going to get tested for AIDS. Anita and I were beside ourselves with worry. In the early 1990s, there were many deaths from AIDS. We couldn't take this terrible possibility lightly.

On a certain day, Tony was to call at 9 A.M., Manila time, to give Anita the test results. She was anxiously awaiting that call when she heard the fax machine printing a fax. Her heart sank as she realized she had left the fax on and therefore could not receive the phone call. She glanced at the fax, which was from a woman who knew nothing about Tony. The woman had written, "You probably don't remember me, but we have met. In my dream last night, you were very distressed about your son, Tony. I woke up and felt a strong need to pray for you." Anita cried out, "Oh God, No!" She knew instantly that Tony would be soon be calling with devastating news.

Just then, the phone rang again and it was Tony. When Anita answered, she just said, "I know, I know, God just told me." They cried together. It was no surprise to me, but I had never wanted my fears confirmed. I loved Tony as my own son, and Rick and I shared the same hobby—we were both train buffs. Now the big question hanging between us was, how long did they have to live? We had no idea, nor did anyone else. I told Anita she could fly home any time she felt she had to. I could not leave the ministry for long, however; it was still very fragile.

Anita wrestled with the situation. On the one hand, she wanted to head for the airport and be with her son, but she sensed God saying, *Wait! Trust Me!* It was only by His grace that she was able to obey. For Anita, the world we lived in was now an unbearably long distance from California. And for both of us, life had drastically changed.

One morning I woke up to find my whole world had turned to gray. My first thought was that all the diseases I'd suffered in the Philippines had affected my eyes—I could no longer see color. Our red floor was gray and all the furniture was gray. Then I became aware that I was breathing dust, and when I looked behind me, I saw I had left footprints on the floor. When I went into the kitchen, our housekeeper was sweeping up buckets of this gray material.

"Trini, what happened? What is this?" I asked.

"Mt. Pinatubo erupted," she informed me. "And Mt. Mayan also," she added.

We lived between these two active volcanoes; each was about 60 miles from our house. Days later, we drove to a seminar, which we had scheduled in Baguio City, very close to Mt. Pinatubo. On a journey I will never forget, as we got higher up the mountain road to Baguio, we could look into the massive crater of Mt. Pinatubo—about 20 miles away—and see fire shooting forth. A kind of mushroom cloud extended high into the sky above the mountain. To this day, when I open some of my reference books, ashes fall out.

A local woman named Flor came twice a week to do the laundry for our team. She was a sweet, lovable lady and we all became friends. One day, Anita and I decided to go visit her. To our amazement, we found she lived with several of her children in the middle of a field. Other similar "squatters" lived here and there around the field. Flor's "house" consisted of a few bamboo poles pushed into the ground, with a blue tarp as a cover. At that moment, Anita and I decided we had to help Flor get a better place to live. While we mulled over exactly what we could do, a typhoon ripped through our area and Flor lost her blue tarp. Whatever remained of her meager belongings was now exposed to the wind and rain.

I drew up a plan for a small portable house that would be bolted together; it would have one door and one window. Romi, our house guard, put it together. Since Flor was living on someone else's land, she might have to move quickly at any moment. In fact, it wasn't long before she was evicted. Thankfully, the house could be disassembled and reassembled easily.

After several other moves, Flor found a piece of railroad land quite close to our house. That little house then begat several additions, but one of them was a little too close to the railroad track and was demolished by a passing boxcar.

By our third year, we had opened the third residential house for our live-in program. This house had a water pump in the back yard. Since the residents needed showers, we constructed an outbuilding out of cinder block and capped it with a thick concrete roof, on which we placed a 100-gallon tank. We ran a hose from the water pump to the top of the tank. The sun shining on the tank heated the water, and the tank's height provided water pressure for showers. However, no one wanted to fill the tank; it took about a half hour of strenuous pumping. So whenever someone broke one of the house rules, they got tank-pumping duty.

Several nights a week, I went to visit the live-in house. All the streets were dark because the electricity did not come on until after midnight. The house was about a mile from ours, but I was not afraid to walk that distance in the dark. Not, that is, until one of our neighbors mentioned that someone had seen a cobra in the street the night before!

Between our illnesses, the needy world around us, erupting volcanoes, dangerous crimes in our area (Anita was robbed at gunpoint on a bus), the train wreck, and now a cobra, returning to our pleasant little cottage in California was sounding better and better. We had an agreement with Exodus that at the end of three years, we would place the ministry in Philippine hands and return home. In the third year, Exodus sent over a board member to appraise the ministry. At that time, we had two group meetings going, one with 50 group members in central Manila, and one with 35 members in northern Manila.

After the board member returned home, Exodus informed us that they wanted us to stay another two years. Anita simply said, "No, I can't do that. Sorry, but I have to get back to Tony."

I negotiated with Exodus and we agreed that I would stay another year on my own. It proved to be a very difficult year for me without Anita. She went back to do part-time work in the Love in Action office, and also took care of Rick, who was getting worse every day. Thanks to some new medication he was receiving, Tony had recovered enough to work part-time, but he was chronically exhausted. During this period, Anita and I both knew we should not be using the telephone to communicate, since each call was over a hundred dollars, but every now and then, we simply had to hear each other's voice.

At my first group meeting in Pacita years before, I had found the man I wanted to train to be our director after I returned to America. Rudy was a brilliant young man; he had completed four years of college by age nineteen, and he was now in seminary. During my four years in Manila, I had made Rudy Assistant Director and could trust him to run much of the ministry. I had also met Gilbert, who came along in my second year there. He, too, was studying for the ministry. Both were capable of heading up Bagong Pag-asa, our New Hope operation.

As my time to leave approached, I felt confident that I had done a good job in Manila. We had a live-in house, good leadership, and the ministry was growing at a rapid pace. After returning to California from Manila, I planned to take a year off to relax and recuperate, and then head for Hong Kong to start a ministry there. The work in Manila was exhilarating but exhausting. I often arrived home at one or two in the morning after our group meetings in central Manila. I thought it was time for a break.

One day, a pastor called from Church of the Open Door, in San Rafael. Steve announced, "Love in Action is moving to Memphis! What do you think about that?"

Sometimes Steve joked around, so I honestly did not believe him. "Steve," I said, "if this is true, have Mike Riley call me to verify it." Mike is our Senior Pastor and I had worked with him for years.

Mike called. "Frank, it's true, they are moving."

This was devastating news. Would there no longer be an ex-gay ministry in the San Francisco area? Could I do anything to keep this from happening? Would God want me to start a completely new ministry in San Rafael to replace Love in

Action? What did this mean for my plans for a sabbatical, and for a future ministry in Hong Kong?

I knew there had been some unrest between Love in Action and the church. When our men had been asked to disperse to various other churches in the area, many had felt unwanted by Open Door. A symptom of homosexuality is sensitivity toward rejection. Many men and women who struggle with same-sex attraction perceive rejection, even when there is none. As the months and years had passed, bitterness toward our church had grown in some of them.

I called John Smid immediately. He explained he had found a mega-church in Memphis that would finance the move, provide office space, and support the ministry in many ways. John added that he felt the men in the program needed to relate to straight men in the church, and that our local church simply did not have a large enough congregation for that. My guess was that those involved in Love in Action were feeling a bit unsupported. Because I was in Manila, I felt help-less to change the situation.

"Can you wait a year?" I asked John. "I'm so tired, I need a rest..."

John said it was not possible, that the plans were already confirmed, and they would be leaving in December, now only a few months away.

At least I was feeling good about the Philippine ministry, which made the uncertainty and disappointment I would be facing at home seem less devastating. As for Anita, she was far from devastated. She felt all this was answered prayer and that God had everything under control. She was not anxious to begin all over again in Hong Kong, and now she would be able to watch over Tony; we were afraid his health could deteriorate at any time. She did feel bad for me, that my plans had been disrupted. Knowing that I had now served 22 years without any time off, she was hoping I could find some time to rest.

By this time, I had completed my contract with Exodus. I had spent four years in Manila and was leaving the ministry in Philippine hands, as agreed. I purchased my ticket to San Francisco, shipped all my books and possessions back to San Rafael, and turned our house over to the ministry so they could use it as a live-in residence for men. Then, during my last week before my departure, the young man I had selected to direct the Manila ministry came in to see me. He had come to tell me he'd had a sexual fall.

I simply couldn't believe what I was hearing. I had felt he'd previously had an emotionally dependent relationship with a missionary from Europe, but that man had returned to Europe and I thought the relationship was over. What I didn't know was that another ministry had sent Rudy to Europe, to represent them at a conference. Rudy's friend was at the conference, and things had rapidly moved from emotional to sexual. I told Rudy I would have to suspend him from leadership, but I certainly didn't want to do it. I gave him a three-month's suspension, which I knew was much too short. I didn't know what else I could do. I was too devastated to think clearly. One of my other leaders went to the ministry board and told them about Rudy's fall. They promptly gave him a five-year suspension.

Thankfully, I still had Gilbert, and he was the equal of Rudy. I called Gilbert and told him I was giving him the directorship of New Hope Manila. He was pleased that I had confidence in him and accepted. However, he wanted to run the decision by his pastor. It was now only two days before my departure. Gilbert got back to me and said his pastor had given him a choice: either go with New Hope, or stay in his church and ultimately become a pastor for that denomination. Gilbert said he had chosen his church. He would no longer be connected with New Hope.

For Gilbert it was perhaps a good decision, as he now has a loving family and a very successful, growing church. But for me, it seemed like the end of the world. I had trained only these two leaders for directorship, and now both were out of the picture. I had to get on that plane. I turned to Sam, our live-in house leader and said, "It seems the ministry is in your hands." Our farewell amounted to me saying something like, "Goodbye and good luck." As it turned out, Sam kept the ministry going for the next ten years! It was a bewildering responsibility to place on his shoulders, but he rose to the challenge.

It was a fretful plane ride home. All my plans were upside down. I was having very mixed feelings about Rudy, both sorrow and anger. The ministry I had worked so hard to establish in the Philippines was now in jeopardy; both of my carefully trained leaders were gone. It seemed very unlikely that I would be able to enjoy the year of rest I so badly needed. Love in Action would be gone in just two weeks, leaving the San Francisco area without an ex-gay ministry. I wondered which I would be facing—foreclosure or bankruptcy—as I now had two empty residences. Rick was about to die any day, and Tony's health was still very fragile. I had no idea just how much worse things were to get before they began to get better.

As 1994 had worn on, Rick had developed dementia. I'd had a friendly relationship with Rick, but he had resented Anita, often calling her "Church Lady." It had been difficult for Rick to allow Anita to take care of him; and of course, it was difficult for Anita to care for someone who continually made sarcastic remarks about her. Anita knew, however, that what she did for Rick helped Tony by taking a load off his shoulders—a load he was not strong enough to bear. Now, as Rick's mind slipped away, he was much nicer to Anita, probably forgetting who she was.

As the time for my return to California had approached, Anita had been facing it with both anticipation and dread. She wondered how she could continue to take care of Rick and be a wife to me, as well. That problem would soon to be resolved, with Anita operating in crisis mode. She later wrote:

I was a woman with a mission I felt in total control of my emotions. Rick now had only days to live and the deathbed-watch was intense, but it seemed it would be all over before Frank's return. Only then could I be the wife Frank needed, and I was trusting God to work it all out.

The staff at Love in Action saw things differently. They saw me as kind of a wreck operating on borrowed energy. They were praying that Rick would last until Frank returned, so he could be there for me when Rick finally passed away.

I left Rick, and went to pick up Frank at the airport. Tony said I wasn't needed that night, and that he would watch Rick. But at 3 A.M., the telephone rang, and I instantly knew what the message was going to be.

Tony said, "Rick just died, can you come?"

I was up and dressed in a flash, and out the door. I took care of everything, even getting the hospital bed removed from their living room.

When I returned home, however, I was like a punctured balloon; I was exhausted. Frank wanted pampering, but I was not able to be what he wanted me to be at that time. The church pastors helped him to see that we both were "home from the wars" and would both need to take time to get our strength back.

Anita had moved back into our little cottage on her return, but my garden—my pride and joy—was in ruins. *It looks a lot like my life right now*, I thought. It had been years since the garden had received any attention. There was about a foot of debris over the patio areas, the trees hadn't been trimmed, and everything was overgrown. A skeleton crew was managing both our live-in houses. Most of the leaders were already in Memphis, and John Smid would be leaving in just a few days. My income was now limited to a mortgage I held. I had huge monthly payments to make on the apartment building and the live-in house, both of which would soon be empty.

I felt compelled to keep an active ministry in San Rafael, and I talked this over with the Love in Action staff. They had many applications for their next year's program so they sent a note to all those who had been selected, asking if they would rather come to San Rafael or go to Memphis. Love in Action directed eleven men to us, nine to be in the program and two for leadership, giving us enough men to maintain one-half of the apartment building as a live-in house for our 1995 program. This left us with three units we would need to rent out. New Hope House, in front of our cottage, had eight bedrooms that needed to be rented out. We found eight men who had already completed the Love in Action Program to fill what would now to be called the New Hope Community House.

On December 6, 1994, I watched with an aching heart as a caravan of three trucks and ten cars departed for Memphis, carrying with them everything we had known as Love in Action.

However, the Lord quickly blessed this transition. We immediately re-instituted the Friday Night Drop-in Meetings. We established a new board with eight members, five of whom were local pastors. My good friend and senior pastor, Mike Riley, became Board President of our newly christened "New Hope Ministries." We had hit the ground running.

Yes, it was another new beginning. Once again, we were starting from scratch. We even managed to produce a newsletter starting in January 1995, but we had almost no mailing list, so there were few people to send it to. The three apartments were not in rentable condition—they were in very bad shape, and two of the three kitchens had been removed.

The men of Open Door Church came to the rescue. Several men in our church are contractors, and they banded together to rebuild the kitchens, with no charge for their labor. They did drywalling, plumbing, electrical work, and even some floor replacement. Love in Action had left a small sum to offset the cost of any appliances we would need, but the cost of building materials proved to be staggering. I maxed my credit card, and still had a long way to go. Those were the days when credit cards came in the mail without your ever asking for them, and that was a good thing for me, because it got me through the crisis. As someone who has always been careful about financial decisions, it grieved me to run up card after card, but it served our purpose, and we were able to complete the remodeling.

Even before we were finished, and while there were still piles of debris on the floors, people eagerly paid deposits to rent the apartments. Soon, everything was finished and rented. It took years to pay off the credit cards, but we were now back in business, operating quite well as New Hope Ministries.

Before long, Anita and Bob Davies began collaborating on a new book titled, *Someone I Love is Gay*. Once again, we were all working day and night, but it was an exciting time. I gave up hope for a sabbatical—and haven't given it much thought since. I also had to give up the dream of starting a ministry in Hong Kong, but someone else picked up that dream, and a good ministry thrives there now.

Our residential program always began on New Year's Eve, with the men repenting for past sins and rededicating their lives to the Lord. New Year's Eve, 1995, was covered in prayer. Soon our program was off and running, and within a week, we were on our way to the first program retreat. It was such a joy for me to be back at The Lord's Land retreat center with a new group of men.

In mid-January, the weather was fierce and the waves on the coast were monumental. Instead of hosting retreats under the palm trees in the Philippines, we were now under the giant redwood trees of Northern California once again. And, as if all this activity were not enough, I began to write my next book, *The Church and the Homosexual Issue*, which was intended for pastors. I felt it was urgent to give them instructions on how to help people who want to leave the homosexual lifestyle. Since we still had no support base, Don Kimball donated his time as our Office Manager. He had computer skills and was the only one who knew how to produce the newsletter. It would be two years before we could afford a salary for him. This was also the year we started our annual "Family and Friends" conference, which has always been well attended.

The 20th Exodus Conference was in San Diego that year, and we had a special summit meeting of Exodus International members. We decided to split off the international ministries from Exodus North America. Thus, Exodus International transferred out from under the North American ministry, and became a ministry of its own. Pat Allan of Toronto, Canada, was elected Coordinator and I was elected Board Chairman. We already had Exodus Europe, Exodus Latin America, and Exodus South Pacific. Together, they represented around 50 ministries. Now, Exodus North America became one of the world regions. We were making progress, even though it sometimes seemed like we were taking one step forward and two steps back.

In the year 2000, I learned that I had cancer. I had two operations and the last one was successful. I was told that if I could remain cancer free for five years, it probably would not return. It has now been nine years.

In May of 2001, Anita and I returned to Manila for the 10th anniversary of Bagong Pag-asa (New Hope), Manila. It was a wonderful celebration, but there were rumblings of trouble. The board president took me aside and said he was resigning, that the ministry was going nowhere, shrinking instead of growing. I promised him I would keep an eye on things and give the leaders instructions. The next, year we once again traveled to Manila and it was even more evident the ministry needed revitalizing. I was busy running a Steps Out Program in San Rafael, and could give New Hope, Manila, only a week or so.

Toward the end of 2003, it became apparent that for the first time in 27 years, there would be no residential program next year in San Rafael: we had no applicants. I sought out God's will and came to believe that God had given me this next year to re-establish the Philippine ministry. Since I always advise the men in our program to be specific in their prayer so they will clearly know when God answers, I told the Lord that there were five things that I thought had to happen to make the Philippine ministry viable once again.

First, we needed a central location for group meetings. The ministry was operating from the director's house, some 17 miles south of central Manila.

Second, we had lost our office and needed another one.

Third, the ministry no longer had a financial base, so I wanted to start a parents' group, not only to help parents but also to encourage them to support New Hope financially.

Fourth, I wanted to do a leadership training retreat, in order to develop new leaders for the ministry.

Fifth, to stir up new interest in the ministry, we needed to publish a new book.

I felt sure I heard God say, *I will give you what you ask.*

In 2003, we had established a missionary team in San Rafael, called New Hope Equipping Team, or NET. Now, the team was ready for its first venture, helping reestablish the Philippine ministry. A ministry consultant and close friend of mine, O.B., agreed to go with me to Manila. As we traveled there, we had no idea what we might be facing. There had been virtually no communication from the Manila ministry in years. Whenever I had wanted to check up on them, I'd had to fly over to see how they were doing. Now, I had no idea if the ministry even had a board. I was pleasantly surprised to find that the ministry had a high-caliber group of people as board members.

O.B. presented a one-day training session for the ministry board members. He laid out a five-year plan, with both short-term and long-term goals. After his presentation, I shared what my five prayer requests were. One board member—a business woman—exclaimed, "Oh, I have an office you can use! It's only about three blocks from here. Do you want to go see it now?"

I could hardly believe what I was hearing. That first day, one of my prayers was already answered! We all headed out the door to see this office. To my amazement, it was located in a brand new, 38-story high-rise, near the intersection of two main streets in the financial district. There was no location more prestigious than this. The office was on the 10th floor with a spectacular view of central Manila and the airport. The end wall was all glass. It was extravagant.

Within a week, the NET team arrived and we conducted a one-week seminar on leadership, which sixteen men attended. Now, two of the five prayers had been answered.

After the team left, Anita arrived and we scheduled a Family and Friends seminar. Our director had arranged for us to rent a condo for the duration of our stay in Manila and after we moved in, I found out there was a rooftop conference room available to tenants for a small cost. On the day of the seminar, the room was completely full. After the seminar, we established monthly parents' meetings. My third prayer was answered, and we had been in Manila only about a month.

Our new office was large enough to hold seminars for up to 38 people. Later, we hosted an open house and about 100 people came, so we had used the corridor as an overflow area. That showed us that we could also use the office for weekly group meetings, which answered another prayer.

The only thing left on my prayer list was to publish a book. When I had first arrived on this trip, I had visited OMF Publishers and presented them with the book, *Caring for Gay Loved Ones*, which Anita and I had put together the year before. Within a couple of weeks, they said that they liked the book and were now sending it to the editing department. Before the end of the year, the book was in every major bookstore in the Philippines. The ministry was swamped with calls from people who had bought or been given the book.

God had answered all my prayers within the first year.

I soon realized the ministry badly needed an office manager. We would have to find a person who was called by God, because we could offer very little in the way of salary. One young man, named John Zulueta, had voluntarily helped me organize the parents' seminar. Then he continued to help me organize other meetings and gatherings—sometimes several per week. I felt sure he was the ideal person to be our office manager.

There was one problem. John had a very lucrative job, which paid far more than the average Filipino received as wages. He was a sales representative for a product very much in demand. He was also well educated, and a part-time Christian counselor. I knew God had chosen him, but John didn't want to acknowledge it. He had great plans for the future, and they did not include poverty.

Now it was near the end of 2004, I was preparing to return to California, and still we had no office manager. The Sunday before my departure, John and I attended his church together. The message that day focused on earthly rewards vs. spiritual rewards. The sermon droned on for an hour and a half, but I didn't mind because I could see John was being convicted. He was beginning to realize that God was requiring a sacrifice from him. At the end of the service he began to cry, and went forward for prayer.

As I sat watching, I felt God had given the ministry exactly what it needed—an excellent office manager. But after the service, John said nothing and I didn't want to ask. I wanted God to do the work without my interference. I was scheduled to leave on Friday, and Thursday night we had an open house. All week, I had expected John to say something about the job, but he did not. Thursday night, John and I were alone, cleaning up the mess after the open house. Finally, I inquired, "John, you know I leave tomorrow. Have you made a decision about becoming Office Manager?"

"I haven't slept a night since Sunday," he confessed. "I know the Lord wants me to do this, but I don't want to leave my good job."

"So, what does that mean, John?" I asked, perhaps a little impatiently. "Are you taking the Office Manager position or not?"

John stared at me for a moment, and then quietly agreed. "Yes, I will be the Office Manager."

I thought our ministry director would be elated at having such a bright young man to help in the ministry, but no such luck. He apparently saw John as competition. John had no designs on the directorship, especially since there was no pay involved. A day after I left, the Director fired John. John, however, knew that God had called him to this job, so he refused to leave and instead, brought the matter before the board. A year of turmoil followed, which seriously compromised the ministry. I wrote letters; I flew there twice; yet, I could not resolve all the issues. Finally, in April 2006, the Director resigned and John Zulueta became Director of New Hope, Philippines. The attacks were over, and now the ministry could grow with new vigor.

Today, Anita's son Tony is still healthy and is now living with his second partner—a fine, responsible man. We all get along quite well and have agreed to disagree on the issue of homosexuality. Tony is a firm believer in free choice. He believes he has the right to choose a homosexual lifestyle, and others have the right to choose not to lead a homosexual lifestyle. Over the years, he has been quite friendly with our program guys, and even attended the funeral of one of them.

Thinking about Tony and his partner brings back memories of my own journey from homosexual behavior to a new life in Christ. Anita and I pray constantly that Tony and his partner will someday embark on that same journey and find the joy, peace, and happiness that I and so many other ex-gays have found. It is true that some did not succeed in this transition, and gave up the fight. It is our prayer that they will return to the battle and eventually find victory. Nevertheless, whether they succeed or not, we have loved them all.

If there is one thing that irks me, it is when the gay community calls us hateful. I came from that world myself, and I love my brothers and sisters who are still in the gay lifestyle. I would like to help them find Jesus and change, but I respect their decision to continue in the lifestyle. I know too much about their wounding and rejection to judge or reject them. In fact, I have faced just about everything they have.

When I entered the gay world, homosexuality was illegal. I can never forget the lynching of two men who had preyed on a young boy in my community when I was just a child. A few years later when I was still a teen, police were regularly raiding the gay hangouts I frequented. I remember hiding, listening to the heavy footsteps of the police, and the terrifying clamor as the cops hauled men away in paddy wagons. It was just like a scene out of a Nazi movie. I fully understand why homosexual activists are so consumed with their rights. I also understand why most of them have no interest in change. Change is very difficult. I have never said it was easy.

The choice to become obedient to Jesus and leave homosexuality behind is probably one of the most difficult decisions a person would ever make. However, I do wish the gay activists would be as tolerant as they are asking us to be. In the late 1970s and early 1980s, I had a good relationship with the pastors of the gay church. I would occasionally have lunch with them, and explained that we were not a political organization that opposed them. We only wanted to help those who had become disenchanted with the gay lifestyle and truly wanted to change.

At first, they seemed to understand. One pastor actually called me to say, "Hey, I've got this crazy guy who wants out of the lifestyle and I'm sending him to you." But within a few years, every gay pastor I was friendly with was dead, and in their places were lesbians. These women wanted to fight. On one occasion, they invaded my old office, which Exodus was now using, and let loose about a thousand crickets, shouting, "A plague on you!" Later, we learned that they call themselves, "The Lesbian Avengers."

I do not judge their lives or their behavior. That is not my job. Listen to Saint Paul in 1ˢᵗ Corinthians 5:12, "What business is it of mine to judge those outside the church? Are you not to judge those inside? God will judge those outside."

Tragically, it is true that many within the Christian community have been harshly judgmental of homosexuals. The "Reverend" Fred Phelps and his "God Hates Fags" website is an extreme example of such hatred. One day, I was in San Francisco and his team was on Market Street carrying signs that read: "Thank God for AIDS." I tried to talk with a couple of the group members, but they would not speak to me. When Rev. Phelps was asked if any gays had repented through his protesting, his alleged reply was, "Who cares?" As sad as it was, at least he was being honest.

Other Christians often project a very subtle rejection. However, in effect, they too are saying, "Who cares?" perhaps not verbally, but with their actions. Even today, when a young person talks to a pastor or church counselor, and confesses struggling with homosexual feelings and temptations, all too often, he or she is asked to leave the church.

On several talk shows, I have been asked, "Does God love gays?" The answer is, "Of course, God loves gays. God is not willing that any should perish." The next question is always, "Are gays going to hell?" That is not my decision to make. God alone will make that decision. There are Scriptures indicating that those who identify themselves as gay are in great jeopardy. Nevertheless, no matter what kind of sins we participate in, up until our last breath, we have the option of repenting and turning to God.

I have seen many gays return to Christ on their death bed. That is enough to convince me that it's not over until it's over.

Frank on a Philippine adventure at age 64. (1993)

Epilogue

As I said at the beginning of the book, I am now 80 years old. I am slightly deaf and also have a problem with what is called "low-vision," or macular degeneration. I have completed 36 years of ex-gay ministry. It has been a wild adventure, and one I would not have wanted to miss. There has never been a dull moment, although sometimes I have wished for just that! I have enjoyed almost every minute I've spent in ministry.

The joy of my life is my wife, Anita. Anita has not only completed a missing part of the ministry, working with women and parents, but she has also completed my life. We have literally been to the ends of the earth together, experiencing one new adventure after another. Hardly a day goes by that I don't thank the Lord for such a precious gift. She is my partner and my delight.

And there's more. What joy I feel when I see the transformation of so many men and women, who have found new life through ministries in which I've been privileged to be involved! So many brave and courageous people have trusted the Lord enough to walk into the unknown. Surprisingly, every so often I receive a call from those who left our ministry and returned to the gay lifestyle. It took a little longer for them, but now they, too, are enjoying a changed life. Around the world there are thousands (perhaps even tens of thousands) of people who have found the life-changing power of Christ.

I have been called the father of ex-gay ministry, but I firmly believe God initiated the ex-gay work Himself. The year 1973, when God called me to ministry, was not only the year of Roe vs. Wade, which made abortion legal, it was also the year of the American Psychiatric Association's declaration that homosexuality is normal, and its creation of class 302, "Ego-Dystonic Homosexuality." This new category pronounced anyone not completely satisfied with his/her homosexual nature to be disordered. In other words, if you didn't like being gay, something was wrong with you! The APA's decision radically changed the world we live in. Most governments responded to this decision by removing all laws against homosexuality and placing homosexuals in a minority class with special rights.

We read in Isaiah 59:19, "When the enemy shall come in like a flood, the Spirit of the Lord will lift up a standard." I believe my call—and God's call to others—was the lifting up of a standard after that decision. Many were called to fight abortion on demand, and others were called to ex-gay ministry.

It was God who called me. I did not create the idea of ex-gay ministry. In fact, to some extent, I wanted to run the other way, like Jonah. I have always considered the ministries I have been involved in to be God's ministries, with me as His servant. I try not to run ahead of Him. I try to be a good steward of what He has given me. I try to have His compassion on those who reject what we are doing, and on those who in many ways have betrayed us. I am fully aware that I was just as disobedient as those who fight ex-gay ministry.

Every day, I am thankful the Lord brought me out of such an unrewarding life, and gave me the helpmate I was always searching for. Every morning, I ask Him for instructions for that day. I try to live a surrendered life. I have visions for the future, but they are frequently denied, and my plans must give way to His plans. I have found Him faithful to answer prayers that are within His will. My experience in revitalizing the Manila ministry was awesome. He answered every prayer, because my will and His will were in line. He does give us the desires of our hearts, but that can be a two-edged sword. If there is evil in our hearts, He may allow us to wallow in that evil until we are saturated with it, and want to be set free. That's when He comes to our rescue.

It is undeniably true—the way out of homosexuality is difficult. However, for those who fully surrender to God's will and are willing to take an active, God-directed part in their own healing, both new life and a very exciting journey lie ahead. We have counseled and ministered to thousands of men and women throughout the years. Those who have found this new life were the ones who developed a strong personal relationship with the Lord.

Some come to seek knowledge, but knowledge will never open the door to change. Others imagine that hard work will bring change, that somehow God will honor their efforts by miraculously producing instant inner change. God does honor our efforts, but only if accompanied by a close relationship with Him. We can never first clean ourselves up and then come to God, because God's standard is absolute perfection. ("You, therefore, must be perfect, as your heavenly Father is perfect," Matthew 5:48.) First, we come to God in repentance. Then, He does the cleaning up.

There are seasons in life. Sometime after puberty, certain men and women encounter the gay lifestyle and think they have found everything they were ever looking for. It is a season for exploring passions and flaunting youth. But that season ends much too quickly. After the spark of youth is gone, many enter a season of searching for true intimacy.

This is where the hard reality of the gay lifestyle surfaces. Some may find partners, but few ever find a partner who remains true. They either have an open relationship, or they settle for anonymous sexual encounters. Many enter into a mid-life crisis. The body is no longer attractive; the gay lifestyle reveals itself to be shallow and empty. The question becomes, "What lies ahead?" Some return to the faith of their youth; they are the fortunate few. Others remain celibate, often not by choice but by lack of opportunity. They enjoy their friends, but long for a deeper intimacy than friendship.

Today, I am in my final season of life. I am surrounded by those I love and who love me: Anita, my wife; Howard, my faithful right-hand man who takes good care of me; and Mike Riley, my friend and Senior Pastor. Mike and I have been through much together in the last 30-some years. Mike has steadfastly served Church of the Open Door since it began. There are a host of others: O.B., my good friend and accountability partner, for one—along with so many who support me, both personally and in ministry.

I have the satisfaction of knowing that Love in Action, which I founded in 1973, is doing well and achieved new heights while it was in the very capable hands of John Smid. John recently began a new ministry, Grace Rivers, which teaches churches how to minister through healthier relationships and authenticity.

It is a great joy to me that God hand-picked Ron Smith to be my successor as Director of New Hope Ministries. Ron came to New Hope in the fall of 2001, immediately after leaving his lover of 17 years. He enrolled in our pre-program while waiting for the 2002 Steps Out Program to begin—as it always did—on New Year's Eve.

About four weeks into the new program, we had a worship/prayer night with a guest worship leader who, to our surprise, brought her parents along. Each man had his turn in the "hot seat" (a chair in the middle of the room), while the whole group prayed over him. When it was Ron's turn to be prayed for, our guest's father spoke out prophetically, "You will be the next torch-bearer." None of us knew what to think. Mostly we dismissed it as unlikely and premature for one so recently out of the gay lifestyle.

This prophecy placed Ron in an awkward position with the other guys, much like when Joseph told his brothers they would bow down to him. Although none of us took it very seriously, I couldn't get it out of my mind. I began to note that Ron had that special relationship with God that is a prerequisite for Christian leadership.

After finishing our program, Ron stayed on as a leadership trainee. He then joined our NET (New Hope Equipping Team) and made two missionary trips, one to help me revitalize my Manila leadership, and the other to a sister ministry in Quito, Ecuador.

Ron returned to Florida to finish his Bachelor's degree in Leadership and Ministry. He then came back to San Rafael in 2008 to work on his Master's of Divinity at Golden Gate Baptist Seminary. By this time, I felt confident the prophecy had been from God. I made Ron the Director of New Hope Ministries in April, 2009, and I then moved into partial retirement as New Hope's CEO. At last, I found that time of rest I had so long wanted and needed.

Ron is now doing all the daily work, and God has opened new doors for him that were never opened for me. I look forward to New Hope's renewal, and watch with great anticipation to see where God will lead this ministry.

Mike, the young man who led me back to the Lord, has also continued to serve God all these years. He is a very successful business man and a faithful servant in his church. We still remain close friends.

As they say, "This is as good as it gets." I can testify that what God puts together is very good indeed. So, if you are suffering in an empty, unrewarding life—please hear me. I have one very important thing to say to you: TRY JESUS!

Frank and Anita at the twenty-fifth anniversary of
Love in Action, in Memphis. (1998)

Frank in Muir Woods at age 79. (2008)

Frank, in his corn field at age 80. (2009)

Frank and Anita enjoying their
retirement, (2008)

Contact Information

New Hope Ministries
P.O. Box 10246
San Rafael, CA 94912
(415) 453-6475
info@newhope123.org

Exodus International
P.O. Box 540119
Orlando, FL 32854
(888) 264-0877
www.exodusinternational.org

Love in Action
P.O. Box 343418
Bartlett, TN 38184-3418
(877) 320-5217
tommycorman@lovein
action.org
www.lovinaction.org